Handled with Discretion

Handled with Discretion

Ethical Issues in Police Decision Making

Edited by
JOHN KLEINIG

ROWMAN & LITTLEFIELD PUBLISHERS, INC.
Lanham • Boulder • New York • London

ROWMAN & LITTLEFIELD PUBLISHERS, INC.

Published in the United States of America
by Rowman & Littlefield Publishers, Inc.
4720 Boston Way, Lanham, Maryland 20706

3 Henrietta Street
London WC2E 8LU, England

British Cataloging-in-Publication Information Available

Library of Congress Cataloging-in-Publication Data

Handled with discretion : ethical issues in police decision making / edited by
John Kleinig.
p. cm.
"Papers . . . first presented at an intensive workshop held from May 4–6, 1995
at John Jay College of Criminal Justice, City University of New York"—Ack.
Includes bibliographical references and index.
1. Police discretion—Congresses. 2. Police ethics—Congresses. I. Kleinig,
John, 1942–
HV7936.D54H35   1996   174'.93632—dc20   96-3420   CIP

ISBN 0-8476-8176-9 (cloth : alk. paper)
ISBN 0-8476-8177-7 (pbk. : alk. paper)

Printed in the United States of America

♾ The paper used in this publication meets the minimum requirements of
American National Standard for Information Sciences—Permanence of
Paper for Printed Library Materials, ANSI Z39.48–1984.

Contents

991053

Acknowledgments

The eight papers and responses included in this volume were first presented at an intensive workshop held 4-6 May 1995 at John Jay College of Criminal Justice, City University of New York. Originally conceived as a joint project of the City University's Institute for Criminal Justice Ethics, housed at John Jay College, and the Institute for Philosophy and Public Policy at the University of Maryland, the workshop was generously supported by a grant from the City University of New York.

The contributors to this volume gratefully acknowledge the assistance received from the president of John Jay College, Gerald W. Lynch, and his staff, and particularly from Margaret Leland Smith, the Institute for Criminal Justice Ethics researcher, whose enviable managerial and administrative skills ensured that the workshop was a pleasant as well as a challenging experience. Mary Hapel graciously assisted in preparing the manuscripts for publication.

T. Kenneth Moran and Benjamin Bowling, of John Jay College, and Neil Richards, from the Police Staff College, Bramshill, U.K., also enhanced the workshop discussions with their presence.

Introduction

Handling Discretion with Discretion

John Kleinig

Criticisms of the way in which police exercise their authority are neither new nor uncommon. Police are vested with considerable formal (de jure) and physical (de facto) power, and that power may be drawn upon in circumstances that are both complex and pressing. It is not surprising, therefore, that their decisions should attract public scrutiny and even criticism.

In public debates over the use of their power, police officials have often claimed that exercises of police power are circumscribed by law and departmental regulation. In other words, police must work "by the book." If we are to believe Samuel Walker, until thirty years ago such claims were also accepted by social scientists: the disposition of individual encounters with the criminal justice system could be "read off" from the formal mechanisms that were in place to deal with them.[1] But then, in an American Bar Foundation (ABF) survey of 1956, it was "discovered" that at each stage of an individual's encounter with the criminal justice system the outcome was determined by a decision that was essentially "discretionary" in character.[2] What emerged from the encounter between citizen and law enforcement official often bore little relation to what might have been expected from a simple reading of the formal requirements.

The discovery of discretion should not have surprised those who found it. Although the public presentation of police decision making may have tended to emphasize its rule-bound character, it has always been recognized by the police themselves that their work could not be too tightly circumscribed by rules and regulations. Indeed, in the very first modern-day police manual – written in 1829 for Sir Robert Peel's London Metropolitan Police – Rowan and Mayne make it clear that their *General Instructions* "are not to be understood as containing rules of conduct applicable to every variety of circumstances that may occur in the performance of their duty; something must necessarily be left to the intelligence and discretion of individuals."[3]

Nevertheless, the findings of the ABF survey pose several critical questions. Was what was supposedly discovered really discretion? Or was it, perhaps, something more general – unregulated decision making – of which discretionary decisions constituted only a subset? With regard to discretionary judgments and decisions, what forms do they take? And what justification, if any, can be provided for such judgments and decisions by police? What limitations or constraints should be placed upon their exercises of discretion?

To a considerable degree, the essays included in this volume take as their point of departure – and object of criticism – the work of Kenneth Culp Davis. In two works, *Discretionary Justice: A Preliminary Inquiry* and *Police Discretion*, Davis frames most of the subsequent discussion.[4] *Discretionary Justice* acknowledges the reality to which the ABF study pointed, namely, that much decision making in criminal justice is not governed by explicit rules. Law, Davis believes, can take one only so far, many of the decisions confronting agents of justice not being amenable to a simple appeal to rules. Recognizing the potential for injustice – and, indeed, the actual injustice – involved in allowing broad discretion, Davis proposes that discretionary decision making be constrained by administrative rules, rules designed not to eliminate discretion but to structure it. In *Police Discretion*, Davis takes the thesis of *Discretionary Justice* a step further: even where criminal law covers a particular kind of behavior, there may be a place for discretion. The reasons for this are to be found not simply in the manifest impossibility of enforcing all the laws, but "between the lines" of social policy and the administration of justice – in funding practices and "unwritten laws" of judicial practice. As long as such exercises of discretion are constrained by open administrative rules, Davis sees no problem with selective enforcement.

THE NATURE OF DISCRETION

In what is probably the most widely quoted characterization of official discretion, Davis states that "a public officer has discretion whenever the effective limits on his power leave him free to make a choice among possible courses of action or inaction."[5] As an account of discretion, however, it is seriously flawed. For it allows that a police officer who roughs up a vagrant in a back alley is exercising (albeit improperly) his discretion. This is false; the officer has no such discretion. His conduct is forbidden. As Joan McGregor points out, what Davis's account leaves out is a normative dimension that is implicit in the characterization of behavior as discretionary.[6] Discretion is not simply a capacity to make choices – of being effectively free to choose between possible courses of action – but a permission, privilege, or prerogative to use judgment about how to make a practical determination. As such, it has embedded constraints – implicit understandings about the range of choice that is legitimately available to officials as they go about their activities. These constraints may be articulated by reference to institutional, moral, and/or administrative norms, norms that may sometimes be mutually supportive, but which at other times may be in tension.

In articulating this normative dimension, more than one contributor to this volume adverts to Ronald Dworkin's metaphor of discretion – in some of its senses – as the hole in a doughnut, the doughnut ring being constituted by authoritative standards. Discretion, Dworkin writes, "does not exist except as an area left open by a surrounding belt of restriction."[7] The standards relevant to judging exercises of discretion will therefore be relative to the norms that are implicit in the particular ring – the ring of norms governing legal, judicial, police, or other practice. In the case of police, James Fyfe suggests, this ring is constituted primarily by the need to protect life, liberty, and property.[8]

The situation is complicated by the fact that discretion is not a univocal concept. Dworkin himself distinguishes a strong sense of "discretion" – in which an authorized decision maker, in the absence of rules binding her, will have to make her own decision – from two weaker senses. According to one of those weaker senses, a person has discretion when the standards to be applied "cannot be applied mechanically but demand the use of judgment."[9] According to the other, attributing discretion to an official indicates that the person in question "has final authority to make a decision and cannot be reviewed and reversed by any other official."[10] What links them all as discretion, however, is the fact that someone is "charged with making decisions subject to standards set by a particular authority."[11] In no case does discretionary authority amount to license or immunity to criticism. Although governed by norms, discretion may be abused or misused.

Beyond these linked senses is a further one in which discretion means "discernment," that is, sound or wise judgment in practical affairs. This is not the sense we have in mind when asking whether police have too much or too little discretion. Whatever discretion they have in the former senses, we require that they exercise it with discretion, though we have no guarantee that they will do so.[12]

The foregoing complexities of discretion are discussed at length – and added to – by Michael Davis[13] and Joan McGregor.[14] Davis differentiates five senses of discretion – discretion-as-judgment (which is similar to the first of Dworkin's weaker senses); discretion-as-mere-decision (which Davis regards as "uninteresting" and Dworkin eschews altogether); discretion-as-discernment (with which Dworkin does not concern himself, except as a desirable feature of discretionary decisions and those who make them); discretion-as-liberty (similar to Dworkin's strong sense); and discretion-as-license (which is much closer to what Kenneth Culp Davis considers "effective power to choose").

Vidar Halvorsen, in reviewing Davis's essay, remains unconvinced that it is helpful to distinguish discretion-as-license, and suggests moreover that discretion-as-discernment be seen as fundamental, the other so-called senses of discretion being more fruitfully understood as different contexts "in which the exercise of interpretative competence is required."[15]

VARIETIES OF POLICE DISCRETION

Police discretion may encompass issues of scope, interpretation, priority, or tactics. It may focus on the role of police, on the way in which they categorize situations, on the ranking they give to different demands, and on the way in which they choose to accomplish the tasks they undertake.

Scope decisions

Police are often the first recourse of people who encounter some crisis: they are "problem busters." But the mere fact that police are called does not show them to be the appropriate persons to deal with the crisis. The police must exercise a form of discretion in determining whether what is brought to their attention demands their involvement. And just because police are so much more accessible (only three digits away!) than lawyers and judges, they must regularly make decisions about what constitutes their proper business. Should they see it as their task to intervene in civil disputes or lovers' quarrels, to open car doors when the keys have been locked inside, or to inform a spouse that his or her partner has collapsed and died on the street?

Issues in an ongoing debate about the nature and limits of the police role are constantly raised and tested by the questions put to police by the public that seeks them out – or even by the situations they happen upon. What is the police role and how much discretion should police have interpreting it?

Some of these questions are raised acutely by James Fyfe. He shows how a particular conception of their work may encourage police to eschew a proper involvement in domestic altercations. By construing the latter as essentially private, they may seek to avoid any engagement with them, even though – absent the relationships involved – they would otherwise have intervened without hesitation. Thus Dorice Smith's call to the Elyria, Ohio, police to report the beating of her sister by the sister's ex-husband fell on deaf ears, because it was allegedly "a civil matter." And Jeffrey Dahmer's young Laotian victim was returned to Dahmer because of the prejudiced judgment that Sinthasomphone's condition was simply the outcome of a gay-lover engagement.[16]

It is Fyfe's view that in cases in which felonious assault is involved police should have no discretion about whether to act: their primary responsibility is to protect life, rights, and property.[17] Although police should have some discretion about whether to respond to demands that are placed upon them, such discretion cannot be claimed where life is imperiled. A commitment to the privacy or sanctity of domestic relations should not be allowed to erode their more fundamental commitment, as police officers, to the protection of life.

Interpretative decisions

Even when police have determined that a situation is one that demands their attention, there may still be important decisions about its interpretation. Does a particular commotion constitute a "disturbance of the peace"? Does a person who questions a police arrest decision "interfere with police operations"? If a car radio is playing Beethoven loudly, does it constitute "excessive noise"? Does a domestic disturbance call for intervention of a social work or law enforcement kind? These decisions must often be made rapidly, there may not be a clear set of precedents, and if no arrest is involved, there may not be a meaningful review procedure.

Here, too, Fyfe offers some telling observations. If police see their role in family disputes as social workers rather than as law enforcers, they may be tempted to handle such disputes in ways that will leave domestic victims in serious jeopardy. Their discretion, once again, is limited by their primary responsibility to protect life, and when life is at risk, they should have no discretion about the general course of action they should take: to provide protection.[18]

Candace McCoy suggests a different way in which interpretative discretionary decisions may be involved. When police investigators are called upon to interpret the meaning of evidence, their discretion may be clouded by an adversarial stance that they have adopted. Their concern may be to confirm guilt rather than to seek the truth, and thus material evidence may be overlooked or ambiguous data may be improperly classified.[19]

Decisions about priority

Even when police have determined that a matter is appropriately theirs to respond to, and how that matter is to be understood, questions remain about whether to intervene and how much to invest in any response. Police must "prioritize" the situation – consider it in relation to other demands that confront them, determine whether it warrants their intervention, and what resources they should devote to it. When a law enforcement decision comes into conflict with a social welfare decision, how are the priorities to be determined? Do enforcement decisions generally take precedence? Under what conditions, if any, may officers engage in selective enforcement of the law?

No one seriously challenges the idea that police should have some discretion about the priority they give to the demands that confront them. There is, however, considerable controversy about the extent to which that discretionary authority should extend to matters of law enforcement. Although selective enforcement is commonly practiced, and even encouraged,[20] Jeffrey Reiman argues powerfully that it should be rejected as an essentially tyrannous use of state power. Although an ideal world might be ruled by philosopher-kings, capable of discerning and choosing the good on a case-by-case basis, the world we inhabit does not enable us to identify such wise rulers, and we must therefore substitute the rule of law for rule by men: "we must settle for second best – meet and make laws and hold everyone strictly accountable."[21] Recasting this Platonic perception for contemporary consumption, Reiman claims that those who value a free society, and who eschew the idea that there are natural rulers, would choose a society in which the rule of law prevails. It is not the task of those with political power to realize certain general ends, such as freedom, but only to accomplish certain limited tasks as embodied in law. Selective enforcement violates that mandate.

Tactical decisions

Once a decision has been made to devote resources to a situation, police must determine how to handle it. To some extent, of course, the tactics chosen will be a function of the resources that have been invested. But there is more to it than that. A police officer who must intervene in a dispute may have to decide whether to act mediatorially or to "come on strong," whether to ask a question directly or to be more circumspect or even deceptive. Are there similarities here between the tactical decisions of police and courtroom lawyers? Do police owe the same level of zeal to the public as lawyers do to their clients? Do they enjoy the same "immunity" from ordinary moral constraints in zealously serving the public?

Howard Cohen addresses the tactical question at its broadest level: what should generally characterize police discretion when tactical judgments are made? He contends that objectivity is called for in discretionary decision making.[22] Although the appeal to objectivity is intended, negatively, to exclude actions motivated by idiosyncratic personal preference, its positive characterization is more controversial. It may be understood either as an appeal to the impersonal demands of "professional service," or by reference to the interpersonal demands of an articulated community interest in "safety and security for all citizens with minimal encroachment on individual liberty."[23] Following Richard Rorty, Cohen favors the latter.

But, as John Pittman argues, Rortyan solidarity may not be easy to achieve in a community that is deeply divided.[24] Although Cohen believes that the more actively engaged police are with the communities they serve, the more likely it is that they will be able to represent a community-wide interest in their discretionary judgments, Pittman considers that our social order manifests a much more fundamental conflict of interests.

The issue of tactical discretion is raised in a somewhat different way by David Wasserman, Howard McGary, and Arthur Applbaum.[25] Partly because police possess limited resources and wish to use efficiently those that they have, they sometimes profile suspects, and in so doing make use of race-based descriptors. In a society that must still struggle with racial prejudice and discrimination, is it acceptable that police incorporate race-based descriptors into their investigative and protective strategies?[26]

Both Wasserman and McGary suggest that though reliance on race-based profiles cannot – and perhaps should not – be completely purged from police decision making, it should be minimized through police training designed to improve their skills in social discrimination.[27] To the extent that police are able to appeal to other characteristics of people in deciding how to act, they will reduce their reliance on invidious appeals to race. McGary, however, more so than Wasserman, is skeptical of the ability of police to practice increased social discrimination in advance of a more general societal rejection of racist attitudes and practices.[28] Nevertheless, he is not despairing of possibilities for a less troublesome contact between police and the communities they serve.

The complexities and problems of using racial generalizations are spelled out in greater detail by Arthur Applbaum. After bracketing the issue of race, and after distinguishing three significantly different situations in which group-based generalizations might be employed to target an individual, Applbaum asks whether an innocent person who is targeted as a result of a presumably accurate group-based generalization has a ground for complaint. In some cases, he allows, an individual might reasonably complain about the violation of privacy, the insult to dignity, and the undermining of a sense of security. But not always. When the bracket is removed, however, and it is allowed that race is the basis for the group-based generalization, the situation is significantly altered. For so corrupting has racism been in American social life, that respectful targeting is unlikely to be possible.[29]

JUSTIFYING POLICE DISCRETIONARY AUTHORITY

The implicitly normative dimension to police discretion is recognized in speaking of exercises of police discretion as exercises of discretionary *authority*. Whence comes this authority? Is it a creature of law, of popular consent, of tradition, of the demand for moral integrity or authenticity, or of expertise? Does it have some other form of legitimation? Or is it, perhaps, an illegitimately claimed authority? The question goes to the very heart of police power – its normative sources and limits – and provides an essential element in the discussion of discretion. Beyond that, moreover, it is necessary to explore the more specific sources of discretionary authority – in situational demands, in patrol officer competence, and in the penumbra of indeterminacy that attaches to particular rules, concepts, and situations.

Reiman and Cohen articulate one possible justification for police discretionary authority, namely, social contract. For Reiman, this would not require the actual consent of the governed, but only a judgment as to what powers it would be reasonable for people to grant to the police. His own judgment about what discretionary authority it would be reasonable for people to grant excludes selective enforcement, and though other authors might not oppose it so resolutely, several of them suggest that in this area police may claim too much discretion.

Reiman believes that in the prosecution of their limited tasks there is (and should be) no grant of authority to police to enforce the law selectively. The grant of discretion would render the laws "vague and uncertain"; its exercise would constitute a nonrepresentative amendment to the existing law; it would almost surely be used in discriminatory fashion; and it adds to the power of police.[30] Following Montesquieu, Reiman argues that the discretionary activity of selective enforcement violates the doctrine of separation of powers by granting to police legislative as well as executive power.[31]

Reiman's respondent, William Heffernan, finds himself in general agreement with the foregoing position. But because a society or law may sometimes be patently unjust, he is not as resolutely opposed to selective enforcement. In Heffernan's view, the presumption against selective enforcement is grounded in a social division of labor in which we rely on police to enforce the community's laws. Even in a just society, however, where the laws are just, there may be some limited room for selective enforcement. Systemic shortages in resources may make it appropriate for police to promulgate policies of nonenforcement. Heffernan believes that for some forms of selective enforcement, the police might expect to gain community support.[32]

Reiman's rejection of selective enforcement is subtly qualified by his recognition that the task of police is not only law enforcement but also order maintenance, and that sometimes a more immediate goal of order maintenance is better achieved by not arresting when it would be legal to do so.[33] This is an important qualification, and raises a larger question about the way in which police should be expected to balance the various general demands that are placed upon them: the crisis-intervention and welfare demands, along with those of law enforcement and order maintenance.

CONTROLLING AND IMPROVING POLICE
DISCRETIONARY DECISION MAKING

As a form of social recognition, police discretionary authority is sustained by a belief that those who exercise it are accountable for their decisions. Because discretionary decision making involves the exercise of individual judgment, rather than the mechanical application of predetermined rules, it is also subject to undemocratic, unfair, and discriminatory uses.

Several authors show how aspects of the larger culture may impact deleteriously on the exercise of discretion. Racism and sexism, for example, often manifest themselves in police work.[34]

Candace McCoy suggests that there are elements within the culture of the criminal justice system itself that may distort the proper exercise of discretion. She claims that the adversarial character of trial proceedings has corrupted both prosecutorial and police discretion prior to trial. A prosecutor's first ethical duty is to pursue the truth rather than trial advantage, and prosecutorial discretion should be exercised in a manner that reflects this.[35] The same should also hold of police, though McCoy argues that their habitual suspiciousness may prejudice their discretionary decisions during the investigative phase of their work. Detectives, she suggests, tend to work on the assumption that "everyone is guilty unless proven innocent."[36] McCoy's respondent, Robert Jackall, is skeptical of her descriptions of both prosecutors and detectives. He claims that the alliance between prosecutors and police is tenuous at best, and that rather than emphasizing the adversarialness of police, it would be closer to the reality of detective work to say that they see themselves as champions of victims.

A good deal has been written about the various social mechanisms of accountability that exist – internal mechanisms such as the chain of command, administrative rule making, and internal affairs divisions, and external mechanisms such as legislature and judiciary, civilian review and media scrutiny.[37] Not as much attention has been given to the appropriate role of these various mechanisms. What parameters of discretion are properly left to police to set? What parameters should be given some wider (extra-departmental) scrutiny? Is there an "order of scrutiny," like a system of checks and balances, that should determine when an issue of discretion is appropriately handled on a departmental basis and when it should come before some external review process? To answer these questions, we must come to terms with the thorny issues of community and police professionalism. Is there a communal constituency to whom or to which police are ultimately answerable? Is it a consensus? a majority? a tradition? a constitution? And are the decisions that police are called upon to make of a kind that entitles them to whatever privileges may be implied in professional self-regulation?

The increasing commitment to community policing within the United States and elsewhere makes it important that consideration be given not only to the control of police discretion, but also to its enhancement. The more rule-bound and the less challenging police work is, the less it will attract and nurture people who will be creatively involved with the communities in which they work. Yet with greater discretionary powers the possibilities for inequitable treatment and corruption increase. How, then, may police discretionary authority be understood so that responsibility to the community may be fostered?

Fyfe emphasizes the importance of having police set clear goals and priorities for themselves, and he argues that chiefs have a particularly crucial role in seeing that these are implemented. Cohen, Wasserman, and McGary focus on the need for officers to interact with the communities they serve, and point to various mechanisms whereby fruitful engagement may be increased. McCoy looks to a prosecutorially led commitment to non-adversarial fact-finding in pretrial investigations. Each of these options has its merits and problems, and it is likely that effective solutions will need to take account of local conditions as much as any general theoretical considerations.

The chapters presented here should be seen as contributions to an ongoing debate. Although the essays have been revised to take account of the lively and productive discussion that followed their initial presentation, none of the authors would wish to claim that the key ethical questions have been decisively answered. Rather, we hope that the debate here joined will now be joined by many others.

NOTES

An early version of this introduction benefited considerably from the comments of David Wasserman.

1. Samuel Walker, *Taming the System: The Control of Discretion in Criminal Justice, 1950-1990* (New York: Oxford University Press, 1993), p. 6.

2. For a published analysis of part of the survey, see Wayne R. LaFave and Frank J. Remington, *Arrest: The Decision to Take a Suspect into Custody* (Boston: Little Brown & Co., 1967). The material is summarized at length in Samuel Walker, "Origins of the Contemporary Criminal Justice Paradigm: The American Bar Foundation Survey 1953-1969," *Justice Quarterly* 9 (March 1992), pp. 201-30.

3. Charles Rowan and Richard Mayne, *[General] Instructions* (London: HMSO, 1829), pp. 1-2

4. Kenneth Culp Davis, *Discretionary Justice: A Preliminary Inquiry* (Baton Rouge: Louisiana State University Press, 1969); idem, *Police Discretion* (St. Paul: West, 1975).

5. Davis, *Discretionary Justice*, p. 4.

6. Joan McGregor, "From the State of Nature to Mayberry: The Nature of Police Discretion," infra, p. 52.

7. Ronald Dworkin, *Taking Rights Seriously* (Cambridge: Harvard University Press, 1977), p. 31.

8. James J. Fyfe, "Structuring Police Discretion," infra, pp. 198-99.

9. Dworkin, *Taking Rights Seriously*, p. 31.

10. Ibid., p. 32.

11. Ibid., p. 31.

12. The title of this collection trades on this ambiguity.

13. Michael Davis, "Police, Discretion, and Professions," infra, esp. pp. 17-26.

12   John Kleinig

14. McGregor, "From the State of Nature to Mayberry," infra, esp. pp. 49-51.
15. Vidar Halvorsen, "Response," infra, p. 44.
16. Fyfe, "Structuring Police Discretion," p. 192.
17. Ibid., pp. 198-99.
18. Ibid., p. 199.
19. Candace McCoy, "Police, Prosecutors, and Discretion in Investigation," infra, esp. pp. 170-71.
20. See the quotation from the IACP Police Code of Conduct in John Kleinig, "Response," infra, p. 68.
21. Jeffrey Reiman, "Is Police Discretion Justified in a Free Society?" infra, p. 73.
22. Howard Cohen, "Police Discretion and Police Objectivity," infra, p. 92. McCoy, too, emphasizes the importance of objectivity when considering interpretative discretion ("Police, Prosecutors, and Discretion in Investigation," p. 172).
23. Cohen, "Police Discretion and Police Objectivity," p. 103.
24. John P. Pittman, "Response: Rortyan Policing?," infra, pp. 108-9.
25. David Wasserman, "Racial Generalizations and Police Discretion," infra, pp. 115-30; Howard McGary, "Police Discretion and Discrimination," infra, pp. 131-44; Arthur Applbaum, "Racial Generalization, Police Discretion, and Bayesian Contractualism," infra, pp. 145-57.
26. The use of racially based profiles may of course be incorporated into organizational policy, and not be used just to guide discretionary practice. Yet, because such profiles are frequently appealed to in support of discretionary decisions, and racial discrimination constitutes one of the most pressing problems of police discretion, it is appropriately discussed in this context.
27. Wasserman, "Racial Generalizations and Police Discretion," pp. 123-25; McGary, "Police Discretion and Discrimination," p. 139.
28. McGary, "Police Discretion and Discrimination," p. 140.
29. Applbaum, "Racial Generalization," pp. 155-57.
30. Reiman, "Is Police Discretion Justified in a Free Society?" pp. 78-79.
31. Ibid., p. 80.
32. William C. Heffernan, "Response: Police Discretion to Arrest," infra, pp. 88-89.
33. Reiman, "Is Police Discretion Justified in a Free Society?" pp. 71-72.
34. See, e.g., the papers by McGregor, Pittman, Wasserman, and McGary.
35. McCoy, "Police, Prosecutors, and Discretion in Investigation," p. 172.
36. Ibid., p. 164.
37. See, e.g., Herman Goldstein, Policing a Free Society (Cambridge, MA: Ballinger, 1977); Douglas W. Perez, Common Sense about Police Review (Philadelphia: Temple University Press, 1994); Jerome Skolnick and Candace McCoy, "Police Accountability and the Media," ABF Research Journal, no. 3 (summer 1984), pp. 521–57; Gregory Howard Williams, "Police Rulemaking Revisited: New Thoughts on an Old Problem," Law & Contemporary Problems 47, no. 4 (autumn 1984), pp. 123–83.

Chapter 1

Police, Discretion, and Professions

Michael Davis

Discretion has seemed an important problem in criminal justice since its discovery in the 1950s.[1] Why? What was discovered? What made it a problem? These are not rhetorical questions. Police (as well as prosecutors, criminal-court judges, and others with whom they work) seem to be the only group whose discretion has had to be discovered or, being discovered, has been designated a problem.

A decade ago, George Fletcher titled his contribution to a law journal's special issue on the problem "Some Unwise Reflections about Discretion." His reflections were supposedly "unwise" (that is, I think, imprudent) because they should have had the same effect as turning up the lights at a teen party. While all the other contributors were happily finding discretion in the law's dark corners, Fletcher argued that their happiness depended on their engaging in semantic hanky-panky. Discretion is both easy to find and important only if one embraces a loose definition. Return to ordinary usage and most discretion disappears – and most of what remains is uninteresting.[2] There should have been a roar of pain, a barrage of criticism. Instead, there was nothing. Though Fletcher's reflections should have been unwise, they proved merely ineffective. It was as if he had turned up the lights on a party of the blind.

What I propose to do here is to add my unwise reflections to his, hoping the blind will feel the heat even if they do not see the light. I proceed in three stages. First, I try to understand what it is about the police that might make their discretion seem important. Second, I try to say what their discretion is. Though much of what I say paraphrases Fletcher, I do add to his distinctions and argue something he did not, namely, that we should exchange talk of controlling police discretion for talk of standardizing police conduct, as a way to save what is important in the "problem of police discretion" without abusing "discretion." Third, I illustrate the benefits of this exchange by suggesting two useful, but generally over-looked, ways to control discretion that some professions have used to standardize their conduct (without worrying whether the standardization has anything to do with controlling discretion). I hope these suggestions reach those whom Fletcher's reflections missed.

I. POLICE

The police, if they are a profession, are certainly an odd one.[3] Except for the military, they are the only profession that trains members to march, routinely orders them about, and treats obedience as an important virtue. The police have the military's love of rank, weapons, medals, and ceremony (for example, military-style funerals for members). Like the military, the police wear uniforms. In this respect, they are clearly distinct from various bureaus of investigation, including the detectives within their own departments, who do not wear uniforms. Though a beat officer can be promoted to detective, the line between uniformed *officer* and civilian *detective* seems to be important. Like the beat officer, the chief of police often wears a uniform (especially on ceremonial occasions).[4]

Though the uniform, weapons, and ceremonies all suggest a military organization, police differ from the military in several ways. The police generally do not bear themselves with military stiffness (even though the military is an important source of police recruits). The military is an agent of policy, working primarily by applying overwhelming force. Civilians are at best irrelevant and at worst obstacles to military objectives. Police, in contrast, are agents of law working primarily among civilians whom they are supposed to "serve and protect" (as Chicago's patrol cars say). Much of what they do is talk, asking questions, giving warnings, advising, and so on. The police generally work alone or in pairs, seldom in the compact bodies characteristic of combat soldiers (and necessary to maintain discipline among them).[5] In this respect, they resemble fighter pilots rather than soldiers. They also resemble pilots in generally being in close communication with their base.[6] But pilots are well-educated officers. Officers on patrol are in fact the lowest rank in a police department (apart from civilians) – what the military would call "enlisted men" to distinguish them from "officers." Though police officers are increasingly college graduates, they remain "foot soldiers" under the command of sergeants, lieutenants, captains, commanders, and so on. The title "police officer" – like its English counterpart, "constable" – is as etymologically odd as "cleaning lady."[7]

Like many of our professions, the police are a relatively recent invention. They appear in Europe in the late eighteenth century; in the English-speaking world, only in the nineteenth. They replaced "peace officers" – the watch in the cities, the town marshal and deputies, the magistrate, the justice of the peace, the county sheriff, and so on – who did not wear a uniform. These older peace officers would have been known to the locals (which may be one reason they were not uniformed), though like today's police they generally wore a badge of office and considered themselves "bound to do their sworn duty." In addition to these civilians, there were, in an emergency, the heavily armed and uniformed strangers – state militia or federal troops.[8]

Today's municipal police seem to be a union of these two kinds of peace officers (as if the cities were in a permanent emergency).[9] Uniformed and disciplined in a way the watch was not, they nonetheless move about like the watch, following a regular beat and carrying only light weapons (nightstick or pistol). They are not soldiers, though analogies with soldiers are common and often illuminating. Is their purpose to enforce the law, to preserve order, to catch criminals, to discourage crime, to reassure citizens that help is close at hand even in a sea of strangers – or some combination of these or other purposes? I do not know. The purpose of the police – their function or justification – may be as complex and poorly understood as the purpose of any other large institution criminal punishment, for example.

Indeed, it is possible that, like many other institutions, the police have no uncontroversial purpose. The police seem originally to have had as many purposes as organizers.[10] And even if the police originally had a single uncontroversial purpose, policing may have changed so much that they can serve that purpose no longer – or, serving it, can be understood only as serving it along with many others, all competing for the same limited resources. We must, I think, try to understand the problem of police discretion without a philosophy of police (or risk having this brief chapter turn into a book). We must try to understand the problem of police discretion as a product of various side-constraints, both moral and practical – constraints with at least as much urgency and legitimacy as those deriving from any theory of policing's goals or functions.

The uniform may be an important clue. The uniform would, of course, have identified the police as peace officers in the great cities where ordi-

Michael Davis

nary citizens would not know them personally. In this respect, the uniform was more effective than a badge (visible only from the front). But I think there is more to the uniform than that: the uniform would promise standardization. The nineteenth century was the great age of standardization and uniforms, and police attire may represent another attempt to make a previously disorderly process relatively uniform.

II. DISCRETION

Where does discretion come in? One way to look at discretion is as a threat to standardization. Since Kenneth Culp Davis's work on discretion is well known, let us begin with one of the few examples of police discretion he actually gives:

> A statute, an ordinance, and a police manual all provide that a policeman "shall" arrest all known violators of law. A policeman lectures a boy from a middle-class neighborhood, but he arrests a boy from the slums, although he knows that both are equally guilty of violating the same statute. Because the evidence against both boys is clear, the policeman's decision is the only one that counts, for the release of the first boy is permanent and the conviction of the second follows almost automatically. . . . [S]uperiors in the department could know all the facts without disapproving.[11]

What bothers Davis here, it seems, is not only that the officer's conduct is illegal (against statute, ordinance, and manual) and unjust (that is, treats like cases differently), but that "no standard, meaningful or otherwise, guides the policeman's decision."[12] Davis does not, of course, mean that there is no standard to guide the officer. Davis himself lists three: statute, ordinance, and manual. The problem for Davis is that the officer did not have to do as the standards required. They were ineffective. The officer's conduct could be and was, in fact, lawless (in an obvious sense).

We might, then, wonder why Davis counts this as an example of police discretion. Why did not statute, ordinance, and manual triply eliminate the officer's discretion? After all, we do not speak of criminals, even those who commit the perfect crime, as presenting a problem of discretion. How does the police officer of Davis's example differ from an ordinary criminal? What is discretion here?[13] To answer that question, we must consider the senses in which "discretion" is now used. Fletcher distinguishes four: judgment, discernment, liberty, and license (as we may call them).[14] We might as well follow his lead, adding here and there. In each sense, discretion works against standardization; in some, it also works against ordinary usage; but in only one (technical discretion-as-license) does it work against standardization in just the way Davis requires.

Discretion-as-judgment

In *discretion-as-judgment* (Fletcher's "personal input"), "discretionary decisions" are contrasted with decisions that are "routine," "mechanical," "ministerial," or "rule-bound." A routine decision is essentially algorithmic: two clerks, with ordinary competence and the same book of rules, would ordinarily reach the same result.[15] The decision maker contributes nothing special. Her opinion does not matter. Any difference in result would mean that at least one of the decision makers had made an error (something easily shown by examining what they did). Ordinary math problems are routine in this way.

Where judgment is required, the decision is no longer routine. Judgment brings knowledge, skill, and insight to bear in unpredictable ways. Where judgment is necessary, different decision makers, however skilled, may disagree without either being clearly wrong. The judgment is a "matter of [expert] opinion." Over time, we may be able to tell that some decision makers are better than others, but we will not, decision by decision, be able to explain differences in outcome merely by error – or even be able to establish decisively that one decision maker's judgment is better than another's.

This way of explaining the difference between routine decisions and judgment, although accurate, glosses over a distinction that, though unimportant in itself, may cause confusion if unexplicated. We must distinguish between what we may call "habitual" (or "subconscious") and "explicitly" rule-bound decisions. Both exclude discretion-as-judgment; both are routine, mechanical, and so on, but not in the same way. What is the difference? Consider:

The military has traditionally wanted soldiers to obey orders "without hesitation," that is, without thinking about what the order means or why it was given. The ideal soldier is a "killing machine," killing only when, where, and how he is told. Though probably no soldier can (or should) achieve this ideal, approaching it makes sense in the highly coordinated environment of the battlefield. Where there is little time for thought, obeying an officer's order unthinkingly (but appropriately) will generally be better than taking the time to evaluate it. The mind-numbing repetition so characteristic of military life seems well designed to make obedience more or less habitual (to make it possible, as the drill sergeants say, "to do it in your sleep").[16] Habitual obedience, however, is not a substitute for skill or knowledge; it is skill and knowledge. Habit is what gives ordinary soldiers instant access to the complex routines that constitute much of what the military knows. So, for example, a skilled soldier knows how to march in formation with as little thought as he gives to walking.

Although habitual decisions are more or less unthinking, a sort of second nature below the notice of the decision maker, explicitly rule-bound decisions are not. They require a conscious reference to rules. They may even require considerable thought (as in a complex math problem). What distinguishes them from decisions involving judgment is their standardization, for example, their indifference to what the decision maker happens to know (so long as she meets some minimum standard). Tennyson caught explicitly rule-bound decision at its noblest:

"Forward, the Light Brigade!"
Was there a man dismayed?
Not though the soldier knew
    Someone had blundered.
Theirs not to make reply,
Theirs not to reason why,
Theirs but to do or die.
Into the valley of Death
    Rode the six hundred.[17]

The Light Brigade did not charge into massed cannon merely out of a habit of obedience, though habit doubtless helped. Aware that something had gone wrong, they still obeyed because of a certain conception of their role ("Theirs not to reason why,/Theirs but to do or die"). They consciously "worked to rule."

The battlefield repays rule-bound decision, whether habitual or explicit. Close coordination gives the military its distinctive power; and, on a battlefield, that power is usually what counts. Even if a soldier is right about his captain's tactical error, his attempt to do what his captain should have ordered, or even a moment's hesitation while he considers what to do, could throw a large mass of troops into terrified disorder, causing losses far greater than obeying the order would have.[18]

But rule-bound decision, whether habitual or explicit, is not a pure benefit. Indeed, rule-bound decision is the source of the distinctive stupidity of military power, its indifference to local circumstance and individual knowledge ("Orders are orders"). In an environment less regimented than a battlefield, taking into account local conditions not easily foreseen may repay any disorder that nonstandard responses introduce. Military standardization, though still possible, may then be relatively costly. So, for example, training (or instructing) police to arrest "all known violators of law" may mean fewer arrests of serious felons, more innocent bystanders injured, and more time spent outside courtrooms waiting to testify in minor cases than would training (or instructing) police to arrest only when they judge the arrest to be worth the trouble.[19] In some circumstances, rule-bound decision is better than judgment; in others, it is not. We must understand the circumstances to know which. Sometimes we lack that understanding.[20]

Whenever we say that a certain decision does not involve judgment, we implicitly assume a baseline of "ordinary competence." So, for example, when I described ordinary math problems as routine, I was, of course, assuming reasonably intelligent adults. For first-graders, even a simple math problem (say, multiplying 36 by itself) may require judgment, because "six-year-old clerks" would find any algorithm we gave them unintelligible.

This point, though obvious, is important. It suggests that, whatever Davis means by "discretion," he cannot mean discretion-as-judgment. If judgment were involved, then two clerks of ordinary competence (presumably, experienced officers) could reasonably disagree about whether the rules required that both boys be arrested – though Davis, lacking that experience, is certain the rules do require it.[21] Davis would have to explain why we should trust his judgment rather than that of those with (what appears to be) more relevant experience. Since I cannot see why Davis should put himself in that awkward position, I conclude that, whatever Davis means by "discretion," it cannot be discretion-as-judgment.

Discretion-as-mere-decision

We should take care not to conflate discretion-as-judgment with the less interesting sense in which "discretion" is equivalent to "choice" or "decision." Not all choices or decisions require judgment. For example, I do not need judgment to know what answer to put down for a routine math problem (though I must still decide to put down that answer rather than another or none at all). Fletcher's term "decisional autonomy" seems to me unfortunate because it might be interpreted to mean even this *discretion-as-mere-decision*. After all, autonomy (literally "self-rule") may seem to be achieved wherever *I* make the decision, not someone else. I rule, not he. But, it seems to me, this is not yet *self*-rule. I have made no personal contribution. I have just "mechanically" carried out the will of another (though by my own decision). In philosophy, autonomy is generally thought to require (and, on some theories, to consist in) a personal contribution to one's decisions. Not every decision is autonomous.

Though discretion-as-decision seems far from any of Fletcher's four senses, it seems to me common in writing about discretion. Often, a discussion of discretion would lose nothing (and gain both in clarity and compactness) were the word "discretion" and its transforms to be simply deleted wherever they appeared – for example, by striking the "discretionary" in "discretionary choice." What explains the literature's tendency to equate discretion with decision?

At least part of the explanation is that most examples of discretion-as-mere-decision involve another element, that is, finality or even nonaccountability. (Note, for example, Davis's observation that "the policeman's decision is the only one that counts.") Surely (it might be thought), where no one can reverse my decision, or even call me to account for it, I make the decision, not someone else. I have "decisional autonomy" or, at least, a "personal input". We can, I agree, correctly say that I do then have "decisional autonomy" and "personal input", but only in the uninteresting sense in which I have it whenever I make the decision, not someone else (whether I exercise judgment or not). The addition of practical or juridical finality or nonaccountability does not change the standard by which I am supposed to make the decision, only the ways in which the standard can be enforced. The decision may well be rule-bound ("mechanical"), though I make the decision and no one else can reverse it or call me to account for it. Though finality and nonaccountability can open the way for discretion in an interesting sense, it is (as I shall explain) as discretion-as-license, not as discretion-as-mere-decision.[22]

Discretion-as-discernment

Discretion-as-judgment is primarily a feature of particular decisions. (Where there is discretion-as-judgment, the decision in question requires judgment.) *Discretion-as-discernment* is, in contrast, primarily a feature of the decision maker. If the decision maker has discretion-as-discernment, she has a capacity for good judgment; she is "a person of discretion"; she can act discreetly; and her acts (within the appropriate domain) generally show it. A discreet act is simply an act characteristic of a discreet person. Discretion-as-discernment is a good disposition, a virtue.

Like most virtues, discretion-as-discernment may be exercised instantly, without conscious consideration, or only after deliberation; it may resemble the knowledge of habit or the painstaking following of rules. Discreet conduct meets a standard, discretion, but it is not therefore easy to predict. Those who are inexperienced, ill informed, or otherwise rendered undiscerning will, of course, have trouble anticipating much the discreet do. But even the discreet will have some trouble. Good judgment (like art) admits of degrees. Some exercises of judgment are merely satisfactory, some good or excellent, some wonderful. The best judgment may (like the best art) be impossible to anticipate and yet seem inevitable in retrospect. In general, the less good the judgment, the more predictable. But there is no certainty, no single "right answer," since, by definition, good judgment has no algorithm.

Because discretion-as-discernment is good *judgment*, there is a baseline problem for discretion-as-discernment just as for discretion-as-judgment. The problems are distinct, however. Because judgment is a fact about a decision, we can generally resolve its baseline problem decision by decision. But because discernment is a fact about the decision maker, any baseline for discernment must rely on a pattern of decision (a record of good judgments) or features of the person that promise good judgments (sensitivity, intelligence, knowledge, experience, good habits, and so on). How then do we decide in practice which decisions require discretion-as-discernment?

Suppose that a police manual says that handcuffs are to be "tight upon the arrestee's wrists, without cutting off circulation or breaking the skin." For new recruits that rule may be difficult to follow, while for an experienced officer it is easy. Does putting on cuffs require discretion-as-discernment? If we use new recruits as the baseline, the answer seems to be: yes, of course. But what if we use experienced officers? Does the fact that experienced officers find following the rule easy mean that tightening cuffs involves no judgment and so no discernment? Not necessarily. If different officers satisfy the rule in different ways, perhaps even explicitly disagreeing about which way is best, we could conclude that cuffing left room for judgment and, leaving room for that, left room for discernment too. Only if all experienced officers tightened cuffs in the same way would we have to conclude that they had internalized an algorithm – that, even for them, tightening cuffs left no room for discretion-as-discernment.

We have already noted that standardization can substitute for judgment. Because discretion-as-discernment presupposes judgment, standardization can substitute for discretion-as-discernment too. Indeed, the absence of adequate discernment may make standardization by habit or explicit rule necessary. For example, if we have a low opinion of the judgment of certain decision makers, we will want to leave as little to their judgment as possible. We will develop routines for them and hold them to those routines as best we can, tolerating whatever loss of sensitivity to particulars that might entail. Bureaucratization is probably best understood as the result of *over*standardizing administration. Bureaucracy differs from administration in requiring decision makers to "go by the book" even when a person of ordinary good sense could see that "the book" is wrong. Bureaucrats are soldiers armed with pens.[23]

Discretion-as-liberty

My fourth sense of discretion, *discretion-as-liberty*, differs from the first three in being a creature of rules, rather than an ordinary fact about a decision or a decision maker. It is a permission to choose among a certain range of options. Because it is a permission, it de-standardizes in a way that neither discretion-as-judgment nor discretion-as-discernment does. We can sometimes even see or hear the difference. For example, the traditional command "Fire at will" leaves a soldier at liberty to fire in a way the command "Don't fire till you see the whites of their eyes" does not. We have no trouble distinguishing between the ragged roar of firing at will and the sudden burst of firing upon "seeing the whites of their eyes."[24]

Generally, standardization is abandoned for liberty where standardization is too costly (where, that is, the benefits, though significant, do not cover the costs in training, supervision, punishment, and so on) or where standardization is actually detrimental (where, for example, soldiers firing on command would fire more slowly, and with less effect, than soldiers firing at will).

Discretion-as-liberty presupposes something like Ronald Dworkin's distinction between "rules" and "principles." Rules, if they apply, command; they can only be obeyed or disobeyed; if they contradict, one must preempt or both fail as rules. Principles, in contrast, weigh in judgment rather than command. They cannot be obeyed or disobeyed, merely given due consideration. Principles never contradict. To satisfy seemingly contradictory principles, we need only give each due weight in our deliberations.[25]

Discretion-as-liberty presupposes that the rules are rules in Dworkin's sense, that is, that they either explicitly grant permission to choose from a list of alternatives ("fire at will") or tacitly leave the decision maker at liberty (consider, for example, the lack of detail in some police manuals on questions such as when to make an arrest). Discretion-as-liberty does not, however, generally leave the decision maker free to do whatever she wants. Rules are not the only guides to action; principles guide action too.

The decision maker should always give due weight to relevant principles. For example, a soldier ordered to "fire at will" is still open to discipline for not firing at all (where he has a good chance of hitting the enemy). He is supposed to give due weight to the principles of warfare when deciding to fire. Discretion-as-liberty is a way to make room for a certain sort of discernment.[26]

Fletcher suggests that discretion-as-liberty differs from simple liberty, authority, or prerogative in presupposing the possibility of standardizing the conduct in question.[27] I agree. We grant discretion where we expect, overall, a better outcome than we could get by standardizing. Where we cannot standardize the conduct in question, we cannot have discretion. The liberty in question is not discretion but an inherent power, inalienable authority, natural prerogative, or the like. To think of discretion-as-liberty is to think of the liberty in question as a contingent permission ("the hole in the doughnut").

Discretion-as-liberty, however, is more than a contingent permission. We can have discretion only as part of a more general "office," that is, a special structure of powers and duties. I do not now have discretion to lease a car, even though I have the money and a contingent right (contingent, in part at least, because the Illinois legislature could tomorrow take it away by abolishing car leasing). I would, however, have discretion to lease a car if, say, my spouse gave me permission to act as agent of our family: "You decide this one." Even such a minor and transitory office as "family agent for this leasing decision" provides enough structure for discretion-as-liberty.

In ordinary usage, "judgment" has two senses: first, the sense we gave it in discretion-as-judgment (where it is almost a synonym for "opinion"); and second, the sense in which it means "good judgment" (as, for example, when we say someone has reached the "age of judgment"). In contrast, "discretion" seems, as Fletcher notes, not to have that first sense. To show discretion is to show good judgment, to be "discreet" rather than merely to make a judgment.[28] So when we speak of someone "exercising discretion" or just "having discretion" (without implying good judgment), we must mean discretion-as-liberty rather than discretion-as-judgment or discretion-as-mere-decision. We can have permission to choose, and indeed actually use that permission, without showing discretion.

"Discretion" meaning "judgment," then, is a term of art.[29] What is its appeal? Perhaps it is the focus on objective situations (does he have a choice, or even a creative choice?) rather than value judgments (did his choice show good judgment?). Social scientists have, until recently, been afraid of letting value judgments into their research (though they have nonetheless let them in). Perhaps now that they are losing that fear, they will find discretion-as-judgment less appealing. However that may be, discretion-as-judgment – unlike discretion-as-discernment or discretion-as-liberty (but like discretion-as-mere-decision) – seems to be a departure from ordinary usage that is in need of defense.

Discretion-as-license

Discretion-as-license, our last sense of discretion, refers to those situations where discretion exists "in fact" though not "in law." The source of discretion-as-license is not, as in discretion-as-liberty, the assent of rules (explicit or tacit), but a mere opportunity. Discretion-as-license differs from the other forms of discretion in always being "against the rules." Though Fletcher does not subdivide this category, I think we should, calling one sense "technical" and the other "substantive."

Technical discretion-as-license is what Mortimer and Sanford Kadish have called a "discretion to disobey."[30] It is close to discretion-as-liberty because it too presupposes a contingent permission. It differs from discretion-as-liberty only in presupposing permission after the act rather than before, a retroactive authorization. (Here "license" means something between "privilege" and "pardon.") The act in question is merely a "technical" violation of standards in at least two respects. First, once authorized (however retroactively) the conduct in question will cease to be a violation, except in a merely historical sense. Second, though literally contrary to the rules (at the time of the conduct), the conduct in question serves the purpose of the rules; it is lawful "in spirit." Reasonable people would not expect or want the rules to be obeyed in this circumstance. The conduct seems substandard only to those who lack full information or good judgment. Although it is unpredictable with respect to the rules ("law"), it may be predictable with respect to expectations ("order"). It is, then, nonstandard only in a sense – "a legal technicality."

Technical discretion-as-license requires the decision maker to go by the book or to act at her own risk. She has a contingent permission to depart from the rules, a license contingent on events subsequent to her decision. She may be wrong about the facts (for example, that arresting one party to a dispute, without adequate cause, will cool things off). She may also be wrong about how her superiors evaluate the facts. They may not only disagree with her judgment but deny that it fell within the range of competent decision making: "This was not a judgment call." Her decision will then be unlicensed; her conduct will have been "licentious" (the other sense of "license").[31] Her superiors, however, will not treat even such an "error in judgment" as ordinary wrongdoing; it will reflect on her competence, not on her character.

Technical discretion-as-license provides a strong incentive to go by the book while inviting the decision maker to choose a nonstandard course where circumstances *clearly* seem to call for one. Technical discretion-as-license requires discretion-as-discernment to work well.

Technical discretion-as-license has, I think, generally been lumped with the substantive sense (discretion as outright licentiousness). This other sense of discretion-as-license is clear, for example, in the "discretion" John Warner attributed to the police who spent the entire evening drinking in a bar when they were supposed to be patrolling the streets of Milwaukee.[32] To describe their conduct as an exercise of discretion seems to stretch the concept beyond the breaking point. Warner's police were acting contrary to orders without (we may suppose) reason to think that they served the law's purpose or should be treated as if they did. They had no discretion to spend their patrol in a bar. What they had was an opportunity to do so, with impunity, owing to the nonfeasance or misplaced trust of their superiors. Their conduct was virtually indistinguishable from that of an ordinary criminal. They had discretion only insofar as they did their drinking discreetly.[33]

This degenerate sense of discretion should not be dismissed, however, without noting what even it has in common with the other senses. Though "an exercise of discretion" seems the wrong way to describe the decision Warner's police made, describing it in that way does signal that it involves a failure of standardization (which, in fact, it does). The conduct in question was interesting precisely because it was (we may suppose) nonstandard, that is, both substandard and unusual. That even Warner's use of "discretion" involves standardization (or, more exactly, a failure to standardize) is evidence that, however unsatisfactory for that purpose, "police discretion" is a term of art designed to mark conduct falling short of some ideal of standardization. Police discretion is a problem precisely because the term "police discretion" implies an opportunity to standardize in some way or other.

We can, I think, now see that Davis supposed his example of the two boys to involve this licentious discretion. Yet what he actually says suggests something else, namely, discretion to disobey. Davis is, for example, clear that the officer's superiors "could know all the facts without disapproving." In addition, Davis is silent on questions that might be relevant to deciding whether the officer satisfied the spirit of the law. For instance:

Did experience show that giving a warning to a middle-class boy was likely to end his criminal career while doing the same for a slum boy was not? Would the slum boy require a few days in jail, a court appearance, a stern warning from a judge, and perhaps a few months of parole to "learn his lesson"? Were the answer to each of these questions yes, everyone (including the two boys) might be better off had the police officer warned one and arrested the other. Why not individualize justice in this way?

III. PROFESSIONS

To standardize is not simply to set standards but to achieve them (more or less). To standardize is to work at getting a uniformity desired but contrary to the normal course of things. Why standardize? Uniformity, as such, is no more a good than its opposite, variety; and standardizing, as such, is always an expense. A proposal to standardize, then, is always in need of defense, a defense having two parts: first, an explanation of what makes the standardization in question good; and second, an explanation of why that good is worth the cost.

Discussions of police discretion, including Davis's, often seem to assume (a) that variation in police conduct is, by definition, objectionable, (b) that the only way to set standards for police conduct is to state what is desired in rules, and (c) that the primary way to obtain police obedience to standards of any sort is by inspection and punishment. I find all three of these assumptions in need of more defense than they have received. I shall now briefly explain why.

What's wrong with nonstandard police conduct? The police are, it will be said, agents of the law, or "law officers" (as we sometimes call them). They are sworn to uphold the law. As the law's sworn agents, they should – more than anyone else – obey its commands. We ordinary citizens want them to. We especially want them to respect our legal rights.

These arguments are, I think, enough to establish a strong principle of legality governing police conduct. They are not, however, enough to establish an absolute rule. We can easily imagine situations in which we want the police to break the law – for example, to break down a door (technically violating a right of property) in order to save the life of someone inside who has just had a heart attack. Giving a second chance to a boy who will probably use it well, as in Davis's example, may be another example of a situation where other considerations seem to outweigh the principle of legality. We must think carefully, then, about how rule-bound we want the police to be.

Let me make this point another way. The problem of police discretion looks much like Aristotle's problem of the relation between justice and equity. If justice is law, then all conduct that does not satisfy the letter of the law is unjust. Since equity consists in departing from the letter of the law, equity must be unjust. But surely equity is not unjust (though, by definition, it departs from the letter of the law). What, then, is the relation between justice and equity? Aristotle's answer is much like my solution to the problem of police discretion:

> while it is true that equity is just and in some circumstances better than [legal] justice, it is not better than absolute justice. All we can say is that it is better than the error generated by the unqualified language in which absolute justice must be stated.[34]

What we have called technical discretion-as-license, it seems, is what Aristotle would call equitable decision (a justified departure from justified rules).

Understood in this way, the problem of police discretion is not whether the police should ever exercise technical discretion-as-license but how often they should. Interestingly, Davis seems to say something similar: "The proper goal is to eliminate unnecessary discretionary power, not to eliminate all discretionary power."[35] But everything depends on what Davis means by "unnecessary."

Because Davis is concerned with the "effective limits" of law, "necessary discretion" may simply mean "what cannot be eliminated by closer supervision" (or what cannot be eliminated at reasonable cost). That way of understanding "necessary" would treat police discretion as a "necessary evil" to be suppressed, as much as can be, by writing relatively easily enforced rules. The Aristotelian alternative is to interpret "necessary" to mean necessary for absolute justice. That way of understanding the problem would make some police illegality a good, not merely a necessary evil. The problem would then be how to allow for as much of the good as possible (consistent with also achieving other goods the police aim at or, at least, should aim at).

There are two objections to this Aristotelian approach. First, we should (it is said) keep police illegality to a minimum. The line between technical and substantive discretion-as-license is too thin; officers too easily cross the line and it is too hard for others – fellow officers as well as supervisors or the public – to tell which side of the line an officer is on. Second, there are always two no-cost alternatives to technical discretion-as-license: (a) rewriting the rules to create some discretion-as-liberty (for example, by substituting "may" for "shall"); and (b) rewriting the rules to leave decisions of that kind to the officer's judgment (for example, "shall arrest, *except when the officer believes the arrest would not serve the ends of justice*").

I have no doubt that such rewriting would sometimes be a good idea. But I do doubt that such rewriting is often without cost. Davis is quite good on the political barriers to such rewriting, including both issues of liability and the public's view that policing should be more or less a ministerial function.[36] But what Davis seems not to have noticed is that such rewriting may actually mean more bad decisions. Where a police officer bears the burden of showing that his conduct, though illegal, was in the spirit of the law, his burden is generally much heavier than when the conduct is legal and he need show only that. All else being equal, as the burden of proof necessary to justify conduct goes down, the more previously doubtful conduct will become clearly permissible. Although "discretion to disobey" tends to restrict the conduct in question to the clearest cases, discretion-as-liberty or discretion-as-judgment does not. That is certainly a cost to take note of.

If we want police to exercise discretion, whether technical discretion-as-license, discretion-as-liberty, or just discretion-as-discernment, does that mean we must allow police conduct to be lawless in that respect?[37] If "lawless" means "without standard," the answer is no. Even equity has a standard, namely "absolute justice." Equitable judgment is "lawless" only in the sense of being an exception to laws (that is, rules). There is no reason to suppose that we must leave police without standards just because we leave something to their discernment.[38] We can lay down various principles of justice to guide them – "Consult all parties," "Be fair to everyone," "Protect the helpless," and so on. We can also provide principles of interest (policies) – "Try not to cause a riot," "Don't take on more than you can handle," and so. We can even provide examples of good practice (ideals) which they can try to approach.[39]

The crux of the problem of police discretion may now seem to be enforcement. How can we get police to do what they should, especially when the guidance we give them is, in part, not in mandatory rules, violation of which is relatively easy to detect, but in principles and ideals, which cannot be violated, merely given less weight in deliberations than they deserve. How can a police department adequately supervise an officer's deliberations when those deliberations involve judgments about which even experienced officers may disagree (made in circumstances that often do not even allow the deliberations to be recorded)?

The answer, I think, is that a police department cannot adequately supervise such deliberations. Or, at least, it cannot without undue increase in supervisory personnel, bureaucratization, and bad decisions. Police discretion is a problem for those who want to understand police work as essentially ministerial. For those who are willing to recognize that police work is much more than rule following, the problem comes to resemble a problem that every profession faces. You cannot both have the advantages of someone's judgment and completely control what they decide. Insofar as someone must work to rule (that is, exercise only "necessary discretion"), he cannot rule his work (have "decisional autonomy"); insofar as he does rule his work, he cannot simply work to rule. If we agree that police officers know much that their superiors do not, and that we want that knowledge to enter appropriately into their decision making, we have already agreed that we do not want them to work to rule. If we want their discretion (their discretion-as-discernment), we must move away from the military-style, command-and-control hierarchy of today's police organization.[40] We must leave police room for (something like) professional judgment.

Leaving the police room for professional judgment does not mean leaving them alone, without standards and without ways to realize those standards in their common undertaking. Leaving room for professional judgment means merely that we must adopt strategies of standardization that substitute for the close supervision so characteristic of police organization today. Here the professions provide a rich store of alternatives. For our purposes, two illustrations should do. Those who wish for more may look into the literature of professional ethics.

One strategy for helping police to exercise their judgment properly is training designed to help them recognize when they are making equitable decisions, to understand what justifies their making such decisions, and to help them make better ones. Police training probably should include many hours going over situations, evaluating alternatives, giving reasons for them, and having others criticize what the trainees have to say. Police probably need a course in police ethics on the scale of the courses that law students today take in legal ethics, medical students in medical ethics, and ROTC students in military ethics.[41]

Police also need ways to help them integrate such training into daily practice. Although most discussions of police discretion seem to lump police with lawyers, judges, and other government administrators with whom they work, that may be a mistake. Police differ from these occupations in at least one striking way. Police seldom have much time for deliberation. Generally, they must depend on instinct, habit, or memory, rather than, for example, library research, when deciding to make an arrest.

For police, then, rules – especially if they are both complex and often changed – may in practice be the same as no rules at all (except, of course, insofar as they tend to generate paperwork, cynicism about rules, and other signs of bureaucracy). In this respect, police resemble hospital surgeons much more than either resemble lawyers, judges, or the like. Theirs is not a contemplative calling. We might then find suggestive one strategy hospitals have of standardizing surgeon conduct at a relatively high level.

Hospitals generally have a regular, often daily, meeting of surgeons, the mortality and morbidity conference, in which surgeons report on deaths or serious injuries to patients under their care. These reports are presented in the form: "This is what I did. It didn't work. What went wrong? How can I do better next time?" This is not a debriefing under the watchful eyes of supervisors: each surgeon will report to the rest in turn, and each will in turn sit in judgment on the rest. The conference has the effect of reinforcing for everyone present the standards in question, not as a top-down command but as part of their common knowledge. It also allows for the open discussion and evaluation of alternatives. A surgeon will quickly learn whether her failure was "just one of those things" or the result of some act clearly unacceptable to those she respects. She will also get advice about what to do next time, each advisor's guidance offered under the watchful eyes of other experts and subject to their immediate correction, if not the common wisdom. She is not prey to the single offhand comment made in the hall or locker room.[42]

Of course, strategies like extensive ethics training or the morality and morbidity conference could not substitute entirely for today's method of standardizing police by top-down rule and supervision. Even surgeons are subject to criminal law, to other legal controls (especially civil suits for malpractice), and to many hospital regulations. I do not offer these strategies as complete substitutes for rule and supervision but as alternatives deserving consideration where the more restrictive controls – for example, rules discouraging discretion-as-discernment or supervision eliminating technical discretion-as-license – are relatively costly.[43]

The notion of relative cost, of course, is itself a difficult matter. Insofar as the ends of policing are controversial, insofar as people may disagree on the side-constraints morality places on police conduct, and insofar as people disagree about the facts (for example, the relative probability of a middle-class boy and a slum boy responding to a warning in the same way), people may disagree as well about the relative cost of my alternatives. I nonetheless offer them as a way of opening discussion of police discretion to modes of standardization generally ignored.

NOTES

I should like to thank John Kleinig for guiding my reading on police discretion and for many helpful comments on the first draft of this chapter; Vidar Halvorsen for comments that both improved the next draft generally and prevented one significant error; and other members of the workshop out of which this chapter grew for a number of useful discussions.

1. "Prior to the late 1950s, the leading experts in the field [of criminal justice] barely acknowledged its existence, much less saw it as a central problem. The relatively recent discovery of discretion is an important part of the story. . . ." Samuel Walker, *Taming the System: The Control of Discretion in Criminal Justice, 1950-1990* (New York: Oxford University Press, 1993), p. 6.

2. George P. Fletcher, "Some Unwise Reflections about Discretion," *Law & Contemporary Problems* 47 (autumn 1984), pp. 269-86.

3. For reasons to leave open the question of the professional status of police, see Michael Davis, "Do Cops Need a Code of Ethics?" *Criminal Justice Ethics* 10 (summer/fall 1991), pp. 14-28.

4. Nursing, I think, is the only other profession, besides the military, that has an everyday uniform. Why does this most peaceful of occupations resemble the military and police in this way? How important is the traditional role of nurses as merely carrying out doctor's orders? How important is it that, like police, they work largely with strangers who do not choose them? I should perhaps point out that answering these questions answers only one of two questions concerning police uniforms: Why any uniform at all? The other question, perhaps the more interesting one, is: Why is the uniform so distinctly military (as the nurse's uniform is not)? Why not a tie and jacket like an airplane steward? There is actually some empirical research suggesting that changing to such a civilian uniform might be a good idea. See D. F. Gundersen, "Credibility and the Police Uniform," *Journal of Police Science Administration* 15 (1987), pp. 192-95.

5. Riots, hostage situations, and raids seem to be the chief settings where police work in groups in the way the military do. In such settings, police departments today generally call upon specially trained units (for example, SWAT teams). Ordinary police seem to lack the discipline necessary for such quasi-military operations. Interestingly, this does not seem always to have been so. For example, the London Metropolitan Police appear to have initially made their reputation by dispersing large mobs and otherwise preventing urban riots (without loss of life). Until then, such riots had to be put down by troops firing upon the crowds. See Charles Reith, *A New Study of Police History* (Edinburgh: Oliver & Boyd, 1956), esp. pp. 156-59. (What about ordinary crowd control today? Police seem to manage this better than the military, even though large numbers of police are involved, perhaps because ordinary crowds must be treated as citizens, not as enemies.)

6. Even in these days of cheap communications equipment, the military still generally requires soldiers in the field to go through a lieutenant (or other field

officer) to communicate with headquarters. The military has not decentralized communication nearly as much as technology allows. They have tried to preserve the command structure, keeping the flow of information into headquarters manageable.

7. "Constable" is derived from the Latin *comes stabuli* ("count of the stable"), originally the official in charge of the emperor's horses, later the head of the household army. See Eric Partridge, *Origins: A Short Etymological Dictionary of Modern English* (New York: Macmillan, 1958), p. 117.

8. Where do the Texas Rangers fit in? They have become state police, but they were not police, militia, or lawmen when founded in 1835 (that is, about five years after the London Metropolitan Police). "Ranger" originally meant "a horseman who could range across the open plains," something close to what we now mean by "cowboy." Until after the Civil War, Texas Rangers seem to have served exclusively as a paramilitary force protecting the frontier from Indians, units being organized for a short period and then disbanded. They became peace officers relatively late in their history. For more, see Walter Prescott Webb, *The Texas Rangers: A Century of Frontier Defense*, 2d ed. (Austin: University of Texas Press, 1965).

9. Today sheriffs, their deputies, and other rural police generally wear uniforms. Is this simply the country copying the town? Or has the "permanent emergency" spread to the countryside? The answer seems to be both. As the city police became more efficient, the criminals moved out of town, creating new problems for rural law enforcement which seemed best solved by adopting the new strategies that had created the new problem. See, for example, Reith, *Police History*, pp. 195-96.

10. For example, the bill creating the London Metropolitan Police stated "[men] shall be sworn in by one of the said justices to act as constable for preserving the peace, and preventing robberies and other felonies, and apprehending offenders against the peace," while the police commissioners issued a handbook laying down nine principles of police work, the first of which was to "prevent crime and disorder, as an alternative to their repression by military force and severity of legal punishment," and instructing the police to offer "individual service and friendship to all members of the public" – as a means to "seek and to preserve public favor." See Reith, *Police History*, pp. 125, 287-88. The bill creating the Metropolitan Police seems never to have supposed that public service or seeking public favor was a police function (while supposing apprehending offenders to be one).

11. Kenneth Culp Davis, *Discretionary Justice: A Preliminary Inquiry* (Urbana: University of Illinois Press, 1971), p. 218.

12. Ibid., p. 218.

13. The explanation is not some slip of the pen. It is, in part, a product of defining "discretion" not in terms of the juridical limits of law but in terms of its "effective limits." Hence, he is quite willing to admit that "[a] good deal of discretion is illegal or of questionable legality." See ibid., p. 4. Yet, as I shall try to show, the explanation may in part be something more interesting.

14. Compare Fletcher, "Unwise Reflections," esp. p. 270 (discretion as "decisional autonomy," "discernment," and "something granted") and pp. 274-75 (Kenneth Davis's "effective power").

15. Compare Davis, *Discretionary Justice*, p. 106: "The main difference between what we call case law and what we call discretion lies in the presence or absence of

an expectation that the tribunal [*sic*] will strive for consistency."

16. Though "mind-numbing" does seem to me to describe accurately the effect of basic training on new recruits, it does not describe its ultimate effect. Neville Shute, who briefly served as a soldier at the end of World War I, remarks in his *Slide Rule: The Autobiography of an Engineer* (New York: William Morrow, 1954), p. 29: "I know of no life so restful as that of a private solider. In those days it was assumed that he was quite incapable of any rational thought or responsibility; his corporal shepherded him about and told him where to go and what to do. He never had to think for himself about anything at all." Shute was free to think about whatever he wanted. The "numbing" of one part of his mind, that concerned with his job, freed the rest.

17. Alfred, Lord Tennyson, "The Charge of the Light Brigade," in *The Norton Anthology of English Literature*, 6th ed., ed. M. H. Abrams (New York: W. W. Norton, 1993), 2:1133.

18. Compare the drill sergeant's joke: "There are four ways to do things: the right way, the wrong way, the army's way, and my way. You will do things my way."

19. Herman Goldstein, *Policing a Free Society* (Cambridge: Ballinger, 1977), for example, p. 99: "It is ironic that an agency which, by tradition, spells out its operating procedures in infinite detail [specifying, for example, where officers must wear their weapon], leaves vast areas of its most important functioning [for example, when to arrest] to the discretion of individual officers." There is irony only insofar as "important functions" are to resemble operating procedures in repaying the effort of rule making.

20. If we build certainty into the criteria for knowledge, we may have to say "usually" or even "almost always." Two decades ago, Horst Rittel and Melvin Webber argued, in "Dilemmas in a General Theory of Planning," *Policy Sciences* 4 (1973), pp. 155-69, that the "search for scientific bases for confronting problems of social policy is bound to fail, because . . . these problems . . . are [by nature] 'wicked.'" Wicked problems (a) have no definite formulation or stopping rule (though how the problem is formulated affects what solutions will seem appropriate), (b) have so much at stake each time that learning by simple trial-and-error is ruled out, (c) have solutions that are good or bad rather than true or false, with no immediate or ultimate test of success, (d) do not have an enumerable (or exhaustively describable) set of potential conclusions or permissible operations, (e) are essentially unique, and (f) can be considered the symptom of another problem. Most discussions of police discretion seem to assume that the problems the police face, both the department as a whole and individual officers, are tame rather than wicked. Yet, it seems to me, most in fact fit the Rittel and Webber definition of wicked problems.

21. Davis cannot, I think, raise the baseline for judgment high enough to make this decision routine, for two reasons. First, experienced police officers really do seem to represent the right level of competency for the baseline. Second, it is hard to see who could replace them. Certainly, neither professors of law nor police chiefs seem likely to be more competent to make arrest decisions than ordinary police officers.

22. Fletcher's other term for "decisional autonomy," that is, "managerial authority," seems even less well chosen. Managers often have authority to make

routine decisions. They must sign off on many things about which they need exercise no judgment whatever. They are required to decide certain questions so that someone knows about all the decisions of that kind in case "something should come up."

23. To describe a police officer as a "street-level bureaucrat," then, is simply another way of saying that she is a foot soldier with a pen (as well as a gun); but to describe her as a "street-corner politician" is (or at least should be) to say something quite different. Politicians are not bureaucrats. They generally do not obey orders (though they too work in organizations we might call bureaucracies).

24. Unlike the command "ready, aim, fire," the command to "fire when you see the whites of their eyes" leaves to the soldiers' judgment when to fire. The soldier is to judge when he can see the whites of the enemy's eyes clearly enough to fire with good effect (and to fire only then). Though the time of firing is left to the soldier's judgment, the soldier does not have liberty to choose when to fire. He must fire as soon as he judges the enemy close enough. (Of course, even obeying the command "ready, aim, and fire" requires judgment – as well as the decision to obey or not. For example, the soldier should aim so as to hit the target. Taking good aim requires, besides good sight, good judgment about such things as the effects of wind, distance, and cartridge.)

25. Ronald Dworkin, *Taking Rights Seriously* (Cambridge: Harvard University Press, 1977), esp. pp. 15-45.

26. Davis's conception of discretion presupposes that there is a point "where law ends" (*Discretionary Justice*, p. 3). For Davis, then, discretion-as-liberty is, by definition, lawless. This is a conclusion typical of certain legal theories, especially positivism, but not of all. Because Dworkin understands law as a union of rules and principles, law as he understands it never ends. Where there is no statute or other rule to cover a decision, there will still be many relevant principles to provide legal guidance. For Dworkin, discretionary decisions need not be lawless even though no legal rule decides them. How much of the problem of discretion derives from legal positivism?

27. Compare Fletcher, "Unwise Reflections," pp. 282-83.

28. Ibid., p. 277: "There are a host of other words [than discretion] such as 'judgment,' 'interpretation,' and 'personal understanding,' any of which could be invoked to stress the input of persons, whether judge or citizen, who must mold and apply the rule to a set of facts."

29. Ibid., p. 277: "These usages reflect distortions of our language in the effort to underscore aspects of decisionmaking that have gone underappreciated."

30. Mortimer R. Kadish and Sanford H. Kadish, *Discretion to Disobey: A Study of Lawful Departures from Legal Rules* (Stanford: Stanford University Press, 1973).

31. Compare John Kleinig, *The Ethics of Policing* (New York: Cambridge University Press, 1996), p. 91: "although there is some official authorization for police discretion, it is sometimes half-hearted in practice. When something goes wrong, individual discretionary authority is likely to be denied. . . . [T]he discretionary authority of the line officer [is] inherently problematic." I don't think it fair to describe the grant of discretion in question as "half-hearted"; it seems better described as a "full-hearted" grant of discretion-to-disobey, a quite sensible administrative strategy in certain circumstances. Discretion-to-disobey has much the same advantages, and disadvantages, as other outcome-related standards of

conduct (for example, strict liability statutes). Fletcher, in "Unwise Reflections," seems to make a similar mistake (though his focus is not police but courts) – for example, p. 276: "Surely the nature of the decision at the time that it is rendered cannot depend upon subsequent events." Why not?

32. Walker, *Taming the System*, p. 9.

33. This may be an example of discretion-as-mere-decision (though a decision de jure and de facto subject to review).

34. *The Ethics of Aristotle*, trans. J. A. K. Thomson (Baltimore: Penguin, 1962), bk. 5, ch. 10.

35. Davis, *Discretionary Justice*, p. 217.

36. Ibid., esp. pp. 27-51.

37. Perhaps it goes without saying, but let me say it anyway. Not all decisions to act equitably rather than according to strict justice involve judgment (in the sense I have been using it). Some equitable decisions are obvious, or at least obvious to anyone of ordinary intelligence. I should also add that some of these obvious decisions may not be so obvious to someone trained to do otherwise. In the military, for example, the decision to break ranks and flee the field in the face of overwhelming attack may be like this. The ordinary civilian would run without thinking, whereas a veteran might find it a hard choice to make and even wait too long to make it – another baseline problem.

38. Compare discussions of disparity in sentencing (another subject on which K. C. Davis has something to say). For what is wrong with the argument that disparate sentences are necessarily unjust, see Michael Davis, "Sentencing: Must Justice Be Even-Handed?" *Law and Philosophy* 1 (April 1982), pp. 77-117; or Michael Davis, *To Make the Punishment Fit the Crime* (Boulder: Westview, 1992), pp. 179-212.

39. Davis, *Discretionary Justice*, p. 56, note 4, himself distinguishes between "rule," by which he means a specific proposition of law; "principle," by which he means a less specific and broader proposition; and "standard," a still less specific and often rather vague proposition. This distinction seems a muddle. What is the metric of specificity? For example, is "Don't kill" specific and thus a rule, or broad and thus a principle, or so broad as to be vague and thus a standard? I have no idea how to answer that question. I doubt that Davis does. His actual argument seems not to require this distinction (and might have benefited from Dworkin's, especially when trying to explain how rules using examples or illustrations work). So I ignore it.

40. Perhaps that transition has already begun. SWAT teams seem to be on their way out, community policing on its way in.

41. For more on this strategy, see Michael Davis, "The Ethics Boom: What and Why," *Centennial Review* 34 (spring 1990), pp. 163-86.

42. Charles L. Bosk, "Forgive and Remember: Managing Medical Failure," in *Professional Judgment*, ed. Jack Dowie and Arthur Elstein (Cambridge: Cambridge University Press, 1988), pp. 522-43.

43. Community policing seems – in certain versions – to be yet another way to help police standardize their conduct; dialogue with the community helps police to know how to apply abstract standards to local cases.

Response

Vidar Halvorsen

Michael Davis has organized his interesting and stimulating essay around three crucial questions: What is it about the police that might make their discretion seem important? How should police discretion properly be characterized? And how, if ever, should police discretion be controlled?

The second question is the fundamental one, in the sense that how we conceive of discretion is likely to determine why we think it is important and what it is rational for us to do in order to control it. It might, for example, be the case, according to Davis's interpretation of George Fletcher's "unwise reflections," that "discretion is both easy to find and important only if one embraces a loose definition."[1]

I.   WHAT MAKES DISCRETION SEEM IMPORTANT?

Davis doesn't address his three questions in logical priority, but starts instead with the question of why discretion seems so important in policing. I don't think that he fully succeeds in giving a satisfactory answer to this question. The reason, I would argue, is that contrary to what Davis claims we cannot fully understand discretion without a general theory or philosophy of policing:

> We must, I think, try to understand the problem of police discretion without a philosophy of police. . . . We must try to understand the problem of police discretion as a product of various side-constraints, both moral and practical – constraints with at least as much urgency and legitimacy as those deriving from any theory of policing's goals or functions. [15]

A theory of policing, however, is not necessarily a theory of policing's goals or functions. Moreover, any theory, whatever its focus, can hardly do without invoking concepts that embody the moral side-constraints to which

Davis is referring. That this is true, even of theories that explicitly ignore the goals and functions of policing, is observed in what probably is the best theoretical account available, Egon Bittner's conception of police as social enforcers.[2] The functions of the police, as Davis observes, are complex and perhaps also badly understood, but the virtue of Bittner's theory is that it cuts across the varieties of police activities and focuses on what he takes to be the distinctive nature of the means that police are authorized to use – the potential or actual use of coercive force. In his important book *The Idea of Police*, Carl Klockars argues that Bittner's focus on means rather than objectives implies that his model is descriptive or value-neutral. This contrasts with norm-derivative models, which take the purposes or ends of policing as their starting point. Klockars's distinction, however, relies on a subjectivist conception of morality:

> No definition of police will do if it is merely a reflection of the hopes, desires, fears, frustrations, politics, or sense of humor of its author. And any norm-derivative definition of police – any definition of police that tries to define it in terms of its *ends* – will ultimately amount to nothing more than that.[3]

Nevertheless, even Bittner's theory must, I believe, rely on the normative concept of authority to account for, say, the crucial difference between the gunman and the police officer. Klockars tries to explicate this difference in terms of a distinction between legal and moral legitimacy. But this distinction is unsound. Legitimacy is a moralized concept in the sense that it embodies a moral validity claim: to argue that something is legitimate is to argue that something is morally sound and that its moral soundness can be supported by reasons.

Legal legitimacy, then, refers to what Ronald Dworkin has called "law's ambition for itself": its claim to moral validity. True enough, the moral pretensions of law may fail, as when the police in Nazi Germany (Klockars's example) enjoyed legal powers to do morally outrageous things. A distinction in terms of legal and nonlegal powers, however, fails to grasp our intuitive conception of the police officer's use of deadly force as essentially different from the bank robber's. In fact, one might argue that when mere legality becomes the sole basis for the use of coercive force, the legal powers of policing collapse into the nonlegal powers of bank robbing in the sense that both activities must rely exclusively on the mechanics of brute power.

The difference between legal (or nonlegal) powers and legal legitimacy might be further elaborated in terms of the notion of authority. As John Kleinig convincingly argues in his book *The Ethics of Policing*, "authority is centrally and essentially a *normative social relation*, an accorded status."[4] But if authority ultimately relies on moral acceptance and consent, then the coercive practices of policing are in constant need of justifications that can rationally be consented to by the public. And the more discretionary these practices are, the more urgent is the need for sound justifications.

Davis has some interesting observations on similarities and differences between the police and the military, although it is not always clear to me exactly what relevance these observations have for the question of why discretion matters in policing. Anyhow, when Davis refers to the odd characteristics of the police and the military as professions or semi-professions, one could argue that some of these characteristics may seem less odd when they are analyzed from the perspective of Max Weber's theory of bureaucracy. According to Weber, hierarchy and obedience are essential features of modern, bureaucratic organizations.[5] Still, Davis is certainly right in pointing out the peculiar manifestations of hierarchy and obedience in the police and the military.

Any discussion of similarities and differences between the police and the military raises two different types of questions: first, the empirical questions of what these similarities and differences amount to, and second, the normative questions of their adequacy and legitimacy. Both types of questions can focus on at least four different dimensions: (1) the fundamental *objectives* of the police and the military as social institutions; (2) their *organizational structures* and models of command and control; (3) the *social relations* between the police and the military and the communities in which they are located; and (4) the *operational styles* and technologies used by the police and the military in carrying out their tasks. The two types of questions and their four dimensions can, of course, be combined in various ways.

For example, among the several operational ways in which the police differ from the military, one seems to me to be particularly relevant for an understanding of why discretion matters in policing. "The police," says Davis, "generally work alone or in pairs, seldom in the compact bodies characteristic of combat soldiers. . . . In this respect, they resemble fighter pilots rather than soldiers." [14] However, although officers on patrol are, unlike fighter pilots, "the lowest rank in a police department," I find the metaphor Davis uses to describe their predicament, "foot soldiers," misleading. Rather, they are what Michael Lipsky calls "street-level bureaucrats."[6] The fact that they work alone or in pairs among civilians makes their supervision by "sergeants, lieutenants, captains, commanders, and so on" [15] a much more subtle and complicated affair than the military control of "enlisted men."

These complexities of street-level bureaucracy have been analyzed from different perspectives by Michael Brown, in *Working the Street*[7] and Elizabeth Reuss-Ianni, in *Two Cultures of Policing*.[8] According to Brown, in their various interactions with the public on the one hand and their supervisors on the other, street-level bureaucrats must strike a delicate balance between autonomy and control. The individual officer on the beat must constantly mediate between the police organization and its environment, and one consequence of this dual situation is, Brown argues, "that occupants of such roles are likely to have broader powers of discretion than other members of the organization."[9]

Furthermore, even when individual police officers are joined together to form squads, which is the case in paramilitary riot control and antiterrorist operations, we still might question the adequacy of the military command and control models. This is exactly what Peter Waddington does in his systematic study of the dilemmas of armed and public order policing, *The Strong Arm of the Law*.[10] The traditional military differentiation of spheres of command into separate but interconnected levels of strategy, tactics, and implementation breaks down in riot control, Waddington argues, because of the fundamental difference between fighting military battles and policing civil disorders. The reactive nature of much riot control implies that tactical and even strategic decisions must be taken at street level by squad commanders. Evidently, this combination of paramilitary operational styles and nonmilitary command models makes the question of police discretion all the more urgent.

"SWAT teams seem to be on their way out, community policing on its way in," Davis claims. [35 n. 40] Are SWAT teams really on their way out in the United States? I am skeptical. In my own country, the relatively peaceful society of Norway, SWAT training has recently been integrated into the basic training program at the National Police Academy. No doubt community policing is on its way in, although it is sometimes hard to say how much of what is referred to by this elusive phrase is rhetoric and how much is reality. It might be more adequate to conceive of community policing as a general philosophy of policing, comprising all the various functions of police work (including SWAT), rather than as a distinctive function, method, or operational style.

Is "community SWAT policing" a contradiction in terms? Not necessarily. Although we must accept that a few atypical emergency situations call for the paramilitary operational style of SWAT squads, we should not accept that they conceive of their task in terms of warfare. Moreover, we should not accept the secrecy that has surrounded the policy and technology of armed and public order policing in many European countries. If the core of community policing is the attempt to reduce the social remoteness so characteristic of paramilitary policing, then the general principles governing this field must be subject to close public scrutiny. In the European context, Waddington's study represents an important step in the right direction. Furthermore, as Davis rightly points out, community policing might even have an impact on how the police "apply abstract standards to local cases." [35 n. 43]

II. DISCRETION

In the second part of his essay, dealing with the problem of how discretion should properly be characterized, Davis draws on Fletcher's illuminating "unwise reflections" about discretion and elaborates on some of Fletcher's distinctions.

Fletcher extracts four different senses of discretion from four different contexts for talking about or using the concept of discretion. According to Fletcher, in *normal people's* talk "discretion" implies good judgment or wisdom (Davis's discretion-as-discernment), a usage that sometimes is merged with discretion as decisional autonomy. In a second context, this latter sense is explicated further by Fletcher in terms of how *lawyers* talk about discretion as managerial authority (Davis's discretion-as-liberty), implying that conflicting parties "do not have a basis for claiming a right to any particular decision by a judge."[11] Fletcher's third sense of discretion relates to how *legal scholars* tend to use discretion more or less synonymously with "personal input," as opposed to the mechanical application of rules to cases, which generates judicial decisions by means of deductively valid syllogisms. In legal theory, there has been a tendency to reduce this sense of discretion (Davis's discretion-as-judgment) to decisional autonomy or liberty. The most prominent advocate of such reductionism is Herbert Hart. In chapter 7 of *The Concept of Law*,[12] he offers a sketch of what amounts to a highly problematic theory of adjudication. When the deductive model fails to generate judicial decisions, due to the inherent linguistic indeterminacy of law, Hart draws the conclusion that hard cases – that is, cases that cannot be decided by syllogistic conjugations of rules and factual premises – cannot be decided by existing law at all. As far as hard cases are concerned, rule-skepticism is accepted by Hart: there is no law, only autonomous decisions by courts; the courts are creating the law rather than applying it. If standards are involved in judicial discretion, they must be extralegal; they transcend the limits of law.

This conclusion seems implausible. One of the great contributions of Ronald Dworkin to legal theory is to point out that there is more to law than primary and secondary rules; first and foremost, there are principles that may enable judges to reach legally sound decisions even in hard cases. This, moreover, is a point that Davis seems to accept. [22] How much of the problem of discretion, he asks, is derived from legal positivism? [28]

It is unfortunate, however, when Davis claims in his discussion of discretion-as-liberty that this version of discretion "presupposes something like Ronald Dworkin's distinction between 'rules' and 'principles.'" [22] According to Dworkin, rules differ from principles in two important respects. *Logically*, rules (unlike principles) are mechanical, hard-and-fast norms that either determine a decision or contribute nothing to it; *substantially*, principles are important for the justifications of rules and may be invoked when deductive reasoning fails to generate solutions. But there is no necessary connection between the logical and the substantial distinction, and it is an open question whether a legal positivist like Hart can accept principles as part of law (though this is what he seems to have done in subsequent exchanges with Dworkin).

Dworkin, then, has a narrower and more problematic conception of rules than Hart, but a broader and more defensible conception of legal reasoning. Consequently, I fail to see why we cannot appreciate the notion of discretion-as-liberty without presupposing the Dworkinian distinction between rules and principles.

I think it may be worthwhile to compare Davis's and Fletcher's typology with Dworkin's differentiation of three different senses of discretion.[13] Discretion in the first (weak) sense exists whenever a given rule does not deductively determine a particular result, but calls for the use of judgment according to standards inherent in that rule. The example Dworkin gives is that of the sergeant who is told to take the five most experienced men on patrol. Here, experience is the relevant standard, which the sergeant is not free to ignore, although reasonable men may differ on the question of which man is the most experienced.

The sergeant has discretion in the second (weak) sense when his decision is final, that is, when his decision cannot be set aside by some higher authority. The third (strong) sense of discretion implies, on the other hand, that the sergeant is not bound by the standard of experience; rather, he is free to decide whether to take experience into account or to ignore it altogether when he selects his five men. In other words, the first and third senses of discretion are mutually exclusive: the sergeant is either required to take the relevant standard into account or he is not required to do so.

Discretion in the second sense (finality), however, is compatible with discretion in the first (discretion-as-judgment) as well as the third sense (discretion-as-liberty): the sergeant may have the last word, yet that fact does not tell us whether he is bound or not bound by the relevant standard. Consequently, I tend to agree with Davis when he argues that to include finality or nonaccountability among the senses of discretion does not add much to our understanding. [20] Dworkin, however, claims that the three senses of discretion have one interesting feature in common:

> The concept of discretion is at home in only one sort of context; when someone is in general charged with making decisions subject to standards set by a particular authority. Discretion, like the hole in the doughnut, does not exist except as an area left open by a surrounding belt of restriction. It is therefore a relative concept. It always makes sense to ask, "Discretion under which standards?" or "Discretion as to which authority?"[14]

Discretion, in other words, is the creation of rules. Yet it remains unclear exactly what the difference is between discretion in the strong sense and a legally granted permission to make decisions within a given sphere of action. Does it contribute to our understanding of discretion if it is the case that one subcategory ultimately collapses into the category of permission? What does the freedom of discretion-as-liberty consist in? If it consists in the freedom of having the final say, it collapses into triviality; if it is tantamount to the freedom of being unbound by rules and principles, it is an open question whether it should count as discretion at all.

Dworkin, not surprisingly, explicitly rejects the conception of discretion-as-license or discretion as power, the fourth and final sense in Davis's and Fletcher's typology: "We must avoid one tempting confusion. The strong sense of discretion is not tantamount to license, and does not exclude criticism."[15]

Fletcher, moreover, seems to make the same point in his profound and effective criticism of Kenneth Culp Davis: "This fourth sense of the concept interweaves with the other three in rendering discussion of discretionary processes virtually incomprehensible."[16]

Michael Davis, however, seems to accept discretion-as-license as a fruitful notion; at least, he suggests an interesting subdivision of the category into "technical" and "substantive" license, although the latter subcategory is eventually dismissed as "degenerate." The typical situations of technical license seem to be situations in which patrol officers are observing violations of rules and decide either to ignore those violations or, in the words of Michael Brown, "to take an informal action (issue a warning) rather than a formal action (issue a citation)."[17] In contrast to situations of substantive license, in which police officers are merely acting out of reach of their supervisors, decisions to ignore or bend formal requirements are subsequently accepted by superiors. In some European countries (like Norway), a general principle of opportunity, granting the individual police officer the right to decide (within limits) whether or not to invoke the criminal process, has been explicitly recognized as part of the legal system. Does this mean that discretion-as-technical-license has been transformed into strong discretion or discretion-as-liberty?

This is a tricky question. Though he denies strong judicial discretion, Dworkin does not explicitly address the issue of whether or not police officers, unlike judges, are sometimes unbound by standards and principles of law. On Kenneth Culp Davis's external understanding of discretion, the answer must clearly be yes. A defensible rejection of the external perspective must, then, demonstrate the primacy of the internal perspective of judges and its relevance for policing and give a satisfactory account of the status and binding force of principles. That task, however, must be reserved for another occasion.

If we accept the primacy of the internal point of view – that is, the performative point of view of a police officer (or a judge) who is under an obligation to articulate sound reasons or justifications for his or her actions – it could be argued that discretion-as-liberty as well as discretion-as-technical-license must rely on interpretations of the relevant rules in terms of the underlying values or principles that would justify those rules. As Davis himself says, "technical discretion-as-license requires discretion-as-discernment to work well." [25] I agree. My hunch, therefore, is that we can do without it as an explication of the concept of discretion.

In short, the fundamental notion of discretion seems to me to be the notion of discretion-as-discernment; and discretion-as-judgment, discretion-as-liberty, and discretion-as-technical-license (or, for that matter, discretion-as-having-the-final-say) are more properly understood, not as different versions of the concept of discretion, but rather as different contexts or paradigmatic situations in which the exercise of interpretative competence is required.

Some of those contexts or situations confront police officers with difficult questions of justification. I am not primarily thinking of the well-known split-second decisions police sometimes have to make and justify in retrospect, but rather of much less dramatic situations, like the one mentioned by Kenneth Culp Davis, in which a policeman "lectures a boy from a middle-class neighborhood, but he arrests a boy from the slums, although he knows that both are equally guilty of violating the same statute." [cited by Michael Davis, 16]

Michael Davis suggests a possible justification for such a differential distribution of force and coercion in policing: insofar as we accept the fact that poor people are more effectively deterred by arrests than middle-class people, arresting the boy from the slums and lecturing the boy from the middle-class neighborhood are justified in terms of the consequences of those options on crime. "Why not individualize justice in this way?" Davis asks. [26]

It is a well-known challenge to consequentialism that everyday morality does not fit easily with consequentialist reasoning in the allocation of punishment. We do not accept the idea that poor people should be punished more severely than rich people convicted of equally serious crimes, even though punishing poor people may have a greater impact on the level of those crimes. One might argue, however, that the allocation of punishment by courts and the use of coercive force in the pretrial stages of policing are morally different, because the stakes are higher in the former than in the latter case. For example, the evidential standards accepted in policing are raised when cases are taken to court. Such an argument hardly succeeds in justifying differential allocation of enforcement in terms of social class. In a sense, it is misleading when Davis speaks of the *individualization* of justice in the example of the two boys, because the individualizing factor is a social characteristic (poverty) for which the boy from the slums is not responsible. Thus, the problems of police discretion are ultimately linked with the fundamental problems of doing justice in an unjust society.

III. PROFESSIONS

I don't have much to comment on the third and final section of Davis's essay, which deals with the problem of how to control or standardize discretion. I fundamentally agree with most of what Davis has to say here; in particular, I strongly sympathize with his criticism of the widespread assumption that "the primary way to obtain police obedience to standards of any sort is by inspection and punishment." [26]

I find his alternative suggestions – ethics education in police training and the institutionalization of ethical debriefing among police officers as professional equals – very illuminating and important. The first alternative is easier to implement than the second; hierarchy and obedience are, probably, indispensable features of police organizations, and the challenge is to modify that basic structure along the lines suggested by Davis. This seems to be compatible with what Davis is saying about the need for moving "away from the military-style, command-and-control hierarchy of today's police organization." [29]

Although Davis explicitly says that he doesn't "offer these strategies as complete substitutes for rule and supervision," [30] I tend to think that rules and rule following have a more fundamental role to play in policing than Davis seems to acknowledge. Despite the obvious fact that they often do not have much time for deliberation, as Davis points out, police officers frequently find themselves in the occupational role of "street-corner judges."

I have profited much from reading Davis's essay as a stimulating reflection on the complexities involved in that occupational role.

NOTES

1. Michael Davis, "Police, Discretion, and Professions," in this volume, p. 13, referring to George P. Fletcher's "Some Unwise Reflections about Discretion," *Law & Contemporary Problems*, 47, no. 4 (autumn 1984), pp. 269-86. All subsequent page references to Davis's essay are enclosed in brackets in the text.

2. Egon Bittner, "The Capacity to Use Force as the Core of the Police Role," in *Moral Issues in Police Work*, ed. Frederick Elliston and Michael Feldberg (Totowa, NJ: Rowman & Allanheld, 1985), pp. 15-25.

3. Carl B. Klockars, *The Idea of Police* (Beverly Hills: Sage, 1985), p. 9, emphasis in original.

4. John Kleinig, *The Ethics of Policing* (New York: Cambridge University Press, 1996), p. 18, emphasis in original.

5. Max Weber, *The Theory of Social and Economic Organisation*, trans. A. M. Henderson and Talcott Parsons, rev. ed. (London: W. Hodge, 1947).

6. Michael Lipsky, *Street-level Bureaucracy: Dilemmas of the Individual in Public Services* (New York: Russell Sage Foundation, 1980).

7. Michael Brown, *Working the Street: Police Discretion and the Dilemmas of Reform* (New York: Russell Sage Foundation, 1988).

8. Elizabeth Reuss-Ianni, *Two Cultures of Policing: Street Cops and Management Cops* (New Brunswick, NJ: Transaction Books, 1983).

9. Brown, *Working the Street*, p. 29.

10. Peter Waddington, *The Strong Arm of the Law* (New York: Oxford University Press, 1991).

11. Fletcher, "Some Unwise Reflections," p. 271.

12. H. L. A. Hart, *The Concept of Law* (Oxford: Clarendon Press, 1961).

13. Ronald Dworkin, *Taking Rights Seriously* (Cambridge: Harvard University Press, 1977).

14. Ibid., p. 31.

15. Ibid., p. 33.

16. Fletcher, "Some Unwise Reflections," p. 276.

17. Brown, *Working the Street*, p. 185.

Chapter 2

From the State of Nature to Mayberry: The Nature of Police Discretion

Joan McGregor

Discretionary decisions of the police have come under constant public criticism. High profile cases such as the videotaped beating of Rodney King and the investigations of the beatings of Nicole Brown Simpson and her later murder permeate daily discussions and have created a national conversation about the discretionary choices of the police. This conversation has included public revelations about issues of, for example, racial discrimination – which show that it is a common experience of African-Americans, in many American cities, to be harassed by the police – and gender discrimination – which show that police have been dismissive in cases of spousal battery. These discussions have led to more and more questions about discretionary decision making by the police. There have been frequent calls to control their discretionary authority by designing rules that will limit their range of options and subject their choices and policies to greater public scrutiny. What is the basis for the criticism of the police's discretionary decision making? What are the standards of evaluation? In answering these questions, we need to be conceptually clear on what it means to have and to exercise discretion, and, I argue, to understand the normative dimensions of police discretionary decision making. The purpose of this essay is to explore the nature of police discretion, with particular attention to its normative parameters. I argue that the normative limits placed on the police may ultimately hinge on the justification of state coercive power. I briefly explore this relationship in the first section. Then I articulate theories of judicial discretion. Judicial discretion is a well-worn topic in the philosophical literature and may prove fruitful for an under-

standing of the nature of police discretion. Finally, I consider the normative constraints on police discretion.

DISCRETION AND LIBERALISM

The question of the nature and legitimate extent of police discretion should
probably be seen within the larger question of the legitimacy of state
authority. One's views about the permissible range of state power and
authority will determine one's views about the appropriate functions and
goals of the police, and possibly the nature and scope of the discretion
granted within those professional and institutional structures. Liberal political theory has provided an account of limited government, one that
protects maximum individual liberty but which is constrained by notions
of equality and justice.[1] As free and equal agents we turn over our right of
self-protection to the state in exchange for the greater security that the state
can provide. Everyone must comply with the laws, and in return the state
provides us with equal protection and treatment under the laws. Many
liberal theorists have used the social contract model to provide the justification for governmental power, including governmental coercion.[2] The
contractualist model of justification of the state and laws asks whether we
as rational and free agents could agree to particular policies and laws in a
hypothetical situation of choice.

Liberals often say salutary things about our government, particularly,
that it is "a nation of laws not men." Presumably, this means that we don't
have individual agents of the government making judgments based upon
their own personal or party prejudices or interests. Yet we give police the
discretionary power to, for example, selectively enforce laws. How is this
practice consistent with being "a nation of laws not men"? Police discretion gives power to individuals. Lord Acton said, and it is often quoted,
that "power tends to corrupt, and absolute power corrupts absolutely." Is
police discretion power that corrupts? Is that power consistent with liberal
ideals of justice and equality? A tyrannical use of force is one that is seen as
unprincipled, capricious, and unpredictable, and it is one in which the
police make personally biased and often self-serving decisions. Discretion
has often been associated with tyranny: Is this association analytic? Oppressive regimes rule in an arbitrary and discriminatory fashion against
selected groups. How is the discretionary decision making of the police in
those "oppressive" regimes different from our own?

Liberals invest a great deal in the rule of law and constitutional government; yet these may be only as effective as the commitment to liberal

values that the police share. In concrete terms, the constitutional protections and stated commitment to liberty and equality for all do not amount to much if police discretion allows the police to enforce laws selectively against powerless minority groups while at the same time failing to protect adequately the interests of members of those groups. There exists a delicate balance between individual freedom and the power of state. Too much power in the hands of police can overwhelm freedom for the individual and thereby undermine the purpose of the state, but the reverse might also undermine the purpose of the state. A full account of police discretion must take account of these larger political questions. But before that can be done we need to be clear about what discretion means and begin to understand its legitimate uses.

WHAT IS THE NATURE OF DISCRETION?

"Discretion" is used in a number of ways and in a variety of contexts. The context in which it is used should tell us something about its meaning. We talk of people reaching "the age of discretion," meaning an age when one can make judgments for oneself, a form of personal autonomy. Along with making judgments, there is the suggestion that one will at that age make choices among reasonable alternatives. There is a wisdom that comes with age. "The better part of valor is discretion," says Falstaff in *Henry IV, Part 1*.[3] Shakespeare understands discretion to be careful or wise judgment. In certain circumstances, "discretion" is used to mean merely judgment, as in "Use your own discretion about the choice of a restaurant." The more standard uses, however, operate within professional and institutional frameworks – for example, the discretion of officials within the criminal justice system, including that of police, judges, prosecutors, parole officers, and juries.

Judicial discretion has been more widely discussed by philosophers than the topic of police discretion; consequently, it may be instructive to consider the different accounts given of judicial discretion. Questions of judicial discretion arise when judges must make decisions about the law. Starting at one end of the continuum, theorists such as Montesquieu argue for what has come to be known as "mechanical jurisprudence," leaving little room for a rich account of discretion in judicial decision making. He said that the judge is nothing more than "the mouth of the law." [4] Judicial decision making means mechanically applying the law, and that does not require complicated thought or judgment. Oliver Wendell Holmes Jr., Jerome Frank, and other twentieth-century legal realists at the other end of the spectrum argue that "[a]ll judges exercise discretion, individualize abstract rules, make law."[5] Judges exercising discretion – as, according to the legal realists, they are continually doing – are making the law as they go. Rules do not determine particular outcomes; judges exercising their discretion decide the outcomes.

H. L. A. Hart rejects the extreme view of the legal realists and also what he takes to be another extreme view, that of the natural law theorists. Instead, he argues for judicial discretion in cases in which the law runs out, in instances where there is no clear rule to cover the case before the court.[6] In those cases, judges exercise their discretion, which amounts to making law or policy where there are no clear laws to bind the judge's decision. This sense of discretion Ronald Dworkin has called "strong discretion."[7]

The strong sense of discretion is, according to Dworkin, to be distinguished from two weaker senses. The first weak sense is used when an official must exercise judgment in applying the standards set for him by an authority. The claim that someone has discretion in the first weak sense is often a comment on the fact that the rule or standard is vague or in some other way difficult to interpret. The second weak sense is used in cases in which no one will review the exercise of judgment. The strong sense of discretion implies that on some issue the decision maker is simply not bound by standards set by the authority in question. In this sense, Dworkin tells us, we say that a sergeant has discretion when he is told to pick for patrol any five men he chooses. Another example Dworkin uses is that of a judge in a dog show who "has discretion to judge airedales before boxers if the rules do not stipulate an order of events."[8] Saying that someone has discretion in the strong sense is different in kind from the weaker senses, since in the stronger case there are no standards to apply. Dworkin, arguing against the positivist, claims that judges are always bound by principle.

Dworkin is dissatisfied with the implications of the strong sense of discretion if it is taken to be operative when judges try hard cases. On Hart's account, according to Dworkin, judges need not enforce preexisting rights, and are not bound by the rule of law. Dworkin argues that judges exercise discretion only in one of the weaker senses of discretion. Judges, on Dworkin's account, must use their judgment and apply principles and rules implicit in the legal system. The rules and legal standards may be vague and/or otherwise difficult to apply, but judges are nevertheless always bound to exercise their discretion within the confines of the preexisting law. They are to find the preexisting rights of the litigants.

More radical and controversial than the earlier legal realists, contemporary advocates of Critical Legal Studies (CLS) suppose that all judges ever do is exercise discretion in a strong sense – a stronger sense than even Dworkin discusses. Dworkin's strong sense of discretion "is not tantamount to license, and does not exclude criticism."[9] He argues that in almost any situation in which a person makes a decision, that decision will legitimately be subject to evaluation under standards of rationality, fairness, and effectiveness. An official's discretion, Dworkin tells us, "means not that he is free to decide without recourse to standards of sense and fairness, but only that his decision is not controlled by a standard furnished by the particular authority we have in mind when we raise the question of discretion."[10] The CLS scholars argue that not only are there opposing rules that would dictate contradictory outcomes to particular cases but the system itself has competing and irreconcilable principles and ideals embedded in it.[11] The judge must make a choice not dictated by law. Descriptively, advocates of CLS argue that most judicial decisions reflect the ideology of the powerful moneyed class in society. Judges use their discretion to support the status quo; they decide cases in a manner consistent with the current power's advantages and interests. Discretion is just unconstrained and unauthorized power. Legal rules do not determine unique legal results.

POLICE DISCRETION

Is there anything we can learn from the analyses of judicial discretion that we can apply to the kind of discretion available to police? Undoubtedly, there are those who defend accounts of police decision making that are similar to those of judicial decision making. There are those who, for example, believe that the police unthinkingly enforce all legal rules, and that police work can be reduced to the mechanical application of rules. At the other extreme, one of the best-known accounts of police discretion was given by Kenneth Culp Davis, who wrote that "a public officer has discretion whenever the effective limits on his power leave him free to make a choice among possible courses of action or inaction."[12] This account makes discretionary whatever acts the police officer is capable of doing, whatever he/she can get away with. If a police officer can get away with beating, harassing, and arresting mostly members of minority groups, then it is within his/her discretion. This account of discretion has affinities with the account held by legal realists and CLS advocates: all claim that decision making is not bound by standards set by the authority in question, even moral ones. Radical theorists claim that police discretion is unconstrained power of the state and the rules that bind police are mere fictions to legitimate the work of the police. Police are just exercising their power against the underclass to maintain order for the powerful class.[13]

Davis's view certainly will not erase fears that police discretion may be indistinguishable from tyrannical uses of power. If it is true to say that we grant police discretionary authority within various parameters, then it would make sense for us to grant them that permission only if it is bounded by some norms. The exercise of discretion must involve choices or courses of action that are *permissible,* not merely possible.[14] Davis's account of discretion leaves out the normative dimension of discretion. Discretion is not simply the "effective" power to choose among alternatives, but an authorization or permission to use one's expertise to make a judgment as to the appropriate course of action. Discretion under this description is constrained by norms drawn from the particular context. In the judicial context, the judge has a certain amount of discretion, which may vary with the type of case. The judge's discretion does not include favoring her relatives in a legal dispute that is before her. Discretion is bounded, the range of legitimate choices is bounded, by norms: professional ones, institutional ones, administrative ones, legal ones, and moral ones. John Kleinig has correctly pointed out that within professional contexts, which are the contexts in which we are most likely to find discretion, discretionary judgments are "primarily those implicit in the practices that constitute the profession and that give it its special claim to professional status."[15] The professions – for example, law, medicine, and engineering – are "constituted by practices that are structured by regulative goals, underwritten by standards of competence, and bound by moral norms that shape the discretionary authority of their practitioners."[16]

In general, discretion is granted in contexts where a person within an institutional role is charged with decision making under a certain authority. Discretionary decisions are always subject to some constraints and standards, if nothing other than the practices that develop within the relevant profession within that institution. In addition, following Dworkin, discretionary decisions may be judged by standards of rationality, efficiency, and/or fairness. Discretion, like the hole in a doughnut, Dworkin tells us, does not exist except as the area left open by a surrounding belt of restriction. The concept of discretion is relative to the context and authority in question, because we will not know what the relevant standards are by which to judge whether the discretion was exercised appropriately until we know the context. The biologist in the field, making decisions about the integrity of an ecological system, would exercise her discretion using the standards of the biological community and not those of economic efficiency. Many of us think that judges, in doling out sentences to offenders, would abuse their discretion were they to appeal to economic standards to set sentences rather than to standards of justice. The meaning of discretion is affected by features of the context, and that context should have its own standards and principles to guide the use of discretion in that context. Different contexts are colored by the background of understood information against which discretion is exercised.

Dworkin's discretion as judgment, his first weak sense, may prove most relevant when discussing police discretion. Sometimes the professional judgments of police officers, though made according to appropriate criteria, might be considered wrong. Someone else assessing the situation might argue that the officer did not in fact follow the criteria or that the criteria supported a judgment in another direction. Police are given instructions, but those instructions are not precise enough to rule out judgment on the part of the officer. Clearly, however, we think that the officer is "bound by standards set by the authority in question." That does not preclude there being standards or principles in a particular context which may come into conflict with one another on given occasions. The standards may also be more or less specific or general, some so general as to lend themselves to a variety of arguments that pull in different directions. But discretion never has the sense of license.

Once we agree that discretion is normative, that it is authorized use of power and not mere power, then we have to find out what police are authorized to do before we can know what norms ought to guide the police use of discretion. What are the police authorized to do, and what is the proper way for them to do it? The view that police are law enforcers, that they are authorized to enforce the law and only enforce the law is too simplistic. To begin with, there are too many laws, and too many violations of those laws. Furthermore, those violations may occur simultaneously. For example, when a bank robbery is taking place and someone is jaywalking we would find it absurd for an officer to give both law violations the same priority. Police have discretion to decide how best to fulfill their authority to enforce the law, and we expect them to use good judgment developed from and informed by their professional expertise when they make such decisions. They have a number of different options regarding how, when, and if to enforce particular laws. Notice what this means: the law is not fully enforced; laws are enforced selectively. Obviously, this can be a source of injustice. Enforcing laws selectively against members of minority groups and the poor is, ceteris paribus, unjust. On the other hand, there are good reasons not to enforce the law fully. For instance, selectively not enforcing the jaywalking law in the above case seems a reasonable course of action.

Probably the most significant fact about police work, and important to unpacking the notion of police discretion, is that police perform various functions: they are authorized to do more than merely enforce the law. Their functions include apprehending criminals, preventing crime or disorder, assisting persons in need, protecting individuals' rights, and keeping the peace. The American Bar Association (ABA), with the endorsement of the International Association of Chiefs of Police (IACP), made the following observation when discussing the function of urban police:

> To achieve optimum police effectiveness, the police should be recognized as having complex and multiple tasks to perform in addition to identifying and apprehending persons committing serious criminal offenses. Such other police tasks include protection of certain rights such as to speak and to assemble, participation either directly or in conjunction with other public and social agencies in the prevention of criminal and delinquent behavior, maintenance of order and control of pedestrian and vehicular traffic, resolution of conflict, and assistance to citizens in need of help such as the person who is mentally ill, the chronic alcoholic, or the drug addict.[17]

In the Police Code of Conduct promulgated by the IACP (1989, 1991), the primary responsibilities of a police officer are described as follows:

> A police officer acts as an official representative of government who is required and trusted to work within the law. The officer's powers and duties are conferred by statute. The fundamental duties of a police officer include serving the community; safeguarding lives and property; protecting the innocent; keeping the peace; and ensuring the rights of all to liberty, equality and justice.[18]

Police do not arrest every lawbreaker. Police also spend varying amounts of time assisting victims of accidents or just giving directions to those in need. Working sports events, concerts, and parades takes up a considerable amount of police time. Within each of these roles or functions police have considerable discretion, room to make various judgments and choices. How police discretion might differ from situation to situation given the function the police are engaged in is a question worth exploring. Does discretion work the same way, for example, when a police officer is fulfilling a community service function that doesn't endanger the officer herself as it would in a case in which the officer is faced with danger, as she sometimes is when making arrests? Some limits on discretion would apply to both cases, but it is not clear that the same norms and standards would pertain in both instances.

Neither statutes nor the ABA and IACP statements explicitly empower police to enforce the law selectively; yet that is often accepted as a reasonable exercise of discretion. For example, the speed limit is fifty-five miles per hour in many areas, yet police in many jurisdictions do not enforce that law unless the offender is going at least ten miles per hour over the limit. The International Association of Chiefs of Police notes within this same statement that "it is important to remember that a timely word of advice rather than arrest . . . can be a more effective means of achieving a desired end." Nowhere in fact does the police chiefs' statement include as a fundamental duty the duty of the police to enforce the law. Rather, the fundamental duties as stated in the Police Code of Conduct are "serving the community; safeguarding lives and property; protecting the innocent; keeping the peace; and ensuring the rights of all to liberty, equality and justice." If police took seriously their task of ensuring the rights of all to liberty, equality, and justice, and if they had been reading their Rawls, they might feel obligated to engage in some far-reaching activities. Law enforcement, then, is a means to achieving these larger social ends, not an end in itself. Nevertheless, none of the general statements described in the Police Code of Conduct helps to clarify how we might unify police authority or discretion.

It should also be noted that there are a number of different levels at which discretion can be exercised within the police organization. We have been focusing on the level of individual police officers making individual choices. But presumably police departments have discretion over where to allocate their resources, and down the line of command there are many discretionary choices that dictate what large numbers of police officers will do.

Admittedly, there are different functions or goals that require the police to exercise discretion both in what functions they are going to perform in a given circumstance and how to perform them. Discretion means that the police must choose not only which means they will employ but also what ends they will pursue: law enforcement, maintenance of order, public service, or "ensuring the rights of all to liberty, equality and justice." A more global question is worth considering: Are these functions or goals unified in some way that makes police discretion authorized by one set of rules or standards? Or is it simply a historical accident that police play all these roles, with the result that there is no unified theory of discretion at work? We might wonder whether there is a meta-principle that could prioritize and make sense of the conflicts that arise among the different roles and functions. This meta-principle would provide police with a vantage point from which to evaluate and criticize their own discretionary choices. Additionally, it would provide the community with an understanding of police choices and a standard of criticism.

DISCRETION AND JUSTICE

What are the normative standards that constrain the police in their use of discretion? We are speaking here of the realm within the hole in the doughnut; the police are circumscribed by many specific rules that preclude particular choices. In that remaining realm, what standards ought to guide their choices? Minimally, when exercising discretion, police must be able to defend their choices on grounds of justice. Satisfying the formal principle of justice would be a good beginning: in treating people and situations differently the police must be willing to say that their differential treatment is justified on the basis of relevant differences. The formal principle of justice claims that you should treat alike or equally individuals who are alike, and should treat in an unlike manner or unequally individuals who are unlike, in proportion to their differences. Discretion is abused when one treats unequally individuals who are relevantly the same or equal or treats equally individuals who are relevantly different or unequal. Of course, what makes two individuals alike or equal is problematic, because police can always cite something that is different about the individuals and the situations in which they are found.

Theorists such as Howard Cohen have argued that police discretionary practices are going to vary from jurisdiction to jurisdiction and that this is a source of injustice.[19] Cohen argues that police discretion is "not authorized, statutes and official department directives do not delegate the police officer the authority to use discretion – there are no published guidelines for its use, no directives outlining the appropriate scope and limits of discretionary action."[20] Does commitment to the formal principle of justice require that all police in every jurisdiction make the same discretionary choices? In what sense would the choices be discretionary if there were a predetermined right answer? Or is it that an individual's behavior is judged to be unjust if that individual's behavior fails to comport with the principle? On Cohen's view, selective enforcement itself would be an injustice. Certainly, we can agree that selective enforcement based upon racial difference alone, for example, is a great source of injustice. There are clearly wrong discretionary choices, those which abuse discretion, and enforcing the laws only against members of racial minority groups is such an abuse. On the other hand, the claim that all jurisdictions should follow the same discretionary practices sounds a lot like saying that there is one uniquely right decision for all jurisdictions. That may be problematic. It is particularly problematic given the different functions that police are expected to fulfill. Different officers may weigh the functions differently and hence arrive at different judgments about the appropriate outcome.

In addition, justice requires equal protection of the laws and an equal opportunity to have one's interests represented and protected. In their treatment of women, for example, police have failed to exercise their discretion in protecting individuals' interests in a way that is consistent with equal protection. Everyone has a right to equal consideration of his or her harms and interests by the police. This does not mean that in fact all harms should be handled in the same way. But serious harms should be treated equally seriously. Police should not discount a harm because it was intraracial, occurred in a poor neighborhood, and/or was perpetrated by a spouse or lover. Consider the treatment of rape victims, in which, until recently it was a common practice to discount the allegations of women victims. The police often tried to trip up the "alleged" victim, for example, by subjecting her to long and humiliating interrogations. As one police detective wrote: "It is always advisable if there is any doubt of the truthfulness of her allegations to call her an outright liar."[21] Police discretion is exercised to decide whether or not there was a crime, whether to investigate a crime, and whether to investigate a crime vigorously. Those decisions are influenced by the police officer's attitudes. Obviously, such discretion can be used legitimately. When, however, their decisions are informed by and reflect a sexist or racist bias, they are not justified. Rape investigators, Gary LaFree found, tended to discount rape allegations where there was evidence that the victim did not conform to conventional moral behavior – as indicated by drinking, style of clothing, apparent sexual lifestyle, and so on.[22] Women do not receive fair treatment if police base their discretionary decisions upon stereotypes about appropriate female behavior which work to the disadvantage of women. Additionally, if police have standards about normal levels of male sexual aggression or acceptable levels of violence in sexual encounters and apply those to rape cases, thereby discounting the woman's charge, then the police do not fairly protect the interests of women. If police bring to bear in their investigations sexist attitudes about the significance of rape, undermining the victim's claim to have been wronged, then women fail to receive equal protection of the laws. Police abuse their discretionary powers when their discretionary choices are informed by sexism rather than by the interests of women.

Another area of abuse of police discretion can be found in domestic violence cases. For many years police did not arrest or did not strictly enforce the law (of, say, assault and battery) when the abuse was perpetrated by a spouse. Research shows that police officers were less likely to arrest in cases of assaults between married couples or lovers than in cases of strangers. "Officers defined the problem as a 'private' matter. In the worst manifestation of this attitude, officers adopted the sexist view that violence by husbands against their wives was not a crime."[23] Feminists have argued that this abuse of police discretion sent a private and public message that the police do not take domestic violence seriously. Abusing one's wife is not legally important. As a result of exposing these abuses in some jurisdictions, police have been mandated to make arrests in domestic violence cases. Selective enforcement in domestic cases is not permissible. Criticism of police discretionary choices in spousal abuse cases has been directed at the fact that police decision making in these cases is not being made in the best interest of the victim or with a due recognition of the message that is being sent to society at large if abusers are not arrested. So in these cases police discretion has been radically constrained in many jurisdictions.

Differential treatment of members of minority groups is probably the largest area of abuse of police discretion. Minority communities throughout the country believe (and they are not statistically wrong about this) that they receive a disproportionate amount of police force and control, but obtain few benefits of police protection or goods of a liberal society. Indeed, a disturbing aspect of this phenomenon is how radically differently the varying groups in society perceive particular incidents of police discretion when minority group members are involved. How is it possible that the videotaped beating of Rodney King could have generated such different conclusions? Some police, many middle-class whites, and the initial jury who acquitted the police of wrongdoing, thought the beating was an appropriate use of police discretion. Others saw it just as clearly as an abuse of discretion – an abuse that is typically directed against members of minority groups.

Police abuse of discretion against minorities in the United States has been constrained by the implementation of a number of significant constitutional rules – the Miranda rule, and prohibitions on the "third degree" and on warrantless searches and seizures, to mention just a few. These rules help to define the constitutional limitations on police discretion. Even with these limitations on police discretionary decision making, however, many questions are left unresolved and open to interpretation: What constitutes interrogation? When is a confession coerced? Do you need a warrant to search garbage left out for collection?

The most fundamental concept of democracy and, possibly, the Constitution is the notion of equality. All participants in a democracy have a basic right to equal treatment from the state. Here Dworkin's distinction between treatment as an equal and equal treatment is relevant. What is important in the context of police work is not necessarily the right to receive the same distribution of some burden or benefit, but treatment as an equal, namely to be treated with the same respect and concern as anybody else. Members of minority groups deserve treatment as equals; they must be guaranteed that their interests will be protected in the same fashion as members of the dominant group, and also that they do not receive a disproportionate amount of police control, including the enforcement of laws against them.

Discretionary decision making is necessary to some degree in police work. A major reason is the plurality of police goals and roles. Complex rules to determine every appropriate choice would be far too complicated to draft – if they could be drafted at all. Some rules or regulations serve to eliminate bad discretionary choices. But the attempt to design rules to constrain all bad discretionary choices with any precision must be doomed to failure because of the infinite number of possible circumstances. What we need is a model that will inform police and the community about the relationship of the police to the community. Different models will have different sets of values implicit in them.

There are two radically different models of police and their relationship to the citizenry.[24] Each model has implicit in it different standards and principles by which the police will judge their own behavior and by which they will be judged by the citizenry. One conception presupposes a kind of Hobbesian "state of nature," where people live in "continual fear, and danger of violent death; and the life of man [is] solitary, poor, nasty, brutish, and short."[25] The police come into this area like an occupying military force. Their major job is to keep order, which they are able to do since they have a monopoly on the use of force. People in the "state of nature" do not trust or share values with the police. Nevertheless, they view the presence of the police as better than their absence. So, for example, when the residents of Chicago public housing wanted the police to have a freer rein in performing searches for guns in their apartment complexes, this did not mean that they necessarily saw the police as their protectors; rather, the residents recognized that they and the police shared an interest in ridding the area of guns. People in a Hobbesian state of nature desire order and peace. The police have their own agenda in policing independent of the interests of the members of the particular community. On this model, police enforce the laws that serve the interests of those with power. Police who perceive themselves along the lines of this quasi-military model often view those with whom they come into contact as the enemy. Loyalty to their fellow officers and superiors is the highest virtue, and often exclusive of other virtues.

A different model might draw its inspiration from *The Andy Griffith Show*, a TV series set in a town where the police exercise their discretion on the basis of shared community values. Everybody in Mayberry shares the same set of goals and values; police officers' judgments about when to arrest or not arrest are informed by values and goals with which the community would agree. On this model, the police live in the community they serve and not only understand the community from an external point of view, but also accept the values of the community from an internal point of view – the values of the community are theirs. On this model, the police work for members of the community and thus they decide, in consultation with the community, what goals they ought to pursue and what roles they ought to play. Decisions to arrest or not arrest would be grounded in a rationale that members of the community could accept. This might be called a communitarian model of policing. The community could, for example, decide that all teenage curfew violators ought to be arrested because it wanted to deter other teenagers from curfew violation and wanted to send a clear message that it valued having underage children off the streets late at night. On this model, police clearly work for the community and must be responsive to the needs and interests of that community. One could imagine communities having associations with the police analogous to Parent-Teacher Associations, jointly establishing goals and programs.

The communitarian model is certainly consistent with the larger framework of liberal society. The liberal constraints function as baselines or background conditions and the hole of discretionary decision making is defined by community values. The community values could not be that police arrest only minority group members – that would violate the liberal protection of being treated as an equal. Racist communities could not enforce their racist beliefs. Analogously, communities that thought that wife beating was acceptable could not expect solidarity from the police. Nevertheless, beyond the concerns of positively violating the rights of minorities or women, or others, there are areas where particular communities' concerns could play a significant role. This model is, of course, an idealized one and does not reflect as it stands all the critical issues of policing in pluralistic societies. Whether there are communities like the imaginary Mayberry is questionable. Whether there are communities of shared values that coincide with the jurisdictions of police departments is also doubtful. There are, nevertheless, communities with shared *interests*, even if their values are quite divergent. These shared interests, which may be somewhat different from those of another neighborhood, provide a good starting place for discussions of discretionary choices in the community. Most importantly, this model emphasizes that the police should keep foremost in their thinking that they must justify their discretionary decisions to the people of the community in which they are working. The community's shared interests form a standard to which police should be bound. It is important to note that the police have expertise that the community members do not necessarily have and hence the police may not be in agreement with the community over every issue. Yet police must, at least in principle, be able to provide reasons for their discretionary actions to the community members, reasons that are consistent with the community's interests.

It is obvious which of these models is preferable in a liberal democracy. The so-called communitarian model, in which police and community work together on the acceptable norms of police discretionary decision making, is preferable in a liberal democratic society. The principle that in general should guide police discretionary authority is that their decisions be based upon reasons which members of that community could accept. This returns us to the contractarian justification with which we began. Many of the difficulties in which police find themselves, particularly with regard to minority communities, are generated by the fact that the police fail to have sufficient dialogue with members of those communities to come to some consensus or at least some understanding of the choices police should make in their neighborhoods. Those minority communities do not see the police working in their interests, representing their needs. What we should be able to expect from discretionary decision makers is that they take our interests in account. Who "we" are may depend upon the context. In the police case, "we" are the particular community being policed. We may not, as George Fletcher has suggested, have a right to a particular outcome or a particular decision.[26] But what we do have a right to, according to Fletcher, is that the decision maker use a particular process, that the decision makers focus on the interests of whomever they are accountable to in the decision-making process. Using this analysis of discretion, police, when exercising discretion, must attend to the interests of the people involved in any dispute and the citizens of the community in which they work. There are, obviously, impermissible outcomes that police cannot choose, those that involve a positive injustice to a person. For instance, we have a right not to be singled out for special abuse or harsh treatment on the basis of our race. On the other hand, there are no specific outcomes that we have a right to, that we can claim from the discretionary decision maker. We hire professionals for their expertise and can expect from them that they will make decisions that are in our best interests. And since the roles and goals of policing are varied, we can discuss with police departments "our" (the community's) interests. (Unlike psychiatry, for example, where there is one indisputable goal, getting the patient well, policing has more than one goal.) The citizens are the beneficiaries of the police expertise but not rights-bearers with claims to particular outcomes.[27]

Tyrannical abuses of discretion can be avoided if police reconceptualize their relationship to the citizenry they police. Appealing to shared community interests, and having an ongoing conversation with the members of the community in which they work, will change how police make discretionary choices and how they will evaluate them. If police thought that they had to be responsive to members of the community in which they work, and if they shared values with those people, then their choices would reflect that set of values. What this suggests is that, rather than designing more and more detailed rules which further narrow the range of options that police will have open to them, we should change how police see their work. The virtues of good policing will not, under this model, look like the virtues of the good soldier. Loyalty to one's fellow officers should be valued only if they merit loyalty, that is, only if they do their job well. Doing one's job well is working with the community and building on shared interests or conceptions of value and deciding on goals for the community with members of that community.

NOTES

The discussion of this essay, particularly by my commentator, John Kleinig, greatly enhanced my thinking about the topic of police discretion.

1. See, e.g., John Locke, *Second Treatise of Civil Government*.

2. See John Locke, *Second Treatise*; Thomas Hobbes, *Leviathan*; Immanuel Kant, *The Metaphysical Elements of Justice*; and John Rawls, *A Theory of Justice* (Cambridge: Harvard University Press, 1971).

3. 1 *Henry IV*, Riverside edition, ed. G. Blakemore Evans (Boston: Houghton Mifflin, 1974), 5.4.119-20.

4. Charles-Louis de Montesquieu, *The Spirit of the Laws* (New York: Collier, 1900), sec. 159.

5. Jerome Frank, *Law and the Modern Mind* (New York: Tudor, 1930).

6. H. L. A. Hart, *The Concept of Law* (Oxford: Clarendon Press, 1961).

7. Ronald Dworkin, "The Model of Rules I," in *Taking Rights Seriously* (Cambridge: Harvard University Press, 1977), pp. 32-33.

8. Ibid., p. 32.

9. Ibid., p. 33.

10. Ibid., p. 34.

11. See David Kairys, ed., *The Politics of Law* (New York: Pantheon, 1982); Mark Kelman, *A Guide to Critical Legal Studies* (Cambridge: Harvard University Press, 1987).

12. Kenneth Culp Davis, *Discretionary Justice: A Preliminary Inquiry* (Baton Rouge: Louisiana State University Press, 1969) p. 4.

13. See Harold Pepinsky, *Crime Control Strategies* (New York: Oxford University Press, 1980). Pepinsky provides an empirical and theoretical defense of the claim that law enforcement is literally a political exercise, an exercise of power, and in that exercise those who have more power as citizens are odds-on favorites to avoid the force of law. See also Michael Lynch and W. Byron Groves, *A Primer in Radical Criminology* (New York: Harrow and Heston, 1986), for a discussion of Marxist theories of crime and policing.

14. Henry Hart Jr. and Albert M. Sacks, *The Legal Process: Basic Problems in the Making and Application of Law*, 10th ed. (Cambridge: Harvard Law School, 1958), p. 162.

15. John Kleinig, "Response," infra, p. 65.

16. Ibid.

17. American Bar Association, *The Urban Police Function* (New York: Institute of Judicial Administration, 1973), p. 30.

18. International Association of Chiefs of Police, Police Code of Conduct, in *Professional Law Enforcement Codes: A Documentary Collection*, comp. and ed. John Kleinig with Yurong Zhang (Westport, CT: Greenwood Press, 1993), pp. 115-16. The code was originally intended (1989) to replace the Law Enforcement Code of Ethics but, after protests, was renamed (in 1991) the Police Code of Conduct

19. Howard Cohen, "Authority: The Limits of Discretion," in *Moral Issues in Police Work*, ed. Frederick Elliston and Michael Feldberg (Totowa, NJ: Rowman & Allanheld, 1985), pp. 27-41.

20. Ibid., p. 28.

21. Alan Firth, "Interrogation," *Police Review* 83, no. 4324 (28 November 1975), p. 1507.

22. Gary LaFree, *Rape and Criminal Justice: The Social Construction of Sexual Assault* (Belmont, CA: Wadsworth, 1989), pp. 73, 76.

23. Samuel Walker, *Taming the System* (New York: Oxford University Press, 1993), p. 34.

24. There are obviously other models but I will use these two to make a general point.

25. Thomas Hobbes, *Leviathan*, ch. 13.

26. See George Fletcher, "Some Unwise Reflections about Discretion," *Law & Contemporary Problems* 47 (autumn 1984), pp. 269-86. Fletcher discusses the cases of an investment counselor and a professor. When the investment counselor exer-

cises discretion in deciding where to commit her clients' money or a professor exercises discretion in the selection of reading materials for her course, neither the counselor's clients nor the professor's students have a right to any particular outcome. But the clients and students have a right to a particular process.

27. Ibid., p. 272.

Response

John Kleinig

I am strongly sympathetic to Joan McGregor's view that discretion is to be understood not merely as the effective power to choose how one will act but rather as a normatively constrained sphere of judgment. Discretion is a permission, privilege, or prerogative to use one's own judgment about how to make a practical determination. The discretion that police possess is thus to be seen as a set of practical options bounded by norms.

Her references to radical critiques of judicial and police decision making are also salutary, for they remind us of the ways in which even authorizations of discretion or even individual exercises of discretion may manifest discriminatory values. The interests of race, gender, and class may help to structure discretionary provisions or, more likely, may infect particular exercises of discretion, thus making it important that opportunities for discretionary judgments be accompanied by guidelines and also be regularly monitored.

That much said, I nevertheless have some reservations about, or at least some questions to pose regarding, Professor McGregor's discussion of the norms that should inform or constrain exercises of police discretionary authority. I limit myself to two concerns.

1. In professional contexts, the norms that constrain the making of discretionary judgments are primarily those implicit in the practices that constitute the profession and that give it its special claim to professional status. Law, medicine, architecture, engineering, and so on, are constituted by practices that are structured by regulative goals, underwritten by standards of competence, and bound by moral norms that shape the discretionary authority of their practitioners.

Professor McGregor argues that in a liberal democratic society the normative constraints on police discretionary decision making ought to be reflective of "shared community values."[1]

I am not sure to what extent she believes that this "Mayberry" character-ization accommodates all the norms or values that are appropriately brought to bear on putative exercises of police discretionary authority. I think, for example, that even if we do not see policing as a profession, there might still be internal expectations about the level of competence that should be displayed by discretionary judgments.[2]

But leaving this issue aside, there are, I believe, two related problems with Professor McGregor's Mayberry appeal, problems that she may ac-knowledge, but which still need to be worked out in greater detail. One concerns the presumption that there exists an identifiable community constituted in part by shared values; the other concerns the identification of the relevant community values.

Professor McGregor notes at the beginning of her discussion of norma-tive constraints that within different jurisdictions we might expect police discretion to be exercised differently, though she indicates that within a particular jurisdiction one should expect – for reasons of formal justice – that exercises of discretion will express themselves in relevantly similar ways in relevantly similar cases. What constitutes a "jurisdiction" for these purposes is not specified, though I would be prepared to allow that there might exist jurisdictions characterized by shared community values. Some rural communities would be most likely to qualify.

However, in large urban and even suburban situations – in this country at least – we encounter a serious problem. For here – if we look at the values actually held by urban dwellers – the presumption of a community, let alone a community partially constituted by shared values, seems im-plausible. To see this, we need not appeal only to the competing interests of capital and labor, and the geographical separation of work and resi-dence, but should also take note of the deep rifts caused by ethnic, cultural, and even religious diversity, and the legacies of racial and gender dis-crimination. Even if we wish to exclude some of these manifest values from recognition on the grounds of their incompatibility with the pre-sumptions of liberal democracy, a wide plurality of competing interests and values is nevertheless still likely to remain. In other words, there may not be too much by way of overall community, and such values as charac-terize particular pockets of shared life may not provide the most appropri-ate touchstone for discretionary decisions. The appeal to "community" and its supposedly shared values is thus much more problematic than Professor McGregor acknowledges.

To some extent, Professor McGregor mutes the problem of oppositional diversity by stipulating a liberal democratic community as the arena for police discretionary decision making. This at least allows for a discounting of some of the competing values that will be found to exist. If every member of the community is to be treated as an equal, then certain forms of race, gender, and class discrimination will be excluded from any calculus of community values. However, we should not assume that the appeal to shared goals and values is necessarily connected to a liberal democratic order or, even if there is a liberal democratic order, that it will be possible to discern – except at the most general level – a set of shared goals and values. It is precisely because of the difficulties of identifying the latter that official decision making so often focuses on issues of process rather than on substantive homogeneity.

In the revised version of her essay, Professor McGregor seeks to respond to the problem of diversity by focusing on shared interests rather than shared values. [61] In this way, she believes that some of the concerns that I have expressed might be circumvented. They might. However, the appeal to interests is itself very problematic, since they can be understood either subjectively or objectively. Subjectively, interests are those things in which I have a stake, those things that matter to me; objectively, my interests are constituted by the ingredients of my welfare. Now, although it might be argued that there will be some congruence of people's welfare interests, even in a somewhat fragmented society, I am not so sure that this can be said of their subjective interests. Which interests does Professor McGregor have in mind?

In expressing my concerns here, I do not want to suggest that any appeal to shared community values or interests must be abandoned. Indeed, without some such appeal it is difficult to know how police authority could be justified in the first place. Whatever else we may want to say about policing in a liberal democracy, it serves those over whom it has jurisdiction and it must be responsive to their voices.

It may be, however, that what we should have in mind when we appeal to "shared community values or interests" is not something that can be simply "read off" from the population served but is a much more problematic amalgam constructed from historically legitimated traditions and ideals as much as from the immanent demands and expectations of those who are being policed. The ring of Dworkin's doughnut, in other words, is constituted not only by laws, administrative rules, and other formal constraints, but by the more open-ended prescriptions of political theory, historical tradition, and social aspiration. Of course, this may leave the prospect of a permanent question mark against discretionary decisions; but provided – as I think Professor McGregor agrees – those decisions remain available to the scrutiny of those who could be affected by them, there is still the possibility of their social legitimation or at least acceptance.

My suggestions here are somewhat abstract, and I think their implementation is much more difficult to achieve. Where, as in New York, police officers are not required to live within or even adjacent to the communities they police, there may well be a perceptual problem so far as the ideological shaping of discretionary decision making is concerned. Whether an Irish Catholic officer from an enclave in Bay Ridge is likely to make appropriate discretionary decisions in the West Village, or an officer born and raised in Westchester is likely to do well on the Lower East Side, is not at all certain. Although big city police academies these days try to sensitize their officers to the variety of lifestyles that might be accommodated within a liberal democratic society, it is not clear that they are always very successful in modifying years of habituation or indeed of countering the considerable pressures that will emerge from an ongoing police culture.

2. Without abandoning the difficult task of appealing to community values or interests, I also want to draw attention to a different form of appeal embedded in Professor McGregor's essay that I think may be helpful in structuring discretion. Discretion, as Dworkin notes, is context-relative, and the kind of discretion that is appropriate to police will to a significant extent be structured by the work that is theirs – that is, by their role, with its implicit rights and responsibilities. There is of course an initial problem here, because of uncertainty about the content of the police role and the priority assigned to factors within that role. As Professor McGregor quotes it, the IACP Police Code of Conduct includes among the fundamental duties of a police officer "serving the community; safeguarding lives and property; protecting the innocent; keeping the peace; and ensuring the rights of all to liberty, equality and justice." The same code also draws attention to the importance of discretionary authority, noting, inter alia, that "it is important to remember that a timely word of advice rather than arrest . . . can be a more effective means of achieving a desired end."

I find this account interesting because, although it presents a very demanding set of objectives, it does not explicitly include law enforcement among the "fundamental duties" of a police officer – but it does make an explicit nod in the direction of selective enforcement. This expands the discretionary authority of police in certain respects by subsuming the specific task of law enforcement under more general social ends. And by not requiring full enforcement it acknowledges that discretionary authority may attach (albeit in limited ways) to every dimension of police work.

Yet at the same time, by adverting to the various social ends that it does, the code provides an important (though not a sufficient) constraint on the use of discretion. The hole of police discretion is negotiated not only by reference to liberal democratic values and historical traditions but also by a particular conception of what police are to be about. I do not say that this is sufficient to allow us to "read off" right responses to situations in which discretion is called for – that would defeat the presumption that discretion is required in the first place – but it does give us a way of gauging the size and shape of the doughnut's hole.

NOTES

1. Joan McGregor, "From the State of Nature to Mayberry: The Nature of Police Discretion," in this volume, p. 60. Subsequent page references to McGregor's essay are enclosed in brackets in the text.

2. In her revised essay, Professor McGregor acknowledges the relevance of such internal considerations [52], but she does not show how they might be integrated into the Mayberry model to which she eventually turns.

Chapter 3

Is Police Discretion Justified in a Free Society?

Jeffrey Reiman

By "police discretion" I understand the freedom of police officers to decide whether or not to arrest an individual when the conditions that would legally justify that arrest are present and when the officer can make the arrest without sacrificing other equally or more pressing legal duties. So I do not count as police discretion the choice of which individual to arrest when the arrest of several is similarly legally justified but the arrest of only one is physically possible. And of course I exclude all the other important, and I think inescapable, acts of judgment that police officers must make (for example, deciding whether the conditions legally justifying arrest are present). Our question, then, is this: Is it justifiable in a free society to allow police officers freedom to determine whether or not to arrest someone when they legally and physically can make the arrest ? The short answer is no. The long answer will require a look at the nature of free societies and the sort of law enforcement they demand.

Before proceeding to this, I want to qualify my thesis in one important way. Police are commonly charged with the dual task of enforcing law and maintaining order. In pursuit of the latter aim, they disperse unruly crowds, quiet noisy neighbors, break up fights before they begin, clear the streets of drunks or prostitutes, and so on. In the context of such order maintenance, the police power to arrest is not so much a power to limit citizens' freedom as it is a power to get troublesome individuals to desist from offending behavior or to clear the area. As long as arrest is used only in this way, I think it is acceptable for police to refrain from exercising their arrest power – even where the facts justify its exercise – if they judge that milder means will serve the goal of order maintenance. Thus it seems to me that discretion does have a place here.[1] But when arrest is used to set in motion a series of events aimed at seriously limiting citizens' freedom, or when the threat of arrest itself seriously limits citizens' freedom, I contend that police ought not to have discretion. A brief detour through the history of political philosophy will help explain why.

Plato is well known for the (it is to be hoped!) unrealistic claim, argued at great length in the *Republic*, that a good state will be possible only when philosophers become kings or kings philosophers.[2] In this good state, there are to be few laws, since Plato thinks of laws the way he thinks of medication: more than just a minimum betokens and promotes a permanently sickly constitution. More particularly, the philosopher-king does not need laws because he or she knows the good, and thus can determine in each new case exactly what is right to do. (I'm not being politically correct here; Plato actually argued for equal opportunity for women to become philosopher-kings.) It would make no sense to tie the philosopher-king's hands with laws, since laws bring about only generally good outcomes and they might prevent the philosopher-king from doing exactly what is right in each new particular situation.

But the *Republic* is not Plato's last word. His last dialogue, and thus his last word – at least on the topic of the good state – is the *Laws*. And the title should make clear that here, near the close of his life, Plato took a far more positive view of the role of and need for laws than he did as an idealistic young man. Midway (in content and in time) between the *Republic* and the *Laws*, stands Plato's dialogue called the *Statesman*. In it, we see unfold before our eyes the shift from the rule of the philosopher-king to the rule of law. It will be instructive to see what reasons ground this shift in Plato's views.

The dialogue in the *Statesman* takes place between a character called "the Eleatic stranger," and another called "the younger Socrates" (not to be confused with the Socrates who leads the discussion in the *Republic*). The stranger starts by speaking of the true statesman, the one who possesses the "royal art" of ruling wisely and justly, and young Socrates balks when the stranger suggests that such a statesman may rule without laws. The stranger then explains that

> the best thing of all is not that the law should rule, but that a man should rule, supposing him to have wisdom and the royal power. . . . Because the law does not perfectly comprehend what is noblest and most just for all and therefore cannot enforce what is best. The differences of men and actions,

and the endless irregular movements of human things, do not admit of any universal and simple rule.[3]

The stranger likens the royal art to other arts such as those practiced by physicians or physical trainers. If these individuals truly possess their arts, it would be absurd to bind them by preestablished rules. If a physician gave a prescription to a patient, only later to discover a better way of curing his ailment, we would hardly insist that the physician stick to the earlier treatment. We would allow, even want, him to do just what his art taught him was best in this particular case. So too, the practitioner of the art of ruling. Says the stranger, "Then if the law is not the perfection of right, why are we compelled to make laws at all? The reason of this has next to be investigated."[4]

Turning to this, the stranger points out that, like other arts, the royal art can never be mastered by more than a few individuals. Thus, there may be rulers who falsely claim to have that art and who therefore say that it is for the best that they rule without laws. Such false rulers are called tyrants, and their lawless rule is as bad as the genuine ruler's rule is good. Moreover, the fact that few are likely to possess the royal art, combined with the possibility of tyrants pretending to have it, makes people suspicious of anyone who would rule without law, even those who have the art. People "can never be made to believe that any one can be worthy of such authority. . . ; they fancy that he will be a despot who will wrong and harm and slay whom he pleases."[5] This suspicion creates instability, which, itself invites tyranny as worried citizens flock to demagogues for protection. In short, because there is no clear identifying mark of the true philosopher-king, no one can be allowed to rule without laws. Says the stranger, "as the State is not like a beehive, and has no natural head who is at once recognized to be the superior both in body and in mind, mankind are obliged to meet and make laws. . . ."[6]

Plato calls rule by laws "second best."[7] It cannot do justice (full, complete, perfectly tailored justice) to the complexity and variability of human affairs, in the way that a genuine philosopher-king unconstrained by laws could. But given how few true philosopher-kings there are, how difficult it is to recognize one and above all how dangerous it would be if a phony philosopher-king ruled without laws, we must settle for second best – meet and make laws and hold everyone strictly accountable. Ironically, the laws are good for the same reason that makes them only second best, namely, because they limit the power of the ruler. They protect the citizens from the rulers, and the citizens pay for this protection by giving up the possibility of perfectly good solutions to their complex and variable problems.

Plato teaches, then, three lessons about the rule of law: First, the function of the rule of law is not only to render justice to the citizens, but also to protect them from their governors. Second, the justification of the rule of law cannot be that it produces the best results in every case; its justification is that it gives generally good albeit imperfect results while protecting against tyranny. Law represents, to use a term not found in the Platonic corpus, a trade-off: the possibility of perfect outcomes is traded off for security against the worst outcomes. Third, this trade-off, and thus the rule of law itself, would not be necessary if states were like beehives, in which those who are truly fit to rule are naturally marked and easily recognized.

From these Platonic lessons about the rule of law, we can draw some morals about police discretion, since police discretion begins where the rule of law ends: police discretion is precisely the subjection of law to a human decision beyond the law. Like rule by philosopher-kings unfettered by law, police discretion makes possible a tailoring of justice to the complexity and variability of human affairs. Thus, one moral to draw is that if we give up police discretion, we also give up the possibility of some results that are better than what we get by strict application of the law. The second moral is that if we allow police discretion, we give certain citizens a special discretionary power over others which can be used in tyrannical ways. Consequently, if police discretion is to be justified, we must be confident that it is more likely to be used to arrive at benefits superior to those the rule of law provides than to be used tyrannically. And, finally, this confidence will be rash to the degree in which states are unlike beehives. The final moral, then, is that the less we are able to pick out those who are truly fit to exercise authority, the less confident we should be about allowing discretionary law enforcement.

Though these Platonic morals regarding police discretion continue to have relevance today, for us they are only a starting point. They do not give us the whole moral truth about police discretion – at least, not in terms that are adequate to modern political theory, nor in terms adequate to the project promised in my title. Plato's republic was not, and was not meant to be, a free society. To shift our perspective and look at the problem from the standpoint of the conditions and nature of a free society is to move a greater distance than might immediately be apparent. My purpose, then, in starting with Plato is, in addition to distilling some general truths about the rule of law and its opposite, to use Plato as a backdrop against which the features of modern political theorizing, with its emphasis on the value of freedom, can most clearly be seen. For this, we must shift to modern thinkers like Hobbes and Locke, and contemporaries like Rawls. Though all of these are broadly in the "social contract" tradition, their contractarianism as such is of secondary importance for our concerns. Far more important for our purposes is the way in which they view the state and the task of political philosophy.

Interestingly, both Hobbes and Locke start where the last of the Platonic morals left off. They echo, and in fact extend, Plato's observation that the human society is unlike a beehive, in that there are no naturally marked and thus easily identifiable natural rulers. The crucial chapter 13 of Hobbes's *Leviathan*, the chapter in which he introduces his grim account of the state of nature and the reasons for getting out of it by creating a political commonwealth, begins:

> Nature hath made men so equall, in the faculties of body, and mind; as that though there bee found one man sometimes manifestly stronger in body, or of quicker mind then another; yet when all is reckoned together, the difference between man, and man, is not so considerable, as that one man can thereupon claim to himselfe any benefit, to which another may not pretend, as well as he. For as to the strength of body, the weakest has strength enough to kill the strongest. . . .
>
> And as to the faculties of the mind . . . , I find yet a greater equality amongst men, than that of strength.[8]

And chapter 2 of Locke's *Second Treatise of Civil Government*, the chapter in which he introduces his own not-so-grim view of the state of nature, begins by making the same point as Hobbes:

> To understand political power right, and derive it from its original, we must consider, what state all men are naturally in, and that is, a *state of perfect freedom* to order their actions . . . as they think fit . . . , without asking leave, or depending on the will of any other man.
>
> A *state* also *of equality*, wherein all the power and jurisdiction is reciprocal, no one having more than another; there being nothing more evident, than that creatures of the same species and rank, promiscuously born to all the same advantages of nature, should also be equal one amongst another. . . .[9]

To these modern thinkers, human social life is less like a beehive than even Plato thought. For Plato, we are not like a beehive because natural rulers are not naturally marked and easily recognized. This led to suspicion and fear of a false ruler who might tyrannize people, and from there to preference, albeit reluctant, for the rule of law as second best. For Hobbes and Locke, and I daresay for us as well, we are not like a beehive because there *are* no natural rulers. No one has – by virtue of innate ability or some other trait – natural fitness to rule others. There are no natural rulers to recognize, no queen bees, no philosopher-kings. And this has new and profound implications for understanding the danger of tyranny and the attraction of the rule of law.

In the state of nature, each has authority over herself and none has authority over others. Let us call authority over oneself "personal authority," and authority over others, "political authority." In the state of nature, then, there is no political authority, only everyone's full and equal personal authority. If there is no natural political authority, such political authority as exists is artificial – created by us. It should be clear that personal and political authority are mutually exclusive categories. The creation and enlargement of political authority is necessarily at the expense of personal authority (and vice versa). Since any political authority that exists is humanly created, it is either taken by force from, or freely given by, those over whom it is exercised. Note that this is a claim in political theory, not in psychology. Neither the taking nor the giving of authority need be consciously or intentionally done.

Since political authority detracts from personal authority, it results from either a forced taking or a free giving up of some of an individual's personal authority. If political authority is taken by force, then it has no moral claim on those over whom it is exercised. Consequently, for political authority to be morally legitimate, for it to exercise a claim on citizens, it must be freely given. But the political authority essential to a state cannot be freely given in the form of an actual voluntary donation by citizens: the benefits of a state depend on its already being in existence when people are born so that they can be protected and educated to the point at which they could make the donation. Thus, the test of whether political authority is legitimate becomes the theoretical one of whether it would be *reasonable* for citizens to make this donation. And that question is answered positively if what citizens get from political authority amounts to the best possible bargain for what they give up for it.

Here lies the analytic power and normative force of the social contract: it embodies the terms on which it would be reasonable for humans equal and complete in their personal authority to grant to some individuals political authority over them. This is why it has never been important that the contract and the state of nature are historical fictions. The contract spells out conditions under which citizens' surrender of some of their equal personal authority is reasonable, and thus, though it is the purest fiction, it provides a standard for legitimate political authority over free people.

An important implication of this contractarianism is that legitimate political authority is literally concocted out of the parts of free people's personal authority that they surrender to the political commonwealth. The lawmaker's authority to make laws is derived from the authority that free people have to make decisions about how they should live, and the law enforcer's authority to back laws up with force is derived from the authority that free people have to use force in defense of their authority to govern their own lives, and so on. Thus, Locke says of the extent of the political authority in a legitimate state:

> It is *not*, nor can possibly be absolutely *arbitrary* over the lives and fortunes of the people: for it being but the joint power of every member of society . . . ; it can be no more than those persons had in a state of nature before they entered into society, and gave up to the community.[10]

And Rawls can say of liberal democracies that "political power, which is always coercive power, is the power of the public, that is, of free and equal citizens as a collective body."[11]

A corollary of this point is that authority exercised by political officials beyond that which it would be reasonable for people to surrender in forming a state is illegitimate. And "illegitimate" here means morally indistinguishable from the sorts of invasions that characterized the state of nature and which, once a state exists, are called "tyrannical" or "criminal." If political authority is understood as the authority that free people reasonably deposit in a state; authority exercised beyond that amount is stolen, taken by force. The force may be that of habit or tradition or ignorance, but forced taking rather than free giving it remains. Thus, authority exercised beyond what is rationally granted is morally indistinguishable from tyranny or crime – that is, from the sorts of coercive invasions the avoidance of which makes the state reasonable in the first place. Rather than citizens having an obligation to respect such authority, they have the right to resist it. Says Locke:

> *Where-ever law ends, tyranny begins* . . . ; and whosoever in authority exceeds the power given him by the law, and makes use of the force he has under his command, to compass that upon the subject, which the law allows not, ceases in that to be a magistrate; and, acting without authority, may be opposed, as any other man, who by force invades the right of another.[12]

It should be evident now that the political authority that governs a free society has a very different moral structure from that which governs Plato's republic. This will be clearest if we imagine, contrary to fact, that

Plato's philosopher-king was dedicated, above all, to promoting the freedom of his or her subjects. Then we could picture the philosopher-king's authority as a kind of unlimited, all-purpose power to do whatever is needed to realize, or even maximize, people's freedom. This is not how political authority in a free society should be understood, however. The most important difference is that political authority that is created by free people is not authority to do whatever is necessary to realize any particular goal, even the maximization of freedom. It is rather a specific, limited grant of authority to do certain things, and only certain things.

Another way to put this difference is as follows. The Platonic ruler is authorized to accomplish a goal, and thus his authority is limited not in its scope but only in the purposes to which it can be directed. By contrast, the modern ruler of a free society is authorized to perform certain specified actions, and thus her authority is limited in its scope. The political officials of a free society are not empowered to do whatever is necessary to bring about some overriding purpose, even the maximization of freedom itself. They have only the authority that they have been given, and they must keep within that even if exceeding it would better achieve popular goals. In this respect, we can understand the efforts of the founders of the American republic, first, to list in the Constitution the specific powers granted to the central government, and then, when it became obvious that the central government could not realistically be limited that way, to list in the first ten amendments to the Constitution specific areas in which the government could not tread even in the service of desirable goals.

From this discussion of political authority there follows a very simple conclusion for police discretion: there are only two ways in which it can be justified in a free society, either by explicit grant from the citizens or by showing that it would be reasonable for the citizens to make such a grant. I take it that there has been no such explicit grant to police. Judges, by contrast, are, or at least once were, explicitly given sentencing ranges within which to choose the most just outcome all things considered. But the police are simply and explicitly authorized to enforce the laws that the people's representatives enact, and no more.

Would it, however, be reasonable for the people to grant the police some range of freedom of decision about whether or not to enforce laws when they legally and physically can do so? Here it seems to me that the answer is no. It would not be reasonable for four very important reasons: First, doing so renders the laws themselves vague and uncertain. Rather than stating forthrightly what will and what will not be permitted, laws subject to discretionary enforcement effectively contain the additional wild-card proviso "if a police officer judges it appropriate, and so on." Second, adding this proviso amounts to amending the laws as passed by the people's representatives. Third, police discretionary power is almost certain to be used frequently in ways that discriminate (in effect, if not in intent) against the poor and powerless and unpopular in our society[13] – undermining the legitimacy of the law where it is most in need of legitimacy. Fourth, granting police freedom to decide whether or not to enforce the law gives police officers the opportunity to use that freedom as leverage over other citizens.

Notice that with this fourth reason the danger of tyranny lies not so much in the police officer's power to arrest, and thus limit citizens' liberty, but in the new power police officers have when it is for them to decide whether to arrest. It might be thought that as long as the police arrest only those who are legitimately subject to arrest, then the discretionary power not to arrest only reduces state interference with the individual below what is legitimate – and thus cannot be tyrannical. But this overlooks the fact that discretion to arrest or not is itself a power over citizens, separate from the power to arrest as such. Over and above their power to enforce the laws, discretion gives the police an additional power beyond what the law authorizes, the power to use their law enforcement authority as a threat. That such threats are the common fare of TV police dramas, and sometimes the only means that real cops have to wring information out of small-time drug dealers or prostitutes and the like, hardly shows that this is right or appropriate to the government of a free society. If we are not ready to endorse a law requiring all citizens to give the police whatever information they want, then such use of discretion as leverage to get information amounts to allowing police to exercise a power over some citizens that we would not allow them to exercise over all. Nor does public acceptance of this phenomenon amount to a public grant of the authority to do it. What it suggests, rather, is that most people don't mind if the police treat drug dealers and prostitutes in a tyrannical fashion.

Bear in mind, I do not doubt that treating drug dealers or prostitutes in a tyrannical fashion may be effective in achieving larger goals, such as catching more serious criminals. But political authority in a free society is not an unlimited grant to do whatever is needed to accomplish good goals (as Miranda warnings and search and seizure protections testify). If most people want the police to exercise discretion in enforcing drug or other vice laws, then the people must say so through their representatives, and this will require in turn that the new authority be justified in open public discussion. And, in fact, my opinion is the same about any area in which it might be thought good to grant the police discretion. Put the grant into the law, or forget about it.

Before concluding, I want to draw support for my argument from another modern political theorist who, while not a social contractarian, played an important role in the thinking of the founders of the American republic. I refer to "the celebrated Montesquieu" to whom Madison, writing in *Federalist* paper 47 attributes that "invaluable precept in the science of politics," the doctrine of the separation of powers.

Montesquieu presents this precept in the context of his discussion of the conditions of political liberty. It is interesting that Montesquieu understands this liberty as "a right of doing whatever the laws permit," and not in the Millian sense, as a freedom from laws. Like Locke, Montesquieu speaks from an older, though still modern, tradition, in which freedom exists as long as all are governed by publicly promulgated laws and only by those laws.[14] He too, then, accepts that the rule of law is the bulwark of liberty. About this bulwark and its maintenance, he writes:

> The political liberty of the subject is a tranquility of mind arising from the opinion each person has of his safety. In order to have this liberty, it is requisite the government be so constituted as one man need not be afraid of another.
>
> When the legislative and executive powers are united in the same person . . . , there can be no liberty. . . .
>
> Again there can be no liberty, if the judiciary power be not separated from the legislative and executive. . . . Were it joined to the executive power, the judge might behave with violence and oppression.[15]

Police discretion is in effect a mixing of legislative and judiciary power with executive power, and thus likewise a threat to political liberty. It mixes legislative power by deciding which laws really are to be enforced, and it mixes judiciary power by deciding who is to come under the laws that are enforced. Now, though neither Montesquieu nor Madison says so explicitly, I think the idea behind the separation of powers is simply that the more people who have to participate in an act of government, the less likely it is that it will be an evil or tyrannical act. Thus, liberty will be best protected if police, judges, and lawmakers each do what they are mandated to do.

I conclude, then, that police discretion has no rightful place in a free society. Where it appears appropriate, I believe this is so because it compensates for flaws elsewhere in the system. For example, police sometimes hesitate to use their powers of arrest because they know that an arrestee may have to spend the night in a detention cell and will get a potentially damaging arrest record even if he is finally not charged or is eventually acquitted.[16] But this could be dealt with by making sure that there is adequate prosecutorial and judicial staff to process arrestees quickly, and by providing for the expunging of arrest records that do not result in a conviction – something long overdue in a society that believes that people are innocent until proven guilty.

Where such institutional flaws are not the problem, then, I contend that seemingly appropriate exercises of police discretion reflect flaws in our laws. For any area in which it would be good to grant police discretion, it will be possible to spell out the rules governing that discretion and build them into the laws (thus eliminating it as discretion in the sense I have been using it here, that is, as freedom to decide whether to apply the law). It follows, then, that for any area in which it is contended that police should have discretion, this will be either to compensate for institutional flaws or inadequate legal draftsmanship. At best discretion solves a problem at the wrong place in the criminal justice system.[17]

Moreover, to the extent that sections of the public are content with police discretion and do not build it into the laws, a dangerous duplicitousness is at play. The people through their representatives say one thing, and through their tacit acceptance say another. They make categorical laws to vent publicly their moral outrage, and then allow the police effectively to redraft the laws once they are out of public sight.

Earlier and in passing, I suggested that there is a difference between Locke's and Montesquieu's view of the relation between law and liberty and Mill's view. Mill's view is that law limits liberty, and thus to enlarge liberty we should shrink the reach of the law. Locke's and Montesquieu's view is that law limits the arbitrary acts of others, and thus to protect liberty we should insist that officials act according to the laws and exercise no authority beyond them. Both views are correct: the simple fact is that a free society should have few and clear criminal laws which the police should be expected to enforce wherever they apply, whenever it is physically possible to do so, as long as doing so is not in conflict with enforcing even more important laws or with explicit legislative guidelines. The police already have enormous powers over citizens that other citizens lack. They should not be given the additional power of being able to use their authority to arrest at their own discretion.

Moreover, the laws should not express society's moral aspirations, but its real will – the terms on which it is truly prepared to act. If the legislators are making more laws than the police can enforce, they should make fewer laws or employ more police officers. The laws should express the actual treatment that the society wants, and police enforcement of those laws should be as automatic as possible. The reduction of discretion should be carried throughout the system. We should have sentencing guidelines for judges, though I would hope for something quite a bit less brutal than the current combination of guidelines plus mandatory minimum sentences. And we should correct the recent lamentable tendency of this combination to shift discretion from judges (who exercise discretion in open court and who are at least somewhat insulated from political pressures) to prosecutors (who exercise discretion out of public view and who are political through and through). Reasonable sentencing guidelines for judges should be matched with reasonable charging guidelines for prosecutors.[18] If these, as well as reasonable arrest guidelines for police, were built into the law, we would have moved a great distance toward realizing the requirements of a free society as understood by liberal political philosophers from Locke to Rawls.

NOTES

I wish to express my appreciation to the participants in the workshop for their many helpful comments, objections, and recommendations. In particular, I thank Professor William Heffernan of John Jay College for his challenging and useful commentary on this essay.

1. I was convinced of the need to make this qualification of my thesis by Professor James Fyfe of Temple University.

2. *Republic* in *The Dialogues of Plato*, trans. B. Jowett (New York: Random House, 1937), vol. I, p. 737.

3. *Statesman* in *The Dialogues of Plato*, trans. B. Jowett (New York: Random House, 1937), vol. II, p. 322.

4. Ibid.

5. Ibid., p. 329.

6. Ibid.

7. Ibid., p. 325.

8. Thomas Hobbes, *Leviathan* (Buffalo: Prometheus, 1988), p. 63.

9. John Locke, *Second Treatise of Civil Government* (Indianapolis: Hackett, 1980), p. 8, emphasis in original.

10. Ibid., p. 70, emphasis in original.

11. John Rawls, *Political Liberalism* (New York: Columbia University Press, 1993), p. 216.

12. Locke, *Second Treatise*, p. 103, emphasis in original.

13. See, for example, Dennis D. Powell, "A Study of Police Discretion in Six Southern Cities," *Journal of Police Science and Administration* 17, no. 1 (1990), pp. 1-7;

as well as the studies reported in Jeffrey Reiman, *The Rich Get Richer and the Poor Get Prison: Ideology, Class and Criminal Justice,* 4th ed. (Needham, MA: Allyn & Bacon, 1995), pp. 105-8. For a general overview of the problem and recent attempts to solve it, see Samuel Walker, *Taming the System: The Control of Discretion in Criminal Justice, 1950-1990* (New York: Oxford University Press, 1993), esp. ch. 2, "Police Discretion."

14. Writes Locke: "for *law,* in its true notion, is not so much the limitation as *the direction of a free and intelligent agent* to his proper interest, and . . . freedom is not, as we are told, *a liberty for every man to do what he lists:* (for who could be free, when every other man's humour might domineer over him?) but a *liberty* to dispose, and order as he lists, his person, actions, possessions, and his whole property, within the allowance of those laws under which he is, and therein not to be subject to the arbitrary will of another, but freely follow his own" (*Second Treatise,* p. 32, emphasis in original).

15. Charles-Louis de Montesquieu, *The Spirit of the Laws* (New York: Hafner, 1949), pp. 151-52. Interestingly, Montesquieu recommends that judges too be deprived of discretion in applying the law: ". . . judges are no more than the mouth that pronounces the words of the law, mere passive beings, incapable of moderating either its force or its rigor" (p. 159).

16. For a sensitive description of cases in which police hesitate to arrest individuals accused by people of doubtful credibility, see H. Richard Uviller, "The Unworthy Victim: Police Discretion in the Credibility Call," *Law & Contemporary Problems* 47, no. 4 (1984), pp. 15-33.

17. I think the same can be said to those who think that the police ought at least to have discretion not to enforce unjust laws. It is easy enough to point to some outrageously unjust law and say it would be better if police were free not to enforce that law. But we are concerned with general policies. And that implies that what must be argued for is a general right of police to decide which laws are unjust enough not to be enforced. For this to be justified, we would need (at the very least) evidence showing that in general the police will be better judges of the justice of the laws than the legislators who make them – whereas the evidence of discrimination by the police argues in the opposite direction. Moreover, it would most likely better serve the cause of justice if police were to enforce unjust laws so that the society would have to face the consequences of its unjust legislation, than if police correct injustice through publicly invisible acts of nonenforcement. It is the legislature that should correct unjust legislation, not the police – another case in which police discretion corrects for a problem that should be corrected elsewhere. Beyond this, it is, I think, inappropriate to apply to the police the model of justifiable civil disobedience. When private citizens engage in civil disobedience, they characteristically submit to the judgment of the law, and thus they pose no threat to the rule of law itself (this is one reason that their disobedience is *civil*). When police or other public officials fail to enforce the law, then the rule of law itself is undermined. At a minimum, if the police refrain from enforcing a law because they believe it to be unjust, they should make their nonenforcement public, in the way that civil disobedients make their disobedience public. Then we might hope that lawmakers would be pressured to respond by improving the law.

18. An interesting proposal to this effect is made in Note, "Developments in the Law: Race and the Criminal Process," *Harvard Law Review* 101(1988), pp. 1550-51.

Response: Police Discretion to Arrest

William C. Heffernan

On reading Professor Reiman's essay on police discretion, it occurred to me that asking me to serve as his critic was a bit like asking Ozzie to sit in criticism of Harriet. Our differences are relatively modest – or at least we do not differ much in our conclusions about police discretion, for I agree with Professor Reiman that when (1) police officers have the legal authority to arrest someone and (2) they can do so without sacrificing equally or more pressing legal duties, they generally should do so. Moreover, I also agree with an implicit point in Professor Reiman's essay – that the arrest decision just described (and its cousins, the stop-and-frisk and deadly-force decisions) are the distinctive problems in police discretion, that other discretionary issues police confront (for example, how to interpret terms such as "probable cause" or "in custody") are part of a larger complex of issues the police share with other parties interested in the criminal justice system.

But there are at least some points on which we differ. First, I arrive at my distrust of police arrest discretion by following a different chain of reasoning. And second, I am prepared to say only that I distrust this kind of discretion; I am not prepared, as Professor Reiman seems to be, to reject it altogether in law enforcement settings.[1]

In an essay I published a decade ago on police discretion to arrest,[2] I argued against the exercise of such discretion by pointing to the fact that police officers take an oath to enforce the law fully on becoming members of their departments. In the years since that essay's appearance, I've concluded that other issues deserve greater prominence. As I now see matters, three issues must be considered in establishing a framework for thinking about police discretion to arrest.

1. Do the officers under consideration exercise authority in a generally just society?
2. Even if they do, is the law they are charged with enforcing a patently unjust one?
3. Is there a division of labor within the society that justifies citizens in relying on the police to enforce the law?

As I understand him, Professor Reiman has confined his inquiry largely to the first question. If a society is not a generally just one, then, I think he would agree, it is far from clear that officers should enforce its laws. Should a South African police officer during apartheid have arrested a black person who stole from a white landowner to feed his family? Should a policeman in Nazi Germany have arrested a Jew who killed a member of the SS? One may, as a general matter, assert that prohibitions against theft and killing are justifiable but also assert that in the special circumstances of an unjust state a police officer – admittedly, this will be the very rare police officer in such a state – does the right thing by *not* enforcing those prohibitions. In speaking of a "generally just society," I limit my remarks to those political institutions that rational agents, acting from a position of equality, would agree to establish in striking a bargain with one another, a standard that Professor Reiman would probably also endorse.

But a further question must be asked: can generally just political institutions generate patently unjust laws? Professor Reiman doesn't address this question directly, but I think it must be confronted when thinking about police arrest discretion. Consider, for example, America's massive exclusion of political and ethnic refugees during World War II. If an INS official had failed, despite a clear mandate to do so, to enforce an exclusion order against the passengers of a ship carrying such refugees, then, in my opinion, that officer would have merited commendation, not condemnation. Professor Reiman might argue that he is concerned only with the best bargain those living within an already existing political society would be able to make. Because America's exclusion of refugees during the early forties (and in more recent years as well) involved people who were *not* members of our society, he could say that he is not concerned about wrongs done to them. I find this reasoning unpersuasive; indeed, I think my refugee example underscores the problem of using a contractarian approach to justice while continuing to reason in terms of the framework of the nation-state. But even if we confine ourselves to purely domestic laws, we still encounter problems of patent injustice. Consider, for example, the anticontraception law that prevailed in Connecticut for more than eighty years before being struck down by the Supreme Court in *Griswold v. Connecticut*.[3] If an officer had decided not to arrest a married couple despite incontrovertible evidence that they had used contraceptives, I think that officer would also have deserved commendation.[4]

Given this latter example, Professor Reiman might say that he is in fact concerned with the justness of specific laws – that he's concerned with justness from top to bottom, not simply with the justness of the arrangements that establish institutions that pass laws. If this is his concern, then we agree even more than I have supposed – though if this indeed is his concern, it is hard to understand why he speaks approvingly of the rule of law while acknowledging that bad laws must be enforced while adhering to it. In any case, as my examples make clear, I think there are situations in which the specific laws generated by legitimate political institutions are so patently unjust that officers do what is right by *not* enforcing them.

Even if we agree that a society's political institutions are generally just and that the specific law an officer is charged with enforcing is not patently unjust, the question remains why police officers should be the agents enforcing that law. The answer to this is straightforward: in contemporary society, there is a division of labor that justifies citizen reliance on the police to enforce the law. At one time this division of labor wasn't so clear. In the early nineteenth century, when English and American communities depended primarily on constables and night watchmen to enforce the law, an observer would have had to concede that these officials were not paid well and were not carefully trained in the use of force. Moreover, the observer would also have had to concede that these officials operated on largely the same legal footing as private citizens as far as civil liability for false arrests was concerned.

Early-nineteenth-century conditions provide a baseline for thinking about the circumstances that prevail today. In contemporary America, private citizens can point to three factors in arguing that they are entitled to rely on the police to enforce the penal laws of their community. First, contemporary police officers are paid well by comparison with members of other professions. Second, contemporary police officers are extensively trained in the use of force; most private citizens are not. And third, contemporary police enjoy a legally privileged position in the use of force, so even if a private citizen wished to enforce the law by making a citizen's arrest, that person would confront liability risks that police officers do not encounter.[5] Taken together, these points create a strong presumption against the exercise of police discretion in making arrests. Penal and civil-nuisance laws, we can say, generate legitimate citizen expectations about what their community should be like. The division of labor between the citizenry and the police in turn generates a justifiable reliance on the part of citizens that the police will implement the version of a decent community outlined in their jurisdiction's penal and civil-nuisance laws.

But of course I have suggested only that there is a strong presumption against the exercise of arrest discretion. Professor Reiman goes further and states that "police [arrest] discretion has no rightful place in a free society."[6] Whether our disagreement is a serious one is not entirely clear, for in my opinion the prime reason why police can justifiably decline to arrest when they are legally authorized to do so has to do with the conservation of their resources, and it is possible that Professor Reiman agrees with me, given his willingness to tolerate a failure to arrest when there are "equally or more pressing legal duties" confronting an officer. [71] It is possible that he agrees with me, but by no means certain, since Professor Reiman speaks in terms of a single officer and thus seems to be concerned only with those situations in which one officer, or perhaps a small cluster of officers, must make an on-the-spot decision about how to deal with a situation.

My concern, by contrast, is with systemic shortages in police personnel. I agree with Professor Reiman that arrest dilemmas can arise unexpectedly (as when a sergeant fails to assign enough officers to carry out an arrest). However, I think the central dilemma of arrest discretion arises with respect to routine and predictable personnel shortages, a dilemma that must be addressed at the executive rather than the patrol officer level. Given problems faced by many urban police departments, executives can anticipate that their patrol and plainclothes officers will not have time to make all the arrests they are authorized to make while also performing the many other functions they are expected to perform. I am uncertain of Professor Reiman's position on police discretion in this kind of setting. Mine is that when a police department faces systemic manpower shortages its executives can justifiably order officers not to make certain kinds of arrests as a way of insuring that other police services, which the executives deem more essential, are also provided to the public.

I believe, then, that the public's legitimate reliance expectation that police officers will enforce the law can be set aside in the face of systemic personnel shortages. But because this reliance expectation is not only legitimate but important, I also believe that police executives can set it aside only by announcing publicly which laws their officers won't enforce and where they won't enforce them. Think, for example, about prohibitions against simple assault. Besides prohibiting particularly serious instances of assault (such as assault with a deadly weapon), state penal laws typically prohibit simple assault – that is, assault where someone suffers physical harm, but not grave or life-threatening harm.[7] For the reasons outlined earlier, citizens can properly expect that police officers will undertake the unpleasant, sometimes dangerous, job of arresting someone who has been the subject of an assault complaint. If police executives conclude that they don't have the personnel to arrest everyone who is the subject of this complaint, it is essential that they announce publicly the criteria they have established for their officers in making arrest decisions. On hearing about the executives' decision, citizens might well conclude that other kinds of nonenforcement are preferable – or they might decide to increase allocations for the police department so as to insure full enforcement. There will be rough passages in this kind of police-community dialogue. An open debate over underenforcement is far preferable, however, to letting line officers decide for themselves what enforcement decisions to make.

One final point about arrest discretion is worth noting. I have concentrated on discretion not to enforce penal and civil-nuisance laws – Professor Reiman's prime concern as well. Near the end of his essay, however, Professor Reiman turns, without clearly acknowledging that he is doing so, to a different issue: "discretion" to violate constitutional rules of police procedure. I've used quotation marks in talking about this latter issue because I believe, as I think Professor Reiman also does, that no convincing moral argument can be advanced on behalf of police officers' decisions to violate these rules of criminal procedure – to flout search and seizure protections, to compel criminal suspects to incriminate themselves, and so on. A critical distinction between failing to uphold an expectation and actively harming someone can be invoked in support of my position. In failing to arrest someone, an officer does not inflict harm on someone else; the officer simply does not honor an interest citizens have in seeing the law fully enforced. In violating constitutional rights, however, an officer actively inflicts harm on someone else – for example, by beating up a suspect (a Fourth Amendment violation) or compelling a suspect to incriminate himself (a Fifth Amendment violation). I think it important to mark off this issue carefully from the quite different one of nonenforcement of penal and civil-nuisance laws.

NOTES

1. Professor Reiman limits his argument to police arrest discretion in law enforcement, as distinguished from order maintenance, settings. This is an important qualification, for most instances of police arrest discretion center on order maintenance – on violations of ordinances prohibiting drinking in public, disturbing the peace, prostitution, and so on. There are, however, important questions about arrest discretion that arise in the category of law enforcement. I address one of these – discretion to arrest in cases of simple assault – later in the essay.

2. William C. Heffernan, "The Police and Their Rules of Office: An Ethical Analysis," in *Police Ethics: Hard Choices in Law Enforcement*, ed. William C. Heffernan and Timothy Stroup, (New York: John Jay Press, 1985), pp. 3-24.

3. 381 U.S. 479 (1965).

4. In his comprehensive history of Connecticut's anticontraception statute, David Garrow found no incident in which police officers arrested individuals for using contraceptives. Indeed, Garrow reports that Yale Law School professor Vern Countryman, an opponent of the statute who wished to test its constitutionality in court, was turned down by Hamden, Connecticut, police officers when he asked them to take action against a town drugstore that was openly selling contraceptives. See David Garrow, *Liberty and Sexuality: The Right to Privacy and the Making of* Roe v. Wade (New York: Macmillan, 1994), p. 128. It seems reasonable to suppose that the Hamden police had decided not to enforce the statute even against contraception vendors.

5. See *Anderson v. Creighton*, 483 U.S. 635 (1987) (police officers entitled to defense of objectively reasonable mistake about the existence of probable cause in actions for money damages brought in federal courts).

6. Jeffrey Reiman, "Is Police Discretion Justified in a Free Society?" in this volume, p. 80. Subsequent page references to Reiman's article are enclosed in brackets in the text.

7. See, e.g., the Model Penal Code's distinction between simple and aggravated assault at sec. 211.1.

Chapter 4

Police Discretion and Police Objectivity

Howard Cohen

The early literature on police discretion addressed the issue of whether police have discretion at all. The work of Jerome Skolnick, Michael Brown, and others documented the ways in which police exercise discretion and made it clear that police discretion is necessary and useful.[1] Police use discretion in a wide range of circumstances, some of it formally authorized, but much of it simply incorporated in the expectations of the job. In the exploration of police use of discretion two major categories of issues remain to be considered, namely, "domain" issues and "judgment" issues. Discussions of domain have a certain priority since it is important to clarify how much discretion police have and in precisely which circumstances: How are the boundaries of discretion to be defined? Can the domain in which the use of discretion is permitted ever be expressed with precision? May police use discretion in any situation that is not controlled by law or department policy? I mention these questions to acknowledge that there are still domain issues to be resolved, though it is not my intention to discuss them here.

Given that there is a domain (however defined) in which police are authorized to use their discretion, there are further issues of police judgment to be explored. Within the domain of discretion, the officer typically must choose a course of action from an array of alternatives. There are, presumably, real choices among the array. That is, there are options that have the potential of leading to significantly different outcomes. If all permissible options led to the same result or if every possible outcome of a discretionary act were of equal consequence, there would be no "judgment" component in the exploration of discretion.

There should be nothing particularly problematic about this point. Police are granted the use of discretion precisely because we believe that permitting the use of judgment in some situations can lead to better results than setting up an inflexible set of rules, policies, and procedures that cannot be altered because of circumstances. The clear implication of this, of course, is that discretion can be exercised well or poorly. Police judgments can be evaluated in terms of their quality. Some judgments will be better than others, and some officers will make consistently better judgments than other officers. Consequently, we have a stake in the quality of an officer's judgment. The public needs to know both that officers are held accountable for the consequences of their discretionary judgments and that police organizations make an effort to help officers make good judgments. Better discretionary decisions will mean better policing.

Acknowledging the role of judgment in the exercise of discretion raises certain problems for police administrators. Officers are held accountable for following law and policy, but they also need to be held accountable for the use of good judgment in the exercise of their discretion. This is a more difficult task. Holding someone accountable for failing to follow a rule is a somewhat cut-and-dried affair. It may be difficult to gather evidence, but once the evidence is available, it is generally possible to determine whether a rule was followed. By contrast, holding someone accountable for using poor judgment seems more akin to second-guessing or "Monday morning quarterbacking." As long as the officer selected a permissible option (that is, one not prohibited by law or policy), it may seem that the quality of the judgment depended upon the course of subsequent events. Surely the officer thought it was the best option at the time or she wouldn't have selected it. This is not to say that accountability is not possible. But if we do expect administrators to hold officers accountable for their discretionary judgments, then it is important to be able to say something to officers about the elements of good judgment. What does an officer need to do to make good discretionary judgments?

It seems to me that a key element in evaluating discretionary judgments is to determine whether they were made objectively. Focusing on objectivity puts the emphasis on how the judgment was made, rather than on how it turned out. That is, rather than second-guessing consequences, a supervisor can try to determine whether an officer has a good process for formulating judgments and selecting among courses of action. To the extent that these processes can be cultivated, good judgment can be a subject of training.

Unfortunately, the answer to the question of what it means to be objective in police work is not obvious. Nevertheless, this is where I would like to begin. I have argued elsewhere that if we adopt a social contract justification of governmental authority, the elements of a contract model impose a set of standards of behavior on those who choose to govern.[2] Because the contract is conditional, public officials must not undermine the basic terms of the agreement (protection of life, liberty, and property). Because the contract is mandatory, public officials must provide fair access to the benefits and services of social life to all citizens. Because the contract redistributes power from the populace to public officials, those officials hold it as a trust that may not be exploited or abused. Because the contract establishes social roles, those who choose to accept those roles must discharge them as society's agents.

It is the fourth point, that public officials are agents acting in social roles, that is important for understanding objectivity. An officer is a representative of the state. As such, one who becomes an officer must distinguish between his role and himself – the person in the role. John Doe may not approve of a particular law or department policy, but Officer Doe is expected to enforce that law or policy.

Using this distinction, I want to characterize objectivity, initially, as acting from one's role rather than from one's personal preferences, interests, attachments, or inclinations. Objectivity, in this sense, is typically associated with such concepts as impersonality, disinterestedness, dispassionateness, and impartiality. Each of these concepts marks a way of keeping one's self out of one's role. Because there are different ways in which the self can penetrate the role, objectivity would seem to require a range of defenses against the collapse of the distinction.

Notice that I am not suggesting that impersonality, dispassionateness, disinterestedness, and impartiality are all equivalent concepts. Rather, they each point to a different way of locating the source of judgment and action in the role rather than the person. The failure to be objective, then, means permitting one's personal values, interests, or passions to play a significant role in one's professional judgment.

That it is possible, and even likely, that police will bring their personal perspectives into their work is perhaps worth noting. Some might say this is obvious and all too common. In *Two Cultures of Policing*, Elizabeth Reuss-Ianni describes "street cop culture" as almost obsessed with personal self-regard as a principle guiding action.[3] Without listing all twenty-one maxims that she says characterize street cop culture, we can note that "protect your ass," "don't make waves," "know your bosses," "don't trust your bosses to look out for your interests," and "don't trust a new guy until you have checked him out" are, in her view, typical of the attitudes she observed. She goes on to characterize police relations with one another and with the rest of the world as based on a system of "vouching" – that is, personal assurances from a trusted source that a new person can also be trusted.

Whether or not Reuss-Ianni has accurately characterized the police culture, she has provided us with a clear example of how police might fail to be objective in their role. On this model, the personal takes precedence over the professional. Self-interest, rather than citizen interest (or even departmental interest), is the basis of judgment. Treatment of others is dependent on, and conditioned by, personal relationship to the officer. Partisanship, partiality, and prejudice are likely qualities of judgment that would result from this perspective.

Although it is possible to define clear cases in which an officer is not objective because he or she does not act from the perspective of the police role, this standard becomes more difficult to understand as we begin to focus on the question: What is the police role? It should be obvious that this question must be answered if we are to define objectivity as I have proposed.

Here we confront an interesting complication. There is not a single, universally accepted model of the police role that we can work from. Indeed, there are two major contenders as models for policing in America. These are the professional policing model and the community-oriented policing model. I contend that these models lead us to very different conceptions of how an officer is to achieve objectivity.

In the following discussion I develop an association between the professional policing model and a *realist* conception of objectivity, and then contrast that with an association between community-based policing and a *pragmatist* conception of objectivity. In drawing this distinction between approaches to objectivity, I follow Richard Rorty's discussion in *Objectivity, Relativism, and Truth.*[4] Rorty characterizes the realists as construing "truth as correspondence to reality." He characterizes pragmatists as viewing "truth as what is good for *us* to believe." My intent is to show how the injunction to "be objective" leads down these two different paths identified by Rorty – the former in the professional policing model and the latter in the community-based model. My hope is that a clearer understanding of the approach to objectivity associated with each model will, in turn, help clarify how police would exercise their discretionary judgment under the respective models. In the case of community-based policing, I hope that a clearer understanding of how an officer could make objective judgments within that model will address some of the concerns about the model raised by its critics.

By associating a conception of objectivity with a model of policing, I do not mean to assert a necessary connection. I have no doubt that a "pragmatist" might support professional policing or a "realist" might support community-oriented policing for a variety of reasons. One does not, after all, come to a position on how police work should be conducted based on a conception of objectivity; nor does one arrive at a philosophical position on objectivity based on a commitment to a model of policing. Nevertheless, I contend that those who begin with a realist's orientation to objectivity will have a difficult time seeing the value of community-oriented policing. It will appear to be a step back from objectivity. By contrast, those who begin with a pragmatist's orientation to objectivity will recognize community-oriented policing as a strategy for bringing "us" into greater accord.

Let me also emphasize here that I am working with models. These are simplified versions of the approaches to policing that are put into practice in a great variety of ways in jurisdictions across the country. There is significant disagreement in both scholarship and practice about how best to describe and define professional policing and community-based policing. Neither term is a label for a single set of practices. My assumption is that the main outlines of the associations between conceptions of objectivity and the models that I am articulating will withstand internal divergence within the respective models. Details, of course, will need to be revised as the models evolve.

THE PROFESSIONAL MODEL

The professional model of policing is generally regarded as the dominant development in the organization of police agencies in twentieth-century America. George Kelling and Mark Moore identify it as a police strategy that characterized thinking of police administrators and theorists from the 1920s to the 1970s.[5] They characterize professional policing as chiefly focused on crime control. They associate this function with a centralized organization, preventive patrol tactics, and rapid response, and with an officer demeanor that is dispassionate, impersonal, and remote from the public.

A widely acknowledged version of a professional police department is the Los Angeles Police Department under the leadership of Chief William H. Parker. Gerald Woods, in *The Police in Los Angeles: Reform and Profes-*

sionalization,[6] characterizes Parker's notion of professionalism through the following elements:

- a military model of command;
- emphasis on crime suppression rather than crime prevention;
- adoption of modern management principles, including the use of research and planning to achieve goals;
- careful selection and training of personnel;
- no tolerance for corruption;
- insulation from political machines; and
- an overriding commitment to public order through force.

The ideal officer on this model is a person of high integrity – calm, polite, and humorless. Peter Manning describes the officers who function best in this role as "invisible, indirectly available, impersonal and specialist."[7]

How is the police role that is developed in this model to be carried out objectively? It is clear that this model envisions an officer who has separated the personal from the professional. The aggressive stance against corruption and involvement in politics is one sign of this. The model's focus on crime suppression and public order also demands a careful exclusion of personal values or feelings from the police role. Given the reliance on force to accomplish these goals, the professional officer must be a restrained public presence. If officers react to lawbreakers from personal disgust or contempt, they may exercise judgments that lead to the use of excessive force or other illegal behavior. The professional officer exercises objectivity by not becoming enraged and doing bodily violence to a man who beats his spouse, by not "getting even" with neighborhood youth for past incidents when they are taken into custody for breaking a shopkeeper's window, and by not treating shabby people more roughly than the well-groomed.

The most compelling approach to establishing a standard of objectivity on the professional model is to make police behavior, to the greatest extent possible, subject to rules and regulations. Insofar as the police role is defined by its governing laws, policies, and rules, police officers who "go by the book" will not risk substituting their personal desires or interests for the responsibilities of their role. The problem here, of course, is that not all police activity can or should be rule governed. In other words, the use of discretion has an essential place in policework, so there is a domain of police activity that cannot be conducted objectively by following rules.

The best attempt to extend the rule-governed conception of objectivity that is grounded in the professional model into the area of police discretion can be found in Kenneth Culp Davis's *Discretionary Justice: A Preliminary Inquiry*.[8] Davis understands clearly that police (and other government officials) must have the authority to use discretion if the government is to avoid doing injustice to individuals in a variety of circumstances. Nevertheless, an extensive delegation of discretionary authority also concerns him, precisely because it introduces opportunities for personal prejudice and personal interest to undermine governmental purposes. Davis attempts to solve this problem in two parts. First, he argues that the use of discretion must be confined to situations where it is truly required. Wherever a law, a rule, or a policy can address the "business at hand," it ought to be our preference. Davis favors "optimum" discretion: "When [discretion] is too broad, justice may suffer from arbitrariness or inequality. When it is too narrow, justice may suffer from insufficient individualizing." He proposed the maxim: "A rule is undesirable when discretion will serve better." Davis observes, however, that in practice there are many areas of discretion that could well be subject to rules.[9]

Once discretion is properly confined to situations in which it is truly needed, there remains the problem of controlling judgment within its legitimate domain. Davis argues that discretion can be "structured" and "checked" to bring its use into conformity with the goals of the law. By structuring discretion he means that administrators can "regularize it, organize it, produce order in it, so that their decisions affecting individual parties will achieve a higher quality of justice."[10] This is accomplished, according to Davis, by "open plans, open policy statements, open rules, open findings, open reasons, open precedents and fair informal procedure."[11]

Checking discretion is a matter of accountability. Davis says:

> The most usual checking authority is a superior of the officer who acts initially, who in turn may be checked by his superior in a hierarchical organization. But checking may also be effective when it is by a colleague on the same level, by one or more subordinates, by legislators to whom interested parties often petition, by legislative committees or their staffs, by an official critic known as an ombudsman, by private organizations, by the press, by an administrative appellate tribunal, or by a reviewing court.[12]

The value of checking discretion is that it creates pressure for consistency, and consistency is an element of justice.

My point here is that the model of the professional officer works best with a standard of objectivity that is grounded in rules. Where it is not possible to refer to rules, as in situations where the use of discretionary judgment is appropriate, the closer that judgment can approximate rule-like behavior, the better. Absent the possibility of invoking a rule, judgment that meets a standard of individualized justice is the next best outcome. Yet here, too, the effort is to find an external standard against which the officer's judgment can be compared. Embedded in Davis's conception of discretion is a realist's notion of objectivity.

This idea of objectivity as controlled, professional detachment combined with careful attention to laws, rules, and policies, and strict scrutiny of limited discretionary authority, may seem quite plausible within the model of professional policing. Law enforcement, crime detection, and criminal apprehension are core police activities under the model and appear to be the kind of activities that can proceed by the book. Supervisors can write manuals that will permit officers to administer their judgments and take action according to an established set of rules and procedures. Within the context of law enforcement, the range of officer discretion is bounded by the possibility of having to bring a case to court. An officer who wishes to see a suspect in court runs some risk if he plays fast and loose with the rules of evidence or the rules of procedure.

Even where police activity is not so carefully circumscribed by law – in the functions related to the maintenance of public order – the police are to function, in Michael Brown's words, as "street-level bureaucrats." That is, they are to maintain a level of detachment from the citizenry they police. Their role is to represent the state and implement its standards of justice.

As a dispenser of law and justice, the objective professional police officer is insulated from the policed community. John Locke used the metaphor of the umpire to signify the way in which government officials are not part of the people they govern. This conception of the police as a breed apart is both challenged and undermined by an alternative model of policing that has gained currency in recent years. This is the model of community-oriented policing.

COMMUNITY-ORIENTED POLICING

Kelling and Moore identify the late 1970s and early 1980s as the period in which a number of police departments explicitly acknowledged public order maintenance and community service as central to the police mission.[13] By contrast to the professional policing model, community-based policing – as characterized by Kelling and Moore – has a service-provider function; operates in a decentralized organization to bring police decision makers closer to the citizens who are policed; relies on foot patrol to create interpersonal contact; and is oriented toward improving citizen satisfaction with their personal security and safety. Jack Greene and Ralph Taylor, in a cautionary article about community-oriented policing, characterize it as an alternative developed to address what they call the failures of bureaucratic policing.[14] They describe the last ten to fifteen years of policing as "the anti-bureaucracy era." The community-oriented alternative, they say, is "based on the theory that a well tended community has less crime than an untended one." David Bayley, another gentle critic, identifies four central elements of community-oriented policing:

- community-based crime prevention;
- proactive servicing (rather than emergency response);
- public participation in planning and supervision of police operations; and
- a shift of command responsibility to lower ranks.[15]

Mollie Weatheritt, an advocate, says community policing is about "changing the ethos of policing to emphasize notions of service, flexibility, consumer responsiveness, conciliation, consultation and negotiation."[16] Chris Murphy, another supporter, says that "community policing advocates a broad social role for police and enhanced community responsibility and participation in policing."[17] Robert Trojanowicz and Bonnie Bucqueroux define community-oriented policing as a philosophy and organizational strategy that promotes a new partnership between people and their police. They go on to say that police and citizens should cooperate to identify, prioritize, and solve contemporary problems.[18]

Although each of these characterizations of community-oriented policing differs somewhat in the identification of key defining elements, all of them imply a deconstruction of the wall of impersonality that the professional model built between the police and the public. This is stated explicitly by Timothy Oettmeier and Lee Brown in their account of Houston's Neighborhood-Oriented Policing (NOP) program:

> For too long, police officers have hidden behind a shroud of professionalism that is characterized by anonymity. . . . The philosophy of NOP . . . recognizes the necessity of abandoning the non-involvement syndrome that has become imbedded in the definition of professional policing.[19]

This call for change has significant implications for objectivity as impersonal adherence to rules and structured exercise of discretion. Indeed, it appears to go so far as to reintroduce the personal into police judgment. But I think it is fair to ask: In abandoning noninvolvement do the police run the risk of abandoning objectivity?

To make sense of community-oriented policing in a way that does not simply revert to encouraging police to follow their personal prejudices in their judgments, we need to articulate a concept of objectivity that is more in accord with the police role – as that role is understood by proponents of community-oriented policing. Contemporary thinking about the police suggests that American policing is well under way in its transition from the professional or bureaucratic model to the community model. Scholars have identified a broad range of departments of all sizes – urban, suburban, and rural – that have embraced one notion or another of community-oriented policing. These departments have formally accepted what has been the de facto role of the police for some time, giving primacy to community service and community safety. They have taken on this role by creating closer relationships between the police and the policed.

Here, it seems to me, Richard Rorty's discussion of objectivity is quite helpful. Rorty advocates reinterpreting objectivity in Deweyan fashion:

> If one reinterprets objectivity as intersubjectivity, or as solidarity, in the ways I suggest below, then one will drop the question of how to get in touch with "mind-independent and language-independent reality."[20]

> For pragmatists, the desire for objectivity is not the desire to escape the limitations of one's community, but simply the desire for as much intersubjective agreement as possible, the desire to extend the reference of "us" as far as we can.[21]

Rorty goes on to develop the contrast between realist objectivity and pragmatist objectivity (solidarity) in this way:

> For the realist thinks that the whole point of philosophical thought is to detach oneself from the particular community and look down at it from a more universal standpoint. . . . But the pragmatist, dominated by the desire for solidarity, can only be criticized for taking his own community *too* seriously. He can only be criticized for ethnocentrism, not relativism. . . . To be ethnocentric is to divide the human race into the people to whom one must justify one's beliefs and the others. The first group – one's *ethnos* – comprises those who share enough of one's beliefs to make fruitful conversation possible.[22]

To apply Rorty's thought to the issue at hand, then, the challenge for police to be objective is to find a common perspective with the policed from which to make discretionary judgments. This, in turn, suggests a level of shared belief in how community life can be conducted to make "fruitful conversation possible." In other words, seen in this way, the divergence between the professional and the community-based models of policing is a divergence about the level of engagement with the community that is required for police to make objective discretionary judgments.

Rorty's pragmatist conception of objectivity contains a challenge to extend our *ethnos*, and this challenge may strike a sensitive note in some police departments. For community-oriented policing to be effective, there must be a community that encompasses both the police and the policed. If the gulf is too wide or if the police are seen, and see themselves, as an occupying army, there may be slim prospects for pragmatic objectivity – to say nothing of community-oriented policing. This is an issue for some departments more than others, but the reports on experiments with community-oriented policing suggest that even in some urban, poor, racially isolated neighborhoods, officers and residents have been able to find common interests.

It is not my intention to defend Rorty's conception of objectivity over a realist's conception. In any event, such a defense – in its own terms – would need to be pragmatic and evolutionary. Time will tell whether officers making discretionary judgments within the framework of community-oriented policing can find a way to avoid being personal, passionate, and prejudiced in their perspective. What is of more immediate concern is to explore whether there are mechanisms to put this concept of objectivity into practice.

My question now is this: Is there an approach to making discretionary judgments in the community-oriented policing model that is analogous to Davis's approach to making such judgments in the professional policing model? I believe that there is, and that this approach can be illuminated through Jean Jacques Rousseau's conception of citizenship.[23]

Rousseau was particularly attuned to the complexities of trying to determine the common interest of a community – or, as he thought of it, its general will. He argued that the common interest shared among citizens could be identified through the effort of each citizen to find within himself his own interest *as citizen*.

In the arena of politics, Rousseau attributed to each person a "double capacity" of private individual and public citizen. Rather than attempting to reconcile all of a person's differing private individual interests, he argued that each individual possesses a "general will," or an interest sufficiently generalized that, at the most abstract level, the interest of any one citizen is identical with the interest of all of the others (no matter how diverse the community, as long as it is truly a community). Thus, one need only discover one's own general will to learn what is in the best interest of the community as a whole. Of course, one's own conception of the general will is compromised to the extent that it has traces of one's own personal interests in it. It is also compromised by our inclination to put our personal interests ahead of the general interest. Rousseau illustrates this point by describing this overlaying of interests as a multiplicity of "wills" within governing officials, or, "magistrates":

> In the person of the magistrate we can distinguish three essentially different wills: first, the private will of the individual, tending only to his personal advantage; second, the common will of the magistrates, which . . . may be called the corporate will, . . . and in the third place, the will of the people or sovereign will, which is general.
>
> In a perfect act of legislation . . . the general or sovereign will should always predominate and should be the sole guide of all the rest.
>
> According to the natural order, on the other hand, these different wills become more active in proportion as they are concentrated. Thus, the general will is always the weakest, the corporate will second, and the individual will strongest of all: so that, in the government, each member is first of all himself, then a magistrate, and then a citizen – in an order exactly the reverse of what the social system requires.[24]

Rousseau argues that every member of a community has a stake in that community – an interest in it – that is shared with all of the other community members. This interest resides alongside other interests within the individual: personal interests, familial interests, professional interests, club or organizational interests, and so on. A police officer may have the interests of a forty-year-old man (or a thirty-four-year-old woman, or whatever) in a certain socioeconomic station, who is a parent and PTA member (or not), a member of a church, a hunter/fisher, an alumni booster, a Little League coach, and so on. At the next general level, the police officer has an interest, shared with other police officers, of doing his or her assigned job as a member of a governmental enforcement agency. That interest can include doing the job efficiently, safely, and with maximal discretion. It can also include doing the job with adequate pay, fringe benefits, a decent pension, and so on. Officers also have an interest in esprit de corps and public approval of their profession. At the most general level, the police officer has an interest as "citizen" that he or she shares with everyone else in the community. It is an interest in being part of a community that functions well and fulfills the basic conditions of the social contract: safety and security for all citizens with minimal encroachment on individual liberty.

Rousseau recognized that citizens in general, and government officials in particular, were not likely to discern the general will without the help of social institutions that required members of a community to engage one another in the exercise of identifying the general will. To this end, he thought that small democracies had a greater probability of discovering the general will and putting it first. He identifies the characteristics of such states as follows:

> first, a very small State, where the people can readily be got together and where each citizen can know the rest; secondly, great simplicity of manners, . . . next, a large measure of equality in rank and fortune; . . . lastly, little or no luxury. . . .[25]

Within this context it becomes possible to address the question: What is the common interest? Ideally, in an assembly of citizens, "what the people is asked is not exactly whether it approves or rejects the proposal, but whether it is in conformity with the general will. . . . Each man, in giving his vote, states his opinion on that point. . . ." [26]

The role of the officer is to enforce the law, not to make it. But as we know, the officer must also "legislate" when he or she uses discretion. The objectivity issue becomes one of trying to assure that in the use of discretion the officer makes judgments that are in accord with the general will – or community interest – rather than the interest of the police as an agency or the interest of the officer as a person.

How, in light of Rousseau's observations, is the officer to discover the community interest (which is also the officer's interest when other, more specific interests are abstracted away)? The advice I would draw from Rousseau here is that police officers are more likely to act from the general will if they are actively engaged in the communities they police, know the citizenry to talk to them, and have occasions for dealing with the citizenry on their own level and in their own organizations. While this does not entirely reproduce Rousseau's conditions of small democracies, it brings us closer to the notion of the police and the policed having things in common as citizens.

Through discussion of issues of community concern, community members with a variety of perspectives have a chance to compare theirs to others' and to press one another to defend their conceptions of the common interest. To the extent that community members are equals (at least in terms of their community membership or citizenship, if not their financial standing) and to the extent that they bring to the assembly a good faith willingness to attempt to set aside their personal interests, they improve the chances of discovering their common interest. If they actually vote on issues, Rousseau suggests, they will have the best chance of accurately representing the general will (or community interest).

A problem that Rousseau's critics have discerned in this approach to identifying the general will is the problem of exclusion or inclusion of persons as community members. If a community is identified in narrow or elitist terms, it may formulate a conception of the general will that is oppressive, and not at all in the interest of persons who are not counted as community members but who may, nevertheless, live side by side with them. One thinks of the treatment of black people in segregated communities.

There is no prescribed set of steps that will assure the mutual discovery of the general will by police and the policed. Engagement in circumstances that are likely to lead to the rational exchange of views, discovery of mutual interests, and articulation of common ground will promote, but cannot guarantee, a sense of community. Whatever strategies take the police in this direction in relation to the policed are worth trying.

Because police are agents of the state, they have an obligation to practice inclusion as they try to develop a community perspective. Even where police work in exclusionary communities, they must acknowledge the membership of all who fall within their jurisdiction. In other words, the general will must be truly general.

How does this translate to community-oriented policing? It suggests that police need to participate with citizens in discussions of their interests. They need to see the community interest from the full range of perspectives that exist in the communities they police, including those views that may not have a voice in community organizations. Rousseau thought of this engagement of one another's perspectives as occurring in an act of legislation. Although we do not legislate together as Rousseau envisioned, there are ways that issues of community interest can be aired in public. If police and citizens had public forums in which they could discuss matters of policy that affect the community; if police and citizens could come to those forums willing to shed their personal or group interests; and if the outcome of those discussions could actually shape policy, we would be most likely to have something that we could confidently say represents our best understanding of the community interest.

The idea of a public forum need not be taken too literally here. Not all members of a community attend public meetings and public events. Some members of a community must be engaged in other places. If police attend community meetings, read community newspapers, meet with community leaders, participate in neighborhood events, and discuss policy issues of community concern in neighborhoods, on street corners, in youth clubs, at senior meetings, and in people's homes, they will be developing the inclusive "solidarity" that Richard Rorty identified as objectivity. In other words, the purpose of all this community interaction is to put the officer in the position of making judgments based on his or her opinion of what is "in conformity with the general will." All of the activities that go into this promote objectivity.

Since all perspectives are not likely to be represented in an organized public forum, community-oriented policing should create forums by encouraging officers to engage citizens where they live – in the shops, on the streets, in community centers, and so on. Here, too, the engagement should be at the level of understanding the community interest. Police officers who operated from those understandings would be operating with objectivity.

Put another way, if we want the police to be objective, it will be necessary to design community-oriented policing programs that encourage genuine police/citizen engagement on policy matters. If these programs are just for show, they will not lead to the understandings that police need in order to be objective. If these programs are politicized by community groups or department administration or local government, they will likewise not lead to understandings that police need to be objective. What this says to me is that we have a stake in fostering and nurturing an authentic community-oriented approach to policing because an important dimension of police ethics depends on it.

NOTES

1. Jerome H. Skolnick, *Justice without Trial* (New York: Wiley, 1966); Michael K. Brown, *Working the Street* (New York: Russell Sage Foundation, 1981).

2. Howard Cohen and Michael Feldberg, *Power and Restraint: The Moral Dimension of Police Work* (New York: Praeger, 1991).

3. Elizabeth Reuss-Ianni, *Two Cultures of Policing* (Brunswick, NJ: Transaction Books, 1983).

4. Richard Rorty, *Objectivity, Relativism, and Truth* (New York: Cambridge University Press, 1991).

5. George Kelling and Mark Moore, "From Political Reform to Community:

The Evolving Strategy of Police," in *Community Policing: Rhetoric or Reality,* ed. Jack R. Greene and Stephen D. Mastrofski (New York: Praeger, 1988).

6. Gerald Woods, *The Police in Los Angeles: Reform and Professionalization* (New York: Garland, 1993), pp. 223-46.

7. Peter K. Manning, "Community Policing as a Drama of Control," in Greene and Mastrofski, *Community Policing,* p. 31.

8. Kenneth Culp Davis, *Discretionary Justice: A Preliminary Inquiry* (Urbana: University of Illinois Press, 1971).

9. Ibid., pp. 52-54.

10. Ibid., p. 97.

11. Ibid., p. 98.

12. Ibid., p. 142.

13. Kelling and Moore, "From Political Reform to Community," p. 6.

14. Jack R. Greene and Ralph Taylor, "Community-Based Policing and Foot Patrol: Issues of Theory and Evaluation," in Greene and Mastrofski, *Community Policing,* pp. 198-199.

15. David Bayley, "Community Policing: A Report from the Devil's Advocate," in Greene and Mastrofski, *Community Policing,* p. 226.

16. Mollie Weatheritt, "Community Policing: Rhetoric or Reality?" in Greene and Mastrofski, *Community Policing,* p. 153.

17. Chris Murphy, "The Development, Impact and Implications of Community Policing in Canada," in Greene and Mastrofski, *Community Policing,* p. 177.

18. Robert Trojanowicz and Bonnie Bucqueroux, *Community Policing: How to Get Started* (Cincinnati: Anderson, 1994).

19. Timothy N. Oettmeier and Lee P. Brown, "Developing a Neighborhood-Oriented Policing Style," in Greene and Mastrofski, *Community Policing,* p. 126.

20. Rorty, *Objectivity, Relativism, and Truth,* p. 13.

21. Ibid., p. 23.

22. Ibid., p. 30.

23. Jean-Jacques Rousseau, *The Social Contract,* trans. G. D. H. Cole (Buffalo: Prometheus, 1988).

24. Ibid., p. 65.

25. Ibid., p. 69.

26. Ibid., p. 107.

Response: Rortyan Policing?

John P. Pittman

Professor Cohen's interesting essay places the discussion of police discretion in the framework of a contrast between two models of policing. I want to examine whether the Rortyan construal of objectivity that Cohen employs strengthens the model of community policing he advocates.

Cohen's discussion contains an implicit endorsement of the community policing model, which he contrasts favorably with what he calls the professional policing model. He suggests that community policing, based on the primacy of community service and an end to the ideals of impersonality, invisibility, and anonymity that professional policing supports through external standards, is more likely to promote effective and ethical police work and is preferable for that reason. Cohen goes on to argue that a Rortyan construal of objectivity is the best way to make sense of the general desideratum of objectivity as the condition for the ethically acceptable use of discretionary authority by police in conditions of community policing. That is, I take the argument to be that community policing is preferable on independent grounds, and not simply because it yields a more workable or better version of what objectivity involves, one construable along Rortyan lines.

In drawing the contrast between realist objectivity in the professional policing model and objectivity as solidarity in the community policing model, Cohen seems to me to run together two separate distinctions, and two senses of "external." Cohen argues that "the model of the professional officer works best with a standard of objectivity that is grounded in rules," and that such a standard has "embedded" in it a realist notion of objectivity. He seems to hold that this is so because a rule always constitutes an "external standard."[1] So he conflates such a "rule-governed conception of objectivity" with a realist notion of objectivity. But there is a significant difference between the way in which a rule might serve as an external standard for evaluating a discretionary judgment and the way in which a "mind-independent and language-independent reality" is taken as the ground of any genuinely objective external standard on the realist conception of objectivity. [100 (quoting Rorty)] A consistent Rortyan – were there such a person – would argue that objectivity is also construable as solidarity in the case of professional policing, and that it is simply a mistake to take the rule-structured version of police objectivity as appealing to an external standard in the strong sense in which the realist does about objectivity. The idea that police should "find a common perspective with the policed from which to make discretionary judgments" [101] is not incompatible with the idea that the "fruitful conversation" between police and community might in part be concerned with the content of rules for the purpose of structuring discretion, that is, of "creat[ing] pressure for consistency, . . . an element of justice." [97] The issue is not whether the space of discretion is to be structured by rules or informed by dialogue with the policed, but of which approach is most likely to achieve the goal: it might be that a combination of the two is most useful. Indeed, there is some reason to think that a combination of community policing and community civilian oversight – acting as an "external standard" – has the best chance of securing the goods of community service and efficient policing.

I think the move to a Rortyan construal of objectivity as solidarity is a problematic one, even if one wants to place an objectivity criterion on discretionary judgment as the fundamental test of such judgment. Cohen argues that the main danger in police discretionary authority is that judgments will be based on "partisanship, partiality, and prejudice." [94] He seems to maintain that the professional policing model, in which the police stand apart, so to speak, from those policed, is more likely to create a wall between police and policed and increase the chances that partisanship at least will become a significant determinant of discretionary judgments. By tearing down the wall, and building bridges, as it were, between police and community, there is a better chance that neither partisanship nor prejudice will get in the way of objective judgments, given the community policing model. But even Cohen's account of community policing makes clear the framework of a persistent gap or distance between the police and the community, a gap *requiring* a dialogue. This is a gap between two parties with distinctly different interests. And it seems clear to me, at least, that this distance is not simply the result of the legacy of the professional policing model's standoffishness.

The distance between the police and the community has to do as much with the widening social inequalities in U.S. society, and the fact that the effects of those inequalities accumulate in an extreme form in specific neighborhoods or communities, as it does with the professionalization of policing. There are also social, political, and ideological forces, forces which have been working for centuries in our country, that create a distance – if that word is adequate here – between police forces and, say, urban African-American communities. Although Cohen tends to describe the problem of conflict of interests in terms of the police officer's personal interest getting in the way of her safeguarding the community interest, it seems to me that the more problematic issue is one concerning a possible conflict of interests between the community as such and the police as a corporate body. That is, there is every reason to think that there would be little or no agreement between the community and the police about what the community interest is. This, I take it, is a real social issue and not merely a problem with Cohen's presentation or formulation of the issue of police discretion.

The problem I have raised is distinct from a "neutral" version of the problem of police discretion. That neutral version – what Professor McGregor has called the "Mayberry" model[2] – concerns the functioning of a fully staffed, well-trained, and well-educated police force, a force with few or no morale problems, in policing a stable, reasonably prosperous community, where the members of the force are drawn from and live in the community, and where the force is representative of that community in terms of race, gender, religion, and sexual orientation, as well as culture and ethnicity. I will not discuss that neutral version, since I take it that Cohen is also not concerned with it: in such a scenario, there would likely be little need for recourse to either the professional policing model or the community policing model. It is worth noting, however, that Cohen himself does not pose the problem in all its complexity but often speaks in a general way, one leaving room for the supposition that the neutral model is the object of discussion. Indeed it is too often the case in discussions of this issue that the theoretical discussion proceeds on a level of abstraction that gives the neutral version room for life. There is often a dramatic gap between the theoretical discussion, which avoids reference to social and racial inequalities and injustices, and the examples used to illustrate the discussion, which are more often than not examples that live only because of the context of social, political, and economic inequalities in which they are set and from which they are derived.[3]

The question I want to pose is whether any police or criminal justice policy or approach can remedy or even begin to address what I take to be an actual deterioration in the conditions for communities as such in the United States. These conditions are also clearly conditions for any kind of "community" or solidarity between police and policed. There are obviously differences, and the conditions for community have not been eroded uniformly throughout U.S. society. There may even be some communities out there that approximate those described by the neutral version. But in the crucial cases, those of people of color in and around the inner cities, the crisis (and thus also the deviation from the neutral version) is severe and unrelieved. But these are just the communities in which the problems surrounding police discretion are greatest. *Hic Rhodus, hic saltus!*[4] If the theory will work, it must work here. But it is just here that the problems confronting the Rortyan solidarity or community-based view are most severe.

The point can be put in the following way: what is required of "community" for it to play the role it does in a Rortyan construal of objectivity as the criterion of acceptable discretionary judgment far exceeds what can plausibly be expected as an outcome of the sort of police policies that Cohen mentions. In this regard, I think the quote from Rorty that invokes ethnocentrism [in Cohen, 100] is crucial and damaging. (It is true that Cohen, following Rorty, mentions inclusion as a desideratum of acceptable ethnocentrism, but inclusion is more problematic the further those that are to be included are from those that are doing the including – I'm speaking of course of social, cultural, and political distance. Requiring the police to try to narrow these differences appears to me to be requiring the impossible.) In another article in the collection that Cohen cites, Rorty responds to some objections raised by the anthropologist Clifford Geertz to Rorty's use of "ethnocentrism." Rorty maintains his view that, lacking any truly objective standards, ethnocentrism is all we have – but at least our ethnocentrism can be an inclusive one. Picking up on Geertz's description of the world as "coming . . . to look more like a Kuwaiti bazaar than an English gentlemen's club," Rorty writes:

> Like Geertz, I have never been in a Kuwaiti bazaar (nor in an English gentlemen's club). So I can give free rein to my fantasies. I picture many of the people in such a bazaar as preferring to die rather than share the beliefs of many of those with whom they are haggling, yet as haggling profitably away nevertheless. Such a bazaar is, obviously, not a community, in the strong approbative sense of "community" used by critics of liberalism like Alasdair MacIntyre and Robert Bellah. You cannot have an old-timey *Gemeinschaft* unless everybody pretty well agrees on who counts as a decent

human being and who does not. But you *can* have a civil society of the bourgeois democratic sort. All you need is the ability to control your feelings when people who strike you as irredeemably different show up at City Hall, or the greengrocers, or the bazaar. When this happens, you smile a lot, make the best deals you can, and, after a hard day's haggling, retreat to your club. There you will be comforted by the companionship of your moral equals.[5]

Irony aside, here we find Rorty taking sides, in effect, with John Rawls against the communitarian critics of liberal political theory. This is, as he says, a matter of rejecting the demand for community in the sense of *Gemeinschaft* and defending the legitimacy – if not the adequacy – of liberal civil society. And it is here that talk of solidarity or community is abandoned in favor of the bazaar or market analogy. Rorty admits that "bourgeois democratic civil society" is not up to the task of creating community, or of assuring that all its citizens agree "on who counts as a decent human being." In this context, resting one's justification of police discretion on "ethnocentrism" seems like a prescription for more tension and conflict, not less. Who gets defined as part of the "us" is not likely to be more inclusive in the streets of New York or Los Angeles than in a Kuwaiti bazaar, I fear.

Rorty's replacement of objectivity with solidarity amounts to the substitution of an actual consensus among "us," our *ethnos* or community, for a "mind-independent external standard." But Rorty is aware of the limits of solidarity, and warns against substituting it for civil society's market relations. Solidarity is not something that can be forced. That is, if civil society splits into divergent and – at best – mutually indifferent or merely tolerant *ethnoi*, who cannot converse because they do not share basic standards of decency, then there are only two institutions that can provide the framework for their coexistence: the market and the liberal (neutral) state.[6]

Given this, we are in a better position to appreciate the resonance of Cohen's assimilation of the professional model to a realist conception of objectivity and of the community policing model to a Rortyan solidarity conception. The rhetorics of these alternative models point precisely to the contrast between public- and private-sector models of policing. In describing professional policing, Cohen invokes the image of "street-level bureaucrats" and adds that "their role is to represent the state." [98] Community policing, by contrast, is characterized by a "service-provider function" aimed at "improving citizen satisfaction" with the quality of the services provided [99]. On the basis of such a contrast, the professional policing model could be seen, in the image of the neutral state, to function by representing an "external standard" relative to the communities policed; the emphasis on service provision and the description of community policing as "anti-bureaucracy" suggests solidarity as the ultimate means to assure consumer satisfaction with community policing. On this reading, Cohen's construal of the difference between the models fits recent political developments, given the resurgence since the 1980s of political programs aimed at eliminating or reducing welfare-state programs and the prevalence of rhetoric that valorizes the privatization of most if not all public-sector functions.

These comments should not be taken to attribute any particular political motivation to Cohen; nor am I trying to assimilate his approach to the political currents to which I just referred. Neither have I been offering a historical account – nor even a sketch of one – of the rise of the community policing model. I have tried only to indicate how Cohen's descriptions of the two models of policing (and I am not challenging the accuracy of those descriptions) fits with the Rortyan views on which Cohen draws.

Cohen acknowledges that "a community that encompasses both the police and the policed" is essential for community policing to be successful [101]. But, given the social realities of police-community relations in civil society that I described above, the prognosis for Cohen's take on community policing seems fairly grim. Rorty seems to me to have a more realistic view of the limits of solidarity than does Cohen.

If these considerations are at all cogent, they suggest that Cohen's Rortyan pragmatist construal of discretionary judgment in the context of community policing represents an unworkable ideal. It is perhaps worth reflecting here that Rousseauian reasons for just this conclusion are almost ready to hand. Though Cohen marshals a Rousseauian framework for presenting his account of Rortyan policing, Rousseau's conception of democratic polity was, as Cohen indicates, explicitly restricted to "very small" states [103], where the restriction signified not merely the absence of strangers but also a society in which there was little or no social, financial, or cultural distance between citizens. That is, Rousseau was addressing the situation of genuine community and not that of an extended civil society. And though Rorty and Rawls continue to write as if the significant differences that plague civil society are differences about "conceptions of the good," I think (and I take Rousseau to share this view) that it is differences – inequalities – in the ownership and control of resources that are fundamental to the tensions and conflicts that create the need for community policing. To the extent that these differences emerge, and become significant, the actual order of the magistracy's interests or wills diverge from the socially required order, as Rousseau would put it. More to the point, there may be no agreement on what the interest of the community is; or, in Cohen's scenario of community policing, the community's version of it may be unacceptable to the police. This is a Rousseauian lesson about the limits of solidarity in civil society. Significant divergences in interest flowing from social and material inequalities, and the political tensions and social conflicts they engender, cannot be ameliorated by enforced solidarity or dialogue. Issues about police discretion cannot ultimately be isolated from a consideration of those constitutive social inequalities, and attempts to provide solutions to a neutral version of these issues are unlikely to be of use in confronting the crises we face.

NOTES

1. Howard Cohen, "Police Discretion and Police Objectivity," in this volume, p. 98. All subsequent page references to Cohen's essay are enclosed in brackets in the text.
2. Joan McGregor, "From the State of Nature to Mayberry: The Nature of Police Discretion," in this volume, pp. 60-61.
3. This becomes clear when one notices that most of the examples discussed by contributors, from Michael Davis's first example of differential treatment of two boys to James Fyfe's discussion of the Dahmer case, mirror contexts constituted by social and racial oppression. This real social constitution of these instances is effaced by posing the issue in the general terms of "police discretion."
4. Lit. "Here's Rhodes, jump here." Hegel quotes the proverb and goes on to say: "It is just as absurd to fancy that a philosophy can transcend its contemporary world as it is to fancy that an individual can overleap his own age, jump over Rhodes. If his theory really goes beyond the world as it is and builds an ideal one as it ought to be, that world exists indeed, but only in his opinions, an unsubstantial element where anything you please may, in fancy, be built" (G. W. F. Hegel, *Philosophy of Right*, trans. T. M. Knox [Oxford: Clarendon Press, 1942], p. 11).
5. Richard Rorty, "On Ethnocentrism: A Reply to Clifford Geertz," in *Objectivity, Relativism, and Truth* (New York: Cambridge University Press, 1991), p. 209.
6. For Rorty's celebration of the liberal state and of Western liberal institutions generally, see, e.g., his *Contingency, Irony, and Solidarity* (New York: Cambridge University Press, 1989), esp. ch. 7.

Chapter 5

I. Racial Generalizations and Police Discretion

David Wasserman

This essay addresses the question of whether the police can reasonably be expected to limit their reliance on generalizations about race and behavior (which I refer to as "racial generalizations") in ways that will significantly reduce the harm done by such generalizations.[1] The question of reasonable expectation is a compound one: First, should the police refrain from making all or some race-based inferences? And second, can they refrain from making those inferences even if they should?

I consider several types of police decisions in which racial generalizations may play a role: decisions to observe or monitor, to stop and frisk, to arrest, and to use deadly force. I focus on the type of information the police may consider in deciding whether the action in question is warranted. I do not address the issue of whether the police should have the discretion to refrain from the action in question even if it is warranted – for example, not to stop and frisk despite reasonable suspicion, not to arrest despite probable cause, or not to use deadly force despite a reasonable belief that it is necessary to prevent the imminent infliction of serious physical injury.[2] Except for decisions to monitor and observe, then, I look only at George Fletcher's and Michael Davis's first two senses of discretion, as judgment and discernment. Determinations of reasonable suspicion, probable cause, and imminent danger are all matters of skilled judgment, not liberty or license. Though all are subject to judicial oversight, that oversight is conducted with considerable deference to the police. But the authority to determine when a given level of force is warranted is never delegated exclusively to the police – they cannot stop, frisk, arrest, or fire "at will."

The concerns I raise about the role of race in the exercise of police discretion might well invite even closer judicial scrutiny. Such scrutiny, however, should be undertaken not with the unrealistic and unreasonable goal of purging racial generalization from police decision making, but of limiting and refining its use. One effective way of pursuing that more modest and appropriate goal might be to prohibit the police from adducing racial generalizations to justify a stop, frisk, arrest, or shooting. Such a prohibition might well encourage the police to use racial generalizations more sparingly and critically, to pay more attention to nonracial details and generalizations. But it might lead as well to increased deception in the official justification of police action. Certainly it would not eliminate the police use of racial generalizations, because, as I argue, that would be an impossible task.

THE HARM OF RACIAL GENERALIZATION IN LAW ENFORCEMENT

Within the past year, uniformed white police officers in Washington, D.C., and New York City have shot black police officers in plainclothes who had been attempting to arrest armed robbers. In both cases, the white officers had apparently assumed that the black man wielding a gun was himself a robber. In both cases, black police officers insisted that a white officer out of uniform in that situation would never have been shot. In *The Rage of a Privileged Class*, Ellis Cose recounts several chillingly similar incidents in the recent past.[3]

For every shooting, there are countless indignities. A black male law student, near the top of his class and clerking for a federal judge, gets stopped four times by Newark police because "he fits somebody's profile"; a black male associate at a leading Los Angeles law firm is driving with a white female colleague to a firm brunch in a wealthy neighborhood when he is pulled over, thrown to the ground, handcuffed, and accused of abduction, then released without apology after his passenger explains the situation. A *Washington Post* columnist finds that of seven middle-class black male acquaintances, all but one have been stopped by police while engaged in innocent pursuits; the one who has not is so fair-skinned that he is often taken for white.[4] Cose tells of his own questioning by police on suspicion of burglary when he sat in his car after dropping off a friend at a posh apartment building, an encounter made brief and civil, he suspects, only by his conservative suit and business card. Most poignantly, he describes his experience in Marshall Field's when he was twelve or thirteen, in search of a Mother's Day gift:

While wandering from one section of the store to another, I gradually became aware that someone was shadowing me. That someone, I ascertained, was a plainclothes security guard. Apparently, I fit his profile of a shoplifter. I roamed through the store, trying to ignore him, but he was determined not to be ignored. Little by little he made his surveillance more obvious, until we were practically walking in lockstep. His tactics unsettled me so much that I could no longer concentrate on shopping.[5]

Cose maintains that "whites can afford to shrug off such encounters because it never occurs to them that a white skin might be taken as a sign of criminality";[6] he concludes that "as long as the dominant message sent to impressionable black boys is that they are expected to turn into savage criminals, nothing will stop substantial numbers of them from doing just that."[7] Obviously, the attitudes and conduct of the police do much to convey that message.

Making or acting on such racial generalizations assumes what is often called "guilt by association." But that phrase fails to capture the gravity of the moral offense. It is far less demeaning to incur suspicion because of one's accidental or voluntary associations than because of one's race. It is, for example, merely annoying to become an object of close police scrutiny because one attended an opera at which gunshots were fired. It is profoundly demeaning to be subject to close police scrutiny because one is a black male youth.

Although police scrutiny of both the operagoer and the black youth is based on the behavior of other individuals in the group with which each is associated, there are obvious, critical differences between the two cases. First, the group with which the operagoer is associated is a transient one, and the suspicion he is under is equally transient; in contrast, when a young black man reaches adolescence, he becomes, in Marita Golden's phrase, a "permanent suspect." Second, the operagoer's association with the others in the audience is voluntary (even if it is not "knowing" in the relevant way); the young man's racial affiliation is not. Third, the police do not assume that any given operagoer has a propensity to violence, while they may well make that assumption about any given young black man. A policeman questioning the operagoer regards him as an "improbable" suspect; the policeman questioning a young black man on an urban street where there has just been a shooting is likely to see him as an entirely appropriate suspect, as someone who probably has engaged, or will engage, in this kind of violence even if he did not on this occasion. (Cynical probation officers have a saying that "there are no good boys, only future referrals."[8]

The police can hardly ignore the fact that the majority of crimes in many urban settings, particularly violent crimes, are committed by young black men, and that a significant minority of the young black men they encounter in those settings have engaged in some form of criminal activity. Michael Levin argues that this baseline information justifies the police in acting differently toward black youth, in the absence of more specific information. He offers a hypothetical involving police reliance on "naked" group probability information:

> A policeman on his beat sees three adolescent black males enter store 1 and three adolescent Chinese males enter store 2. He wants to take preventative action against shoplifting by making his presence known, but he has time for just one deterrent saunter – walking past one store will leave time for the other to be victimized. What should he do?[9]

Here, if the officer chooses to saunter by store 1, he is basing his decision simply on his belief that the black youth are more likely to shoplift – he has not had the opportunity to learn anything about either group, other than age, sex, and race, that would affect the odds of their shoplifting (such as reports of racial or ethnic gang activity in the area). The officer may have the discretion to walk anywhere in his beat he chooses – discretion in Davis's third sense of "liberty." Yet, in other contexts, we hold that such discretion cannot be exercised on the basis of "suspect factors" like race and gender.

We might take a position about police discretion similar to Charles Nesson's position on jury discretion – that it serves the valuable social function of relegating unacceptable but unavoidable factors such as group probability rates to a "black box." Situations like Levin's are unsettling on this account just because the lack of informational camouflage threatens to expose our reliance on those factors. But this is a deeply cynical position, which assumes that we cannot afford, and should not be required, to reveal the real reasons for state action. It thus offends the publicity principle. As I argue below, the conjunction of race with other factors often makes a reliance on race less objectionable not by disguising it, but by giving the individual an opportunity to opt out. The extent of the mitigation depends on the extent of the opportunity. In Levin's hypothetical, there are no other factors, and no opportunity for the individual black youths to exempt themselves from the racial generalization. But do we really want the officer to flip a coin to decide which store to saunter by?

AN EXCLUSIONARY RULE

Our discomfort with the officer's reliance on a naked racial generalization is matched by our reluctance to deny it to him. The critic to whom Levin's hypothetical is addressed, Jonathan Adler, responds that the officer need not flip a coin; that the police can rely on group-based probabilities in deciding whom to observe, but not whom to arrest. A "saunter" is not a sufficiently intrusive action to preclude police reliance on group probability rates. In contrast, "random searches of blacks or their cars" would be sufficiently intrusive.[10] In effect, the police officer's decision about where to saunter is no more problematic than the police department's decision about where to place its officers. It is the use of force against an individual which requires a more particularized justification.[11]

Adler takes the position that the police cannot use group probability rates to justify "an interference with autonomy." Such an exclusionary rule has ample precedent. The Equal Protection Clause of the Constitution has been held to bar state agents, and private agents entrusted with important social decisions, from considering certain statistical information regardless of its relevance. Thus, the Supreme Court has barred the use of race and gender in underwriting, even though both race and gender may have some predictive value. Excluding race and gender from underwriting decisions has a social cost in higher premiums; excluding race from police decisions may have a social cost in reduced deterrence. In the face of such costs, there are three general reasons for an exclusionary rule: first, the economic, social, and psychological harms caused by a reliance on race and gender; second, the likelihood of overreliance (even experienced underwriters and police officers are likely to regard race and gender as more predictive than they actually are); and third, the likelihood that the reliance on a group generalization masks or expresses simple animosity toward the group, and that it may be impossible to purge the distorting effects of such animosity from generalizations about the group.

Such an exclusionary rule is still problematic, however. On the one hand, it appears too permissive. It still allows the police to use race in deciding whom to observe or follow; it offers no protection against the kind of humiliation suffered by Cose in Marshall Field's. Further, observation often leads to more intrusive police action, when the observed individual confronts the observer or makes a gesture seen as furtive or threatening. Even if the police would respond in the same way to a similar confrontation or gesture by a suspect of any race, they will often be in a position to elicit or observe such conduct only because of the suspect's race.

Moreover, the strength of the rule will depend on how comprehensive a ban it imposes on police reliance on race. Adler argues that "group probability rates *alone* are an insufficient justification" for significant infringements of autonomy like car searches and frisks.[12] But few police operations rely on such naked group rates. Police reliance on race usually comes into play in conjunction with more specific factors, such as similarity to witness descriptions or suspicious conduct. (Of course, race still plays a role in police decisions based on this more specific information, as I discuss in the next section.) A ban on naked racial generalizations would protect against only the most indiscriminate police actions. As such, it would be redundant, since even if the police took full account of the demographics of crime, they would rarely, if ever, have reasonable suspicion that an individual had committed a crime *just* because he was young, black, and male.

On the other hand, the rule would seem unrealistically and unfairly restrictive if it were taken to exclude *all* police reliance on "group probability rates." It would be, to say the least, far more difficult to exclude race in such a context than in underwriting decisions, even if we were determined to do so. An underwriter can consult tables that aggregate race or gender and assess risk by other, permitted, factors. A police officer facing a potentially violent suspect has no race-aggregated tables to rely on. In a situation where he faces a choice between intervening against black and white suspects, he does not have the benefit of the stipulation that the suspects' behavior was the same; the suspects' race might enter into his decision by affecting his judgment of how threatening their conduct was. Even if he were willing to flip a coin when the suspects' behavior was equally threatening, he could hardly avoid being influenced by race in determining whether that condition was satisfied.

EMBEDDED RACIAL GENERALIZATIONS

More important, even if the police made no assumptions about a general propensity to commit crimes, they would face a myriad of situations in which skin color appears to have some value in assessing the likelihood that a crime has been, is being, or is about to be committed. An informal sample of those situations suggests the pervasiveness of racial generalizations in police decisions, the plausibility of many of those generalizations, and the dangers of relying on them.

Sometimes police reliance on race appears uncontroversial. The use of skin color simply for identification purposes is no more problematic than the use of any other kind of identification evidence. I doubt that anyone would object to a police officer observing black youths more closely than white youths immediately after receiving a report that a young black male had committed a robbery in the vicinity. And it certainly seems reasonable for the police to take account of race in matching a suspect to the available description of the perpetrator, in order to decide whether to make an arrest. Still, these uses of racial information may not be as simple, or as innocuous, as they appear. The police in search of a white perpetrator may accord a far more robust presumption of innocence to white youth in the conduct of their investigation, because they assume that the baseline probability of any given white youth being involved in a crime is much lower. For the same reason, they may require a closer match to stop or arrest a white suspect.[13]

Race may also serve as a proxy for other, ostensibly more legitimate considerations. Thus, Peter Ainsworth and Ken Pease note that even the most bias-free police officer patrolling an all-white suburb would have more reason to stop a young black than a young white dressed in a grubby T-shirt and jeans. "It is not the police officer's fault that skin color is a particularly easy marker for strangeness in an area." Still, the officer's action is troubling because of the reason why race is such an easy marker:

> The reason why no black people live in the posh suburb is that black people get a raw deal in employment and education. So the reason you can identify the black youth as a stranger is because, through a history of discrimination, people like him cannot afford to live in an area like that. By stopping the black youth, [the officer] would be adding the insult of a stop to the injury of a long term discrimination against his people.[14]

Race in this context, moreover, is not simply a marker for strangeness. While a white youth in a black neighborhood would also be marked as a stranger, he would not engender the same suspicions as a black youth in a white neighborhood. If he were stopped, it would probably be for a warning about personal safety or for questioning about drugs, not for suspicion of burglary. The officers would assume that white youth do not go into black neighborhoods to commit burglaries, since they can steal better goods less conspicuously in white neighborhoods.

A similar use of race as a social marker was described by a former New York City police officer. Patrolling on Coney Island, he pulled over a young black man driving a large blue Cadillac with a residence sticker from Breezy Point, a gated community which the officer knew was exclusively white.[15] In recounting the incident, he claimed to have reached the conclusion that the car was not owned by its current driver through a simple census, not a racial generalization.[16] But his conclusion that the car was stolen did rely on a behavioral generalization involving race: that the white residents of Breezy Point did not lend their cars to young black men. (In fact, the car was stolen, though it might conceivably have been lent to the black youth for transport to a car wash or a mechanic.)

There is also a wide range of situations in which race may affect the police interpretation of an individual's appearance or behavior. Thus, a certain style of dress may mark a black youth as a gang member, a white youth as a harmless wanna-be; in contrast, a profanity-laced exchange among black youth may be seen as playful, among white youth as volatile.

As the Breezy Point anecdote illustrates, the interplay of race and other features is often complex and highly localized. Consider the significance that race has around Columbia-Presbyterian Hospital, a large training institution surrounded by predominantly Hispanic and black neighborhoods with some of the most active crack trade in New York City. A casually dressed dark-skinned man a block or two from the hospital would probably be an object of greater suspicion than a casually dressed white man, especially if the dark-skinned man was wearing a beeper, but even if he was just strolling down the street or standing next to a stoop. The difference would largely vanish if he was wearing a resident's jacket, but perhaps not if he was wearing an orderly's. A late model car with Jersey plates idling on the curb might well be monitored more closely if the occupants were white than black. These differences would reflect the police belief that almost all the crack dealers in the neighborhood are black or Hispanic; that most residents at Columbia-Presbyterian are white; that residents do not deal crack, while some orderlies may; that much local crack is sold to white suburban youth who drive across the George Washington Bridge; and that white youths are unlikely to have any legitimate business on the side streets of Washington Heights.

Some of these generalizations may rely on outdated or inadequate information, and the processes by which that information is gathered may be infected with bias. But in the absence of a specific claim of inaccuracy or bias, it is difficult to say which, if any, of these generalizations are invalid.

Several features of these generalizations are worth noting. First, they rely heavily on race. Second, they do not associate racial groups with some general tendency to offend, but with highly specific, local, and changing patterns of behavior. Third, an individual of the group subject to the generalization can usually exempt himself from it by changing his dress or behavior. Still, to a neighborhood youngster struggling to avoid the temptations and depredations of street life, these generalizations add the insult of misplaced suspicion to the injury of a poor, crime-ridden environment.

Finally, it seems inevitable that the police will rely excessively and uncritically on such generalizations. Like most generalizations, those about race and behavior tend to be self-perpetuating, because those who rely on them tend to ignore inconsistent or qualifying information. For example, Neil Richards reports that the London Metropolitan Police overlooked major criminal activity by white gangs because they assumed that almost all significant crime was being committed by Afro-Caribbeans and Asians.[17] Moreover, the usual resistance of social generalizations to qualification and disconfirmation may be greatly exacerbated by racial animosity, by the extent to which many police officers are motivated to accept them.

A MORAL DILEMMA

The use of racial and other group generalizations by the police inflicts profound and enduring harm on the individuals in those groups, perpetuating the apparent validity of those generalizations in an insidious cycle. Yet it is neither desirable nor possible for the police to make decisions, even decisions involving the use of force, without relying at least tacitly on some of those generalizations.

I believe that the use of racial generalizations by the police confronts us with a moral dilemma, and that we should direct our efforts to mitigation rather than denial. Ultimately, the effort at mitigation may involve the usual liberal prescriptions for breaking the association between skin color and crime. But on a more modest scale, there may be a great deal that the police can do to mitigate the kind of harm Cose describes. For example, reforms advocated for other reasons, notably increased minority recruitment and community policing, may do much to reduce police reliance on group-based probabilities and thus to reduce the harm in such reliance.

Even if inferences based on group probabilities cannot, and perhaps should not, be entirely purged from police decision making, the police can reduce their impact through what Laurence Thomas calls "acquired social monitoring."[18] Thomas claims, in effect, that the locus of responsibility and blame in the stereotyping debate has been misplaced.[19] What is blameworthy is not, or not so much, that the police use group probability rates, but rather that they fail to acquire the discrimination that would reduce their reliance on those rates. While it may be unreasonable to expect a police officer to increase the risk to herself or others by waiting for a suspect to display the kind of crime-specific conduct that would reduce or eliminate any recourse to racial generalizations, it may be reasonable to expect her department to reduce the frequency with which she has to rely on race, by honing her social discrimination.

As Thomas points out, "the average person has extensive social monitoring skills, as is evidenced by the fact that just about everyone is capable of recognizing flirting behavior. . . . We are so adept at monitoring individuals on the basis of their self-presentational behavior, both attire and body language, that we usually do so easily and rather unreflectively."[20] Thus, as Thomas argues, it does not take great acumen to recognize that several young black men running in tandem in jogging suits represent less of a threat on an urban sidewalk than several casually sauntering young black men in hooded sweatshirts and baggy trousers. Still, even such straightforward social monitoring may be more difficult in general than Thomas suggests. Bradford Cornell describes the complex discrimination involved in a routine judgment about the predatory or opportunistic disposition of an unknown individual:

> [A] young woman walking to a bus stop at night notices that a lone man is already there. The thought occurs to her that the man might behave opportunistically, in the sense that he might hassle, rob, or even attack her. Based on what she can observe, the woman has to decide whether to approach the man or turn around and walk to a more distant bus stop. In making this decision, she will try to decode observable information about the man, including his dress, grooming, mannerisms, age, size and ethnic characteristics.[21]

Cornell argues that such social decoding works far better for members of a person's own racial or cultural group:

> Because people have a strong incentive to disguise opportunistic intent, decoding requires evaluation of subtle distinctions between complex combinations of characteristics. An individual will be able to make such subtle distinctions only if the people to be sorted have a cultural background similar to that of the people he or she was exposed to. . . .[22]

Cornell suggests that the cultural limitations of social decoding lead to a vicious circle: "Decoding problems lead to segregation, which reduces the amount of intimate interaction between two peoples, which in turn increases the decoding problem."[23]

Thomas contends, however, that there is a morally problematic asymmetry in social decoding – oppressed groups can differentiate among their oppressors far better than the reverse. He attributes this difference to the enormous disparity in power between a historically oppressed people and their oppressors. American blacks had to become acutely sensitive to subtle distinctions among American whites, while American whites could afford to be obtuse. Thomas argues that this historical difference makes the lack of social discrimination among predominantly white police forces especially problematic. The law-abiding black youth mistakenly suspected by a white police officer is victimized less by the misbehavior of people with similar complexions than by the culpable indifference of the larger society to details of dress, body language, and behavior that would readily distinguish them.

What Thomas's argument would seem to require is not the wholesale exclusion of race and ethnicity from police decision making, but a concerted effort to overcome intergroup differences in decoding skill of the sort observed by Cornell – particularly those differences that arise from a history of oppression. The more the police rely on characteristics besides race, gender, and age, the less adverse the impact of their generalizations. With regard to young black men, for example, a generalization involving a complex interaction of race, appearance, and behavior may still be regarded as a racial generalization, but its harm is mitigated in two significant respects: First, it does not apply to many or most young black men – to those who do not dress or act in the specified ways. Second, it ascribes an increased probability of criminal activity to other young black men based on details of dress and behavior that are largely under their control; they can exempt themselves from suspicion by altering those details. Of course, it may be difficult or costly for them to do so – damaging to their self-identity or their social standing – and that difficulty and cost must be considered in assessing the reasonableness of the generalization.

Clearly, the social discrimination demanded of a police officer in a multicultural city goes beyond that required of a white citizen to distinguish black joggers and businessmen from black hoodlums, to use one of Thomas's examples. The sheer variety of groups, and the nuances of dress and behavior that distinguish them, require unusual acuity. Moreover, social markers are moving, elusive targets. Not only have some black muggers been reported to dress in jogging and business suits, but more importantly, many law-abiding young black (and white) men consciously or unconsciously mimic a "gangsta" style of dress, speech, and body language.

These difficulties, however, are matters of degree. Social discrimination will always be imperfect, but there is likely to be an enormous difference in the degree of discrimination displayed by a rookie from the suburbs and a veteran officer who has spent years patrolling the neighborhood in which he grew up. Many recent measures designed to improve police effectiveness may also enhance social discrimination and reduce intergroup differences that reinforce segregation. For example, social discrimination can be enhanced by hiring minority officers from high-crime neighborhoods, who will have honed social discrimination as a survival skill; by expanding community policing to allow the officers assigned to an area to become familiar with its individual troublemakers and their styles of dress and behavior; and by using informants not just for tips on specific instances of crime but for information on local patterns of criminal activity and trends in criminal self-display.

This optimism about police reform and social discrimination must be tempered by four considerations. First, a decreased reliance on group stereotypes may lead to an increased reliance on judgments about individual propensities. To the extent that community police are acquainted with individual troublemakers, they will have less need to rely on group generalizations; instead of targeting people because of their race, the police may "round up the usual suspects." Admittedly, a reliance on history and reputation is preferable to a reliance on skin color.[24] But it has significant moral costs: it burdens an individual with his past and tempts him to repeat it, by nullifying the social benefits of self-reform. And it encourages the police to overlook criminal activity by those too young, or too discreet, to have previously come to their attention.

Second, in encouraging law-abiding individuals to exempt themselves from suspicion by avoiding certain kinds of dress and behavior, the police may reduce the value of that dress and behavior as a marker for criminal activity. If it is widely known what dress and behavior provoke police suspicion, the guilty as well as the innocent will be able to avoid suspicion. It is easy, however, to make too much of this problem. Most teenagers of all races are familiar with the styles of dress, speech, and behavior that attract the admiration of their peers and the suspicion of the police. Moreover, those of their peers who really deserve the attention of the police often court it, or at least make little effort to avoid it. Unlike drug couriers, they do not aim to stay as inconspicuous as possible – they strive for respect as much as wealth, and the former requires bravado, defiance, and intimidation in an oppositional culture.

Third, minority recruitment is no panacea. Not only may minority police lose their social decoding skills in their separation from their neighborhoods and their companions, but they may be absorbed into a police culture that ignores or denigrates those monitoring skills, and encourages them to rely on far coarser generalizations. The police establishment may change minority recruits far more than minority recruits change the police establishment.[25]

Finally, there are significant practical limits to the social discrimination that the police can achieve. Two limits are suggested by the Justice Department report on a Kansas City experiment in removing guns from high-crime neighborhoods by vigorous surveillance. First, the familiarity bred by community policing was limited by the mobility of street criminals: "Two thirds of the persons later found carrying guns in the beat resided outside the area."[26] Second, the attempt to particularize gun frisks by the use of race-neutral body language (for example, "frequent touching of the waist," where handguns are often hidden) was unsuccessful, since most suspects rode in cars, and "only 9 percent of the guns were found in pedestrian checks."[27] But these qualifications do not diminish the moral urgency of inculcating social discrimination in the police force; they merely remind us that we must be realistic about the immediate practical impact of heightened social discrimination.

Michael Levin, not surprisingly, challenges the value of social discrimination as a cure or even a palliative for the moral dilemma posed by racial generalization. Levin insists that since specificity does not eliminate race as a factor in social judgment, it offers little or no defense to the charge of racism:

> To see how little specificity helps, the reader might in an experimental spirit pass the following remark the next time the topic of race and crime comes up in conversation. "There is no need to shun all blacks. The ones to watch are black males between the ages of 14 and 25 with baggy pants, expensive running shoes, an in-your-face expression, who use the phrase 'shee-it-muthafuckah' with great frequency. Be careful of teen-age boys who bump you, but especially of black boys who do." I predict this display of social awareness will be called "racist stereotyping."[28]

I suspect that the charge of "racist stereotyping" is less likely to be elicited by the generalization Levin offers than by what I take to be its underlying assumption: that most, or a large majority, of the young black men one encounters meet his description. That assumption is mistaken, and it illustrates the lack of discrimination that Thomas decries. Most young black men simply do not fit that description, even on the No. 3 train above 125th Street, which I rode weekly for several years. There are plenty of intimidating young black men on that train, to be sure. But I believe, based on my own experience, that anyone with a modicum of social discrimination would see that a large majority of young black men on that train are not intimidating and do not wish to be. (That might, admittedly, be cold comfort to a frightened rider who encountered a group that matched Levin's description, but that is not the point.) Levin may have been led to a contrary assumption by the salience of intimidating young black men (the "availability heuristic") or, less charitably, by a reluctance to question impressions that support his position.

If we regard Levin's generalization as one that would in fact exempt from suspicion a significant proportion of young black men in urban settings, I think it would be unreasonable to condemn that generalization as "racist stereotyping." Even if a confrontational style would be regarded as more threatening when it was adopted by black than white youths, a high level of suspicion would be engendered by almost any group of belligerent young men. It is easy enough for a black youth to see how his behavior contributed to the suspicion he faced, even if it might be hard to resist peer pressure to engage in it, as well as the broader pressures of an oppositional culture. It may also be true, as Ellis Cose suggests, that young black men are caught in a dynamic of self-fulfilling expectation that young white men are not: strangers observe them with an initial wariness; they act to fulfill the expectations conveyed by that posture.

Of course, we can do far better than Levin's generalization. Years ago, riding around the Thirty-second Precinct with two dedicated white police officers with years of anticrime and narcotics experience between them, I was struck by how little of the boisterous, confrontational "street theater" we witnessed alarmed or even interested them. They had learned, or appeared to have learned, how to distinguish behavior intended to look threatening from behavior that really was threatening. A young black man on the streets of North Harlem did not need to act or dress like a choirboy or a bookworm to escape their suspicion. This social discrimination was not a matter of racial sensitivity; it was, as they say, merely good police work.

The acquisition of transracial social monitoring skills by the police would make it easier for them to exempt a broad range of young black men from the suspicion they now face simply because of their skin color, age, and sex. Of course, there is no guarantee that individual police officers would be motivated to acquire or apply such monitoring skills. But, as my ride through the Thirty-second Precinct suggested, improving social discrimination is a way of conserving energy and enhancing personal safety. While sharper discrimination will hardly eliminate racial differences in police suspicion, it should help to mitigate the harms caused by blanket suspicion. No one who takes those harms seriously will regard this as a trivial gain.

NOTES

As my endnote attributions indicate, in revising this essay I have benefited greatly from the comments and suggestions of other workshop participants.

1. In using the term "racial generalization," I mean to include summaries of statistical information (however accurate) of the form: "Almost all the muggings in this neighborhood are committed by black males between the ages of 14 and 25," as well as verbal approximations of regression equations of the form: "X is more likely to commit a mugging in this neighborhood if he is black[, given that he is between 14 and 25 and is wearing running shoes]" and "X is likely to commit a mugging in this neighborhood, given that he is a black male [between the ages of 14 and 25 wearing running shoes]."

2. These decisions may also be affected by the race of the suspect, of course, and they may also involve generalizations in which the suspect's race plays some role, for example, about the differential preventive or deterrent impact of a given intervention. We could require the police to intervene whenever the criterion for intervention was satisfied, but such a blanket rule would be circumvented or undermined were the police to take race into account in determining if that criterion had been satisfied.

3. Ellis Cose, *The Rage of a Privileged Class* (New York: HarperCollins, 1993) These tragic mistakes are idiosyncratic in one respect. They arise in part from a technical problem – the difficulty that plainclothes officers have had in quickly identifying themselves to their uniformed brethren. This problem has little to do with race. But these incidents also suggest the extent to which a man with black skin, whatever his vocation and status, is at greater risk of deadly mistakes in judgment. Moreover, the details of some of these incidents, with suspects shot repeatedly in the back or on the ground, suggest that black skin may still inspire loathing as well as fear.

4. Donna Britt, "Assumptions Take a Beating," *Washington Post*, 2 June 1995, p. C1, col. 1.

5. Cose, *The Rage of a Privileged Class*, p. 68.

6. Ibid., p. 104.

7. Ibid., p. 110.

8. The suspicion faced by the operagoers is similar to that faced by the men in two British communities where brutal sex killings occurred; the police, lacking clues but certain that the perpetrator was local, "invited" all the young and middle-aged men in the community to give blood for DNA typing. Because the imposition was brief and nonrecurring, and the suspicion based on geography rather than propensity, no offense was taken.

9. Michael Levin, "Reply to Adler, Cox, and Corlett," *Journal of Social Philosophy* 25, no. 1 (spring 1994), p. 9.

10. Jonathan E. Adler, "More on Race and Crime: Levin's Reply," *Journal of Social Philosophy* 25, no. 2 (fall 1994), p. 108.

11. Levin argues that Adler's concession puts him on a slippery slope: "Once Adler lets race figure in some decisions, such as which store deserves a stroll-by, he cannot just arbitrarily ban the use of race in more serious decisions, including the taking of more invasive measures. [I]f race is equally predictive in other contexts, it should be practically relevant there too" ibid.,(p. 116). This is, however, even less plausible than most slippery slope arguments. Our constitutional

jurisprudence provides a clear stopping point at the use of force. Thus, the police use of force is circumscribed in a way that other police actions are not, though there will, of course, be borderline cases in which it is unclear whether a given police action involves force.

12. Adler, "More on Race and Crime," p. 108, emphasis added.

13. A significant racial disparity in the threshold for finding a match is suggested by a recent incident in which Metro-North police officers frisked a senior vice president of *Black Enterprise* magazine as he got off a commuter train to go to his office in midtown Manhattan (*New York Times*, 8 May 1995). The police had a report of a gun-carrying black man on that commuter line who was well dressed, about five feet ten inches tall, with a mustache and an athletic build, sometimes carrying a briefcase. The magazine executive was well dressed and athletic, and held a briefcase. But he was also six feet four inches tall, with no mustache. These discrepancies might well have precluded the frisk of a white commuter; the police may have seen them as less significant for a black commuter, given the paucity of well-dressed, athletic, briefcase-toting black men on that line.

14. Peter B. Ainsworth and Ken Pease, *Police Work* (London and New York: The British Psychological Society and Methuen, 1987), p. 101.

15. The former officer is Professor James Fyfe; the story was related at the Workshop on Ethical Issues in Police Discretion, held at John Jay College in New York City, 6-8 May 1995.

16. The driver could conceivably have bought the car from a resident without removing the sticker.

17. This example was related at the Workshop on Ethical Issues in Police Discretion.

18. Laurence Thomas, "Statistical Badness," *Journal of Social Philosophy* 23, no. 1 (spring 1992), pp. 38-39.

19. Thomas focuses on civilian conduct, not police conduct; I am applying his critique to the latter.

20. Ibid., p. 38.

21. Bradford Cornell, "A Hypothesis Regarding the Origins of Ethnic Discrimination," *Rationality and Science* 7, no. 1 (January 1995), p. 6.

22. Ibid., pp. 18-19.

23. Ibid., p. 23.

24. As Mark Kelman observes in contrasting group affiliation and past misconduct as grounds for denying employment, "those denied an opportunity as a result of past misdeeds are at least not being punished for a mere propensity or set of background demographic characteristics, but for something they have presumably chosen to do during their lives" (Mark Kelman to Dr. Michael Feuer, Office of Technology Assessment, U.S. Congress, memorandum, 26 June 1990,"A General Framework for Evaluating Classification Errors, with Special Reference to Integrity Testing," p. 9).

25. I owe this point to James Fyfe.

26. Lawrence W. Sherman, James W. Shaw, and Dennis P. Rogan, *The Kansas City Gun Experiment*, National Institute of Justice Research Brief, January 1995, p. 4. This particular practical barrier may have a technological fix, however, in the recent development of hand-held "aim and shoot" metal detectors – assuming that they can detect the metal of a gun within the metal casing of a car.

27. Ibid.

28. Levin, "Reply to Adler, Cox, and Corlett," p. 7.

Chapter 5

II. Police Discretion and Discrimination

Howard McGary

The philosopher and legal scholar Ronald Dworkin gives the following account of discretion:

> What does it mean in ordinary life to say that someone "has discretion"? The first thing to notice is that the concept is out of place in all but very special contexts. For example, you would not say that I either do or do not have discretion to choose a house for my family. It is not true that I have "no discretion" in making that choice, and yet it would be almost equally misleading to say that I do have discretion. The concept of discretion is at home in only one sort of context; when someone is in general charged with making decisions subject to standards set by a particular authority.[1]

Discretion is exercised at every level of police work, from the administration of justice by high police officials to the cop on the beat. Police administrators have the discretion to decide what policies should determine their duties. For example, they can decide to place greater emphasis on crime prevention than on the apprehension of criminals. Individual police officers also have a great deal of discretion, however, in the performance of their day-to-day activities. A. J. Reiss writes: "Most police officers work most of the time without direct supervision. Their discretionary decisions, thus, are not generally open to review by supervisors. . . ."[2] Police officers have discretion in enforcing clearly stated laws, as well as the authority and discretion to settle disputes that do not clearly involve violations of the law.

In this discussion I explore the following question: Can police discretion justify the use of a person's age, race, religion, and sex in determining who should be subjected to police authority? There is a popular belief that most police work is done strictly by the book. In other words, where there are clear laws and clear violations of these laws, police ticket or arrest those people who violate the laws. But even those people who have this rosy view of police work must reluctantly admit that sometimes police officers are uncertain about what the law requires and whether a particular individual has, in fact, violated the law.[3] There are also cases, however, where the police officer is certain that the law has been broken and knows who violated the law, but determines that more harm than good would be served by arresting the lawbreaker.

It is wishful thinking to believe that all police officers know the laws and mechanically apply them in a fair and impartial manner. This is an overly optimistic view of police work. In fact, I would go so far as to say that a very large percentage of police work is discretionary. If this is true, we can hope only that police discretion operates in accordance with the constraints of justice and the spirit of the law.

Let us begin our examination by considering the following case:

> A police officer is parked on the side of a busy highway with a posted speed limit of fifty-five miles per hour. She observes a group of motorists who are exceeding the speed limit, but it is impossible for the officer to pull over all of the speeders. So she decides to pull over the violators that are close to her police vehicle.

Is this case of police discretion in line with the constraints of justice and the spirit of the law? The rule the officer appears to be following is: Ticket speeders who are nearest to the officer's vehicle. Given that the officer cannot apprehend all of the speeding motorists, and it would defeat the purpose of having speeding laws to let them all go, this rule of thumb employed by the officer seems fair and reasonable.

What about the motorists who are pulled over for speeding? Do they have a legitimate complaint? Is the officer using her discretionary powers properly or is she unjustly discriminating against this subgroup of speeders? Clearly on one level she is not. Members of the subgroup broke the law by speeding. Because they have broken the law, on a retributivist account of punishment they deserve to be ticketed. According to a retributivist, a person deserves punishment only if he or she is responsible or accountable for some illegal act.[4] So, on the retributivist account, one might argue that members of the subgroup of speeders are getting what they deserve even though they are singled out for ticketing.

But the officer could appeal to another principle of punishment to justify the use of her discretionary powers in this manner. She could adopt a utilitarian point of view. On this theory of punishment, we punish only if punishing promotes greater utility than any of the available alternatives.[5] Thus, people may be punished even when they are not responsible for their illegal acts. The officer could use this rationale to justify her decision to stop some, but not all, of the speeders if doing so promoted greater utility. But is it reasonable to think that the officer's decision to stop some, but not all, of the speeders promotes greater utility than letting them all go? I think so.

But the utilitarian and the retributivist justifications of punishment are not the only theories that we can employ to justify the officer's actions. We could also employ what the legal philosopher Joel Feinberg calls the notion of comparative justice.[6] According to the basic principle of comparative justice, "likes should be treated alike." So, in the context of punishment, when people commit like crimes they should be punished in a like manner.

If one embraces the notion of comparative justice, one could argue that we should stop either all of the speeders or none of the speeders. But I think Feinberg would say that this would be a premature conclusion. For the complete principle of comparative justice is: "Treat all men alike until it can be shown that there are relevant differences between them."[7]

The basic principle of comparative justice has a strong egalitarian element: the presumption that equals should be treated as equals. According to this principle, objective standards of justice are logically affected by comparisons between the parties. The critics of comparative justice, however, argue that justice does not require that we compare individuals with each other, only with objective standards. Thus, according to noncomparative justice, we do not treat individuals justly because we treat them alike, we treat them justly because we are following some objective standard.

Equal treatment does not necessarily entail justice. The former Green Bay Packers tackle Henry Jordan made the following remark about his coach, Vincent Lombardi: "He treated us all the same. Like dogs." The critics of comparative justice warn us that this principle is at best a formal principle because it fails to specify what we should actually do when confronted with specific circumstances. In order to determine what we should do in specific circumstances, we must rely on some material principle that can tell us what to do in specific cases. In the case of our speeders, we might be on solid ground in stopping some, but not all, of them, if we can show that there is some morally relevant reason for treating likes differently.

But what about more controversial cases? How should a conscientious police officer decide what to do in cases involving generalizations about race, sex, age, and so forth? There are two general approaches that I would like to explore briefly. The first is the Bayesian approach. According to this approach, a rational decision is one that is based on the maximization of expected utility. The Bayesian approach uses axioms that allow for the determination of subjective probabilities, and then uses these probabilities to calculate expected utility. This approach is not uncontroversial, even though it has a long history of application in normative and descriptive decision theory. A primary criticism of this approach has been that it is too comprehensive because most decisions, including rational ones, are made on the basis of less than complete information about the alternative courses of action available to agents.

In our case involving the police officer who wants to determine what her policy should be for pulling over speeding motorists, her primary aim is to select the lawbreakers from a given set of motorists. In some cases this is quite obvious. In other cases, the officer must make inferences about who from the given set of motorists are lawbreakers. But given that police officers in actual practice have some discretion about how and when to apply the law, they might employ the Bayesian approach in cases where there is no question in the officer's mind about who the lawbreakers are. My discussion of the use of police discretion in the first section of this essay assumes a Bayesian approach to decision making. At the end of the essay I briefly consider how a contractarian approach might handle these issues.

The contractarian asks: What would rational self-interested parties agree to in real and hypothetical situations under conditions of uncertainty? The basic idea here is not what will maximize utility or promote the greatest happiness for all, but what rational self-interested parties would agree to. According to contractarians, their approach avoids a popular objection to the Bayesian approach, namely, that in its pursuit of the common good the Bayesian approach fails to respect the rights of individuals. In fact, the political philosopher John Rawls has forcefully argued that the right (the just) must be prior to the good. He endorses the Kantian idea that persons should not be regarded as mere means.[8] A contractarian would argue that a just decision or procedure should not be based simply on how much social utility is expected to result from the decision, but on whether rational individuals, under conditions of fairness, would choose to harm or violate the rights of certain individuals in order to maximize social utility for all. Rawls and other contractarians insist that the contractarian approach respects the rights of individuals at the same time that it allows for an appropriate regard for the common good.[9]

THE BAYESIAN APPROACH

The police officer pulls some, but not all, of the speeders over for ticketing for what she considers morally relevant reasons. She calculates that ticketing some of the speeders is in line with an objective standard and that the reason offered for not holding all of the speeders to this standard is that it is not possible to do so. The speeders who are ticketed are not singled out because of something that is beyond their control. If they decide to speed again, they can change their relative position in the group of speeders. Where they are ticketed today for speeding, they might be spared tomorrow. The characteristics that are used to single out speeders are not thought to be "suspect." (Suspect characteristics are characteristics that are thought not to be within the actors' control, and they have a long history of being used as a basis for inflicting harm on innocent persons. Race and gender have been designated as clearly suspect characteristics in our society.) So, in our speeding case, the strong deterrent value of ticketing some speeders overrides the harm caused by not treating all the speeders in the same way.

But let us make a slight modification to our speeders case. Suppose the motorists who are singled out for ticketing are selected because they are members of a particular race or sex. Have they been unjustly discriminated against? Can the police officer provide a rationale that will allow her to employ suspect characteristics in her decision making? Is this a decision rule that the officer could reasonably adopt?

I do not think so. It is doubtful whether a rule that singles out speeders on the basis of their race or sex can be justified by reference to some objective standard of justice. Given the history of racism and sexism in this country, the disutility and unfairness created by such a rule would seem to outweigh any of the advantages to be derived from such a rule. But legal theory and practice does not categorically rule out the use of suspect characteristics. The law says that when these characteristics are employed in decision making, compelling state interests must be served by doing so. The worry is that in this case it is hard to see how some compelling interests are served by police officers following such a rule.

What if we add a further dimension to our case? Suppose the highway that our speeding motorists are traveling is known for drug trafficking. And let us further suppose that a particular racial group includes a high percentage of persons who have been arrested for drug offenses. Would these facts change our position about the use of race in deciding who should be pulled over for ticketing? I do not think they should. Yet some people have argued that we can and should use statistical arguments to draw inferences about what should be done to particular persons.[10] By the use of statistical reasoning, then, does the police officer have a morally relevant reason for pulling over motorists from only one racial group because there is a greater statistical probability that members of this group will be drug offenders?

Ours is a hypothetical case, but lawyers for nineteen minority motorists stopped for drug and weapons charges on the New Jersey Turnpike have argued that the state police use racial profiles to target black and Latino motorists. According to these lawyers, black motorists on the southern-most twenty-six-mile portion of the turnpike were 500 percent more likely to be stopped by the state police than were white motorists. Although blacks represented only 15 percent of all the motorists violating traffic laws, they represented 46 percent of the motorists stopped between January 1988 and April 1991. The nineteen motorists claimed that such a practice violated their constitutional rights.[11]

This alleged discriminatory practice by state police is not restricted to New Jersey. A Hispanic man traveling on Route 84, just over the Connecticut border, was stopped for a cracked windshield and within minutes his vehicle was searched for drugs. Lawyers for the Hispanic motorist argued that Hispanics are illegally targeted for drug searches on Route 84, a major thoroughfare from New York to Boston. According to the attorneys, Hispanic motorists are stopped by the state police more often than other motorists and often they are interrogated and searched without cause.[12] In such cases, is a person's race ever a relevant characteristic for police stops and searches?

I don't think so. First, even if we assume that – actually – statistical arguments can be used to draw particular conclusions from general claims, it does not follow that in our specific example such an inference would be valid. Let us consider a slightly modified example taken from the work of the philosopher Laurence Thomas.[13] If we know that nine out of ten Acme cars are defective, then clearly it is rational to infer that it would be unwise to take the chance of buying an Acme automobile. So far so good. Doesn't our police officer employ similar reasoning when it comes to our speeding motorists? Suppose that 90 percent of known drug offenders are members of a particular racial group. Wouldn't this fact provide the officer with rational grounds for inferring that she is justified in pulling over only members of this racial group? I do not think that an objective noncomparative standard of justice would justify the officer's actions. But if we adopt the principle of comparative justice, we might discover a morally relevant reason for pulling over only speeders from this particular racial group. What would such reasons look like?

The officer's claim that she has a morally relevant reason for stopping only members of a particular race because there is a high probability that members of this group are drug offenders is false. This is not a good reason unless we add the further premises that (1) there is a high probability that stopping only speeders from this group would maximize arrests for drug offenses; (2) the benefit from maximizing such arrests would outweigh the disadvantage caused by the negative deterrent effect on speeders who are not members of this group; and (3) the specter of racism that this practice would raise in a society with a known history of racial discrimination would not cause the general level of racism in the society to increase. It is doubtful that all these premises are true and that such a rule would be the most rational alternative available to the officer. It is indeed questionable whether this is a rational alternative at all. So if likes should be treated alike unless there is some morally relevant reason for treating them differently, then the alleged differences cited above do not seem to qualify as morally relevant differences.

In the examples above, we did not immediately reject our police officer's use of her discretion in a way that appeared to discriminate on the basis of race. A part of our willingness to allow the officer to single out members of one racial group is that they are wrongdoers. Members of this group cannot claim they did not do anything wrong, but only that they were being unfairly treated when compared to other wrongdoers. But in our assessment of their complaint on grounds of comparative justice, we found the officer's discretionary rule to be invalid when we put her rationale for discriminating against this group into a historical context and then accurately evaluated the utility and disutility of such a discriminatory rule.

Would it make a difference if the race of the police officer and of the group being singled out were identical? In practice it might, because in a society with our racial history it would be hard for many people to believe that the motives of the officer were pure if she was not from the same racial group as those who were singled out for ticketing. We should not ignore this reality because to do would be to fail to appreciate the harmful negative consequences that can flow from people's perceptions. If we are accurately to calculate the efficacy of such a rule, then we cannot ignore people's perceptions about the fairness of the rule. In a society where there has been a long history of racial discrimination, it is difficult for many people to accept that a person is acting from nonracist motives when they engage in a controversial practice that primarily harms members of another racial group. These perceptions must be taken into account in decid-ing whether a particular discretionary rule is fair and wise.

Given our remarks about perceptions, the racial identity of the officer can have a bearing on the effectiveness of such a policy. In certain situations, we might be warranted in adjusting our discretionary practices according to the racial identity of the police officer. For example, in a racially explosive situation it might be better to have officers who are of the same racial group as the participants. They might be better able to bring calm to the situation. Nevertheless, although the race of the police officer could have some bearing in our revised case, I do not think that it is the decisive consideration. Even if the officer and those who felt that they were being unfairly singled out were of the same racial identity, the issue would not be resolved.

What if the group of speeders who are stopped are from different racial backgrounds, but the majority are members of one racial group? Should this alter our conclusion? I think it should. This modification would allow us to salvage some of the deterrent effect of stopping speeders in the first place; this would be so because all races would have reason to believe that if they speed they will be ticketed. But it would not completely resolve the deterrence issue because some speeders could still rationally infer that they had a lesser chance of being stopped for speeding simply by virtue of their racial identities. Therefore, all things considered, even in our modi-fied case it would not be wise or fair for an officer to adopt such a discretionary rule.

But what about cases that do not involve race, in which the officer uses her discretionary powers discriminatorily when it is unclear whether par-ties affected by her actions are guilty or negligent in some way? Consider the following case: A police officer decides to pull over mostly senior citizens at a vehicle inspection stop. Her reason for doing this is that the reaction time for seniors is greater than the reaction time for other drivers, and seniors would therefore be less likely to be able to respond effectively in the case of an emergency situation brought on by some mechanical failure. Is her reasoning sound? We can quibble about whether the typical senior citizen has a lower reaction time than younger drivers and about the connection between slow reaction time and accidents. But let us assume, for the sake of argument, that these claims are true. Would this justify the officer in pulling over senior citizens for inspection more frequently than younger drivers?

In this situation, the officer clearly could have noble motives for pulling over the elderly drivers. She may not wish to harm or disrespect older drivers. In fact, she may want only to protect the seniors and other drivers from possible harms. What should the officer do? Should she pull over only vehicles that have some obvious mechanical problems or should she use some random method for pulling over cars? Why can't she use her discretion and pull over elderly drivers if she thinks that accidents might be reduced by doing so? Do the elderly drivers really have good reasons for objecting to such a practice?

The answer to these questions is unclear. Perhaps we can gain some insight into this case by examining a similar case. During certain hours of the day, some store owners deny teenagers access to their stores. They do so because they believe that teenagers engage in a lot of shoplifting, considerably more than members of other age groups. In both these cases, a generalization about members of a group is used to penalize particular members of that group, even those members who are completely innocent. Laurence Thomas has argued persuasively that the use of suspect characteristics like race and sex often involves a rush to judgment. He argues that there are usually much better social indicators than a person's race for picking out rule violators. For example, he claims that we would be better served by focusing on attire. According to Thomas, very few people are mugged by people in tweed sport coats and ties.[14] Thus it would not be rational to conclude that a person so attired, black or otherwise, would be a mugger. Using parity of reasoning, the same would hold for a person's age. Thomas's point is that our preoccupation with race and other suspect characteristics in American society inhibits our development of needed social monitoring skills. Our lack of interaction with people from various races ill equips us with the skills necessary to distinguish friend from foe. Thomas argues that we would be much better served by developing these social monitoring skills than by relying on statistical generalizations about race and other suspect characteristics to draw conclusions about what particular people will do.

David Wasserman, in his essay in this volume, "Racial Generalizations and Police Discretion," generally supports Thomas's conclusions, but he warns us that we cannot totally do away with the need to depend on generalizations based upon suspect characteristics like race. He argues that a more diversified and experienced police force would make it less likely that a police officer would need to rely on racial sterotypes. He writes:

Years ago, riding around the Thirty-second Precinct with two dedicated white police officers with years of anticrime and narcotics experience between them, I was struck by how little of the boisterous, confrontational "street theater" we witnessed alarmed or even interested them. They had learned, or appeared to have learned, how to distinguish behavior intended to look threatening from behavior that really was threatening.[15]

Wasserman's conclusions are instructive, but I do not think they will completely succeed in changing actual police practice until evils like racism are greatly reduced in our society. Racism produces racial stereotypes. The stereotypes do not cause the racism. But given that the complete elimination of racism is not on the immediate horizon, what do we do for now? Clearly Wasserman's proposals are in the right direction, but alone they will be insufficient to help a responsible police officer who wants to use her discretionary authority in ways that do not discriminate unjustly against some citizens.

What are some of the things that individual police officers can do to reduce the likelihood that they will use their discretionary powers in unjust ways? Individual police officers in their day-to-day activities must strive to be more reflective in their decision making. They must calculate and anticipate the full range of consequences that might ensue from their decisions. I realize that this may be unrealistic in emergencies, or in life and death situations, but most police work does not consist of these types of situations. In most instances, police officers have time to evaluate the various alternatives open to them and to assess the possible consequences of those alternatives.

The claim that police officers never know what the next encounter will bring does not justify rash or uninformed judgments on their part. Erring on the side of caution does not entitle the officer to set aside deliberation in making discretionary decisions that could lead to unjust discrimination. We are not second-guessing police officers in asking them to make well-informed discretionary judgments. Their deliberations should include an awareness of the negative impact on race and other relations caused by discretionary decisions that tend to intensify various divisions in society; a recognition that the discriminatory application of objective standards by the use of suspect characteristics may reduce the deterrent value of having the standards; and a realization that using suspect characteristics in discretionary decision making often means ignoring factors that may have greater reliability in identifying criminal conduct.

THE CONTRACTARIAN APPROACH

A police officer who adopts a contractarian approach is concerned with rights and the integrity of the individual as well as the common good. The officer who follows this approach would be especially concerned to respect the presumption of innocence. If one takes this right seriously, one must have strong reservations about using racial generalizations as the primary reason for arresting or detaining a citizen. This is not to say that statistical inferences can never be used, but simply that the mere fact that a person is a member of a particular racial group is not good reason for the belief that a particular person has committed a crime. A contractarian like Rawls would be willing to sacrifice some expected utility in order to respect important individual rights. The assumption that a person is guilty cuts at that person's integrity. Such a presumption is especially harmful to persons who have a history of marginalization and unjust discrimination. Of course, a Bayesian might be sensitive to such rights, but only in a derivative way. Bayesians respect rights only if doing so promotes greater expected utility than not doing so.

A contractarian would argue that a rational and just police officer should use her discretionary powers in ways that would first respect fundamental rights and then promote social utility. So, for example, in the case of our elderly drivers who are pulled over more often than younger drivers for vehicle inspections, a just police officer would seek to ascertain whether such a practice would violate any fundamental rights. Should these inspections violate the rights of the elderly drivers, some alternative course of action ought to be pursued. For example, instead of stopping elderly drivers disproportionately, we might require that all drivers who have caused serious accidents submit their vehicles to inspection more often than persons who have not caused such accidents. By requiring this, we would judge drivers by their driving records and not by factors beyond their control (like their age). Such an alternative might better serve our desire to protect drivers from car accidents that can be attributed to vehicular failures and at the same time respect citizens' right to the presumption of innocence.

This appears to be a just and reasonable alternative to stopping all elderly drivers at random checkpoints. But even if I am wrong about this particular alternative, it is likely that some modification of this proposal will suffice. I am less optimistic, however, about finding an alternative proposal for our speeding black motorists case. Our elderly drivers case is easier to handle because the objects of our focus are unsafe vehicles. But in our speeding black motorists case, we are concerned with the behavior of the motorists. More specifically, we want to detect speeders who may be trafficking in illegal drugs.

Is there a more just and reasonable alternative for detecting such persons than one that relies on racial generalizations about drug traffickers? One might think so, though finding such a method is more easily said than done. Perhaps we could require all convicted drug traffickers to place an insignia on their vehicles that would identify them as convicted drug traffickers, but there is some question whether such a requirement would pass constitutional muster. Nevertheless, given the New Jersey Supreme Court's decision to uphold Megan's Law (a New Jersey statute that requires convicted child molesters to register with local authorities), there is some reason to believe that a law requiring convicted drug traffickers to place on their vehicles an insignia which identifies them as convicted drug traffickers may be judged constitutional by the present conservative U.S. Supreme Court.

But even were such a requirement to be legal, it is extremely doubtful whether it would assist police officers in picking out speeders who are also drug traffickers. It is highly unlikely that drug traffickers would use their own vehicles. Perhaps we could deny driving privileges to convicted drug traffickers. However, it is very unlikely that this practice would deter police officers from using racial generalizations in a racist society if the majority of convicted drug traffickers were black. Unless we can reduce racism in our society, I doubt whether either the contractarian or Bayesian methods will help a well-intentioned police officer use her discretion in ways that do not discriminate unjustly against members of certain groups.

WHAT CAN POLICE ADMINISTRATORS DO?

What can police administrators do to better enable individual police officers to avoid making discretionary decisions that discriminate unjustly against members of certain groups? In addition to the instructive proposals by Thomas and Wasserman, police departments should work to reduce the "hassle" contact that presently exists between police and particular racial and ethnic groups. A great deal of the discomfort experienced by many ethnic and racial minorities in their contacts with police has nothing to do with police arrests. Even members of these groups who have never been arrested do not have positive impressions of the police. Members of some groups believe that they are hassled rather than served by the police.

I think that these negative police perceptions regarding certain groups can be attributed in part to the way in which police view their role in the community. Do they see themselves more as an occupying army in a foreign land during wartime or as members of a community who are charged with the important responsibility of protecting and serving? Clearly, the way police view their role will have a tremendous bearing on how they do their jobs.

In Detroit, police officials have tried to combat the conception of police as an occupying army by allowing civilians to accompany them on patrol and to visit police precincts to view police in their day-to-day activities. These are useful programs because they foster a better understanding between civilians and the police. But it is also important to create programs that will allow police officers to get involved in the full life of the actual communities they serve.[16]

One way in which communities have attempted to get police more involved in the neighborhoods they serve is by placing a residency requirement on police officers. I do not think that this requirement has adequately addressed the problem, however. If you coerce the police into becoming members of a community, this will breed resentment rather than fraternity. Perhaps a better way to approach this problem would be to create incentives that will encourage police to get involved in community organizations and activities. Police Athletic Leagues, for example, have had a positive impact in this regard. But in times of budgetary crisis these programs are the first to go. Perhaps police, the community, and other public officials need to reevaluate their priorities. Some things that may appear to be tangential to good police work may be more central than we realize. Unjust discrimination involves viewing people as the "other" or as "outsiders." Police officials must do all that they can to combat the alienation that exists between the police and the people they serve. These efforts will require full and open discussion of topics like racism and police involvement in the communities where they work.

NOTES

1. Ronald Dworkin, *Taking Rights Seriously* (Cambridge: Harvard University Press, 1977), p. 31.

2. A. J. Reiss Jr., "Discretionary Justice in the United States," *International Journal of Criminology and Penology* 2, no. 2 (1974), p. 181.

3. Samuel Walker, *Taming the System: The Control of Discretion in Criminal Justice, 1950-1990* (New York: Oxford University Press, 1993), pp. 23-25.

4. H. L. A. Hart, *Punishment and Responsibility* (New York: Oxford University Press, 1973), p. 8.

5. Ibid., pp. 72-83.

6. Joel Feinberg, *Social Philosophy* (Englewood Cliffs, NJ: Prentice-Hall, 1973), pp. 98-99.

7. Ibid., p. 102.

8. John Rawls, *A Theory of Justice* (Cambridge: Harvard University Press, 1971), pp. 179-83.

9. Thomas M. Scanlon, "Contractualism and Utilitarianism," in *Utilitarianism and Beyond*, ed. Amaryta Sen and Bernard Williams (Cambridge: Cambridge University Press, 1982).

10. Michael Levin, "Responses to Race Differences in Crime," *Journal of Social Philosophy* 23, no. 1 (spring 1992), pp. 5-29.

11. Jon Nordheimer, "N.J. Troopers Accused of Bias in Traffic Stops," *Quincy (Massachusetts) Patriot Ledger*, 23 December 1994, p. 1.

12. Jenifer McKim, "Arrest of Hispanic Drivers Challenged," *Boston Globe*, 29 May 1995, p. 15.

13. Laurence Thomas, "Statistical Badness," *Journal of Social Philosophy* 23, no. 1 (spring 1992), p. 31.

14. Ibid., p. 33.

15. David Wasserman, "Racial Generalizations and Police Discretion," in this volume, p. 128.

16. Jack R. Greene and Stephen D. Mastrofski, eds., *Community Policing: Rhetoric or Reality* (New York: Praeger, 1988).

Response: Racial Generalization, Police Discretion, and Bayesian Contractualism

Arthur Isak Applbaum

In these comments, I elaborate upon a few conceptual issues raised by David Wasserman and Howard McGary in their thought-provoking essays on the use of racial generalizations by police.[1] To start, I make two very big bracketing assumptions, and then distinguish three pure cases of statistical generalization. Then, about each of the pure cases, I ask two questions.

TWO BRACKETS

I wish, at least at the start, to set aside two important and perhaps compelling arguments against the use of racial generalizations. The first is that racial generalizations typically are the products of either faulty inference or prejudice, and so acting upon them is irrational. The second is that the persistence of racism and its consequences in America is such a grave injustice and social problem that even the use of accurate and unbiased racial generalizations is repugnant and harmful. I wish to bracket off these arguments, not because I think that they fail, but because they work too well as conversation stoppers. I believe that there is interesting and hard conceptual work to be done about the moral permissibility of using statistical generalizations in police work even when virulent prejudice is not at issue. To do so, some abstraction from the harsh realities of American racism is necessary.

Let us provisionally restrict our attention, then, to those racial generalizations that meet a minimal test of instrumental rationality, in that use of the generalization is a means toward some given objective such as "the efficient apprehension of violators." Generalizations that fail such a test are simply foolish, whether or not they are morally wrong. What is this minimal test of instrumental rationality? For a start, the statistical inference must be accurate. One must have reliable information, and one must ask of that information the right question. The right question is: What is the probability that a person is a violator given that the person fits the generalization? and not: What is the probability that a person fits the generalization given that the person is a violator? Suppose half of all smugglers passing through customs are Ozians. By itself, this does not tell customs officials the proportion of Ozians who are smugglers. To answer the right question, one also would need reliable information on the proportion of travelers who are Ozian and the proportion of travelers who are smugglers. If one out of every thousand travelers is an Ozian, and one out of every ten thousand travelers is a smuggler, the correct Bayesian inference is that one out of every twenty Ozians is a smuggler.[2]

With a false positive rate of 95 percent, can searching all Ozians going through customs be instrumentally rational? One cannot say without knowing more about what counts as a benefit and a cost, given the objective. Again, let us draw this with exceeding narrowness: apprehending violators is a benefit, expending scarce police resources is a cost, and nothing else counts – not fairness, not civil liberties, not the burdens that fall on the innocent false positives, and so forth. Under these assumptions, a generalization is instrumentally rational if the expected net benefit of finding the true positives – the Ozians who are smugglers – exceeds the cost of searching all the false positives – the innocent Ozians. Whether one in twenty is a big number or a little number, and so whether a statistical generalization about Ozians is useful to customs officials, depends on what counts as a cost and benefit. This is the lesson Bayesian decision theory holds for us.[3]

Among the set of search strategies with positive net benefits, some are better than others. There may be a more refined strategy that is more efficient than "Open the luggage of all Ozians"- for example, "Open the luggage of Ozian girls" or "Open the luggage of Ozians with Kansan accents." And presumably there are search criteria for non-Ozians as well, such as "Open the luggage of anyone who crosses the border frequently." If a more refined search strategy is available, not to use it is inefficient. The use of the social monitoring skills that David Wasserman discusses is a good example of a more refined search strategy. If it is instrumentally rational to acquire and employ the skills needed to distinguish the harmless street play of black teens from threatening behavior, to rely on a rougher racial generalization alone is foolish, quite apart from whether it is unfair. If there are even better strategies that make no use of group characteristics at all, so that "Open the luggage of anyone who crosses the border frequently" is more efficient than "Open the luggage of anyone who crosses the border frequently plus all Ozians," then to use the group-based generalization is foolish. But the opposite may be true, and efficiency may demand the inclusion of group-based generalizations.

I am not at all endorsing the view that law enforcement agencies should take "the efficient apprehension of violators" as their sole objective, and I certainly am not endorsing the view that the burdens that befall nonviolators and the moral demands of fairness, liberty, and respect should not shape and constrain police objectives. I have elaborated an extremely narrow view of policing to make this point: since the objective of apprehending violators is at least a part of good policing, and since at least some race-based generalizations are instrumentally rational with respect to this objective, one cannot reject the use of all racial generalizations on the grounds that they are foolish. To reject at least some race-based generalizations, one must show that their use is morally wrong.

THREE CASES

There are at least three conceptually distinct types of cases in which the police might use group-based selection criteria, and a number of mixes of these pure types. In the first, call it *group-based patrol*, the police, searching for as yet undiscovered violations or seeking to deter violations, use statistical inferences from group characteristics to select those who will be subject to heightened scrutiny. Examples: stopping Ozians at customs in order to catch smugglers or shadowing young black males in department stores in order to deter shoplifting.

In the second, call it *group-based enforcement*, the police use some group-based characteristic as a criterion for selecting which known violators will be subject to law enforcement out of a larger set of known violators. Example: out of the set of all speeders, state troopers select young black males for ticketing. Though a group-based characteristic is used, there is no statistical generalization here, and the use of group characteristics has no probative value: it is already known who is and is not speeding.

Distinguish this from a mixed case, enforce-to-patrol, where group-based enforcement is used as a way to implement group-based patrol. Here, minor violations are enforced against known minor violators who fit a group-based generalization in order to search for unknown major violations. Presumably, police engage in this search strategy when they are barred by law or policy from pure group-based patrol. Example: out of the set of all speeders, young black males are ticketed disproportionately so that the police officer can take a look inside the car for signs of drug trafficking.

Call the third pure case *group-based identification:* an unidentified suspect in a known violation is described as having group-based characteristics, so the police stop those who fit the group-based description. In pure group-based identification, no statistical inference is made about the likelihood of criminality among those who fit the description. Assuming that the description of the suspect is accurate, it is simply given that the violation was committed by *someone* fitting the description.[4] The inference here is about the likelihood that someone who fits a description is the particular person described. The difference is seen most clearly when the descriptive characteristics are not otherwise believed to be correlated with criminal behavior. If a thief is described as a tall redheaded woman, the instrumental rationality of stopping tall redheaded women to find this violator turns on the likelihood that any one tall redheaded woman in the vicinity is a particular tall redheaded woman, which – if nothing else is known about the suspect – is simply the reciprocal of the number of tall redheaded women in the vicinity. To find this particular suspect, one does not need to make any inferences about the proportion of tall redheaded women who are thieves.

When the descriptive characteristic is one that is also believed to be correlated with criminality, however, group-based identification may be mixed with group-based patrol. If a suspect is described as a young black male, the likelihood that someone who fits the description is either this particular suspect or some other violator may be high enough to pass the test of instrumental rationality, even if neither likelihood by itself does. Finally, if police are barred from engaging in pure group-based patrol, they may adopt the strategy of identify-to-patrol, and stop those who match the description of a particular suspect in order to implement an instrumentally rational group-based patrol.

Though the mixed cases are no doubt quite common in police practice, I will focus on the three distinct pure types. To the extent that the mixed cases are simply intermediate cases, I leave it to the reader to make the necessary interpolations. (For example, as the incidence of minor violations rises in the general population, enforce-to-patrol approaches the pure search case; as the incidence of major violations rises in the general population, enforce-to-patrol approaches the pure enforcement case.) To the extent that the mixed cases involve police lawbreaking and deception, the wrongs involved are not particular to the topic of statistical generalization.

TWO QUESTIONS

About these three types of case, let us ask two questions. First, does an innocent false positive who is stopped by police because of the use of a group-based generalization have a reasonable complaint? Second, does a true positive, a violator, have a reasonable complaint? If, for a type of generalization, both the violators and nonviolators have good grounds for objecting to their treatment, then that practice clearly lacks moral justification. If nonviolators appear to have a reasonable objection, but violators do not, then perhaps there is some way to answer the objection of the nonviolators. A successful answer to the nonviolators will need to show why it is reasonable for them to accept the treatment to which they are subjected, and that requires showing, among other things, that being subjected to police scrutiny does not involve fundamental disrespect or indignity.

Consider first the pure group-based enforcement case: police who ticket only black speeders. Though those who are stopped are indeed violators, they have a clear objection: fairness requires that those who are alike in the relevant respects be treated alike and that those who are different in the relevant respects be treated differently. Being black is not a difference relevant to whether one should be ticketed, so the unequal treatment is unfair. Indeed, it is difficult to imagine an objective served by such treatment that is not straightforwardly malicious.

In contrast, a violator does not appear to have good grounds for complaint in the case of pure group-based identification. How is his treatment unfair? Like the speeder in the pure enforcement case, he has indeed committed the violation. Unlike the speeder, he is not being singled out from a larger set of violators for unequal treatment, for there is no larger set of violators in this instance – the police are responding to a report of a particular crime. Nor are the police making an inference about the propensity of members of a group to commit crimes, which may fail to treat an individual with respect, for in the pure description case the only inference is about identity, not criminality. Although it is true that those violators whose identifying characteristics are less prevalent in the population are easier to catch than those with more common characteristics, why is this not simply the violator's bad luck, and our good luck, rather than a case of unfairness? Is the tall redheaded thief who is caught treated unfairly because she is easier to catch than medium-height brown-haired thieves? I think not. Fairness does not require equal chances of success for thieves. If the tall redhead has no comparative advantage as a thief, let her choose another line of work.

Now suppose the identifying characteristic is race. Example: a theft by a tall Asian male teenager is reported in a neighborhood where Asians are few. It is instrumentally rational for police to stop all tall Asian male teenagers in the neighborhood because the chances that any one Asian teen is a particular Asian teen are high, and, as it happens, someone stopped by police because he fits the description is in fact that particular Asian teen described – the thief. Why is this too not simply his bad luck? Even if we suppose injustice led to the low numbers of Asians in the neighborhood, has an injustice been done to would-be thieves? Unequal opportunity to live in desirable neighborhoods is an injustice; unequal opportunity to steal from those neighborhoods is bad luck.

Can the violator claim that because, ex ante, the police did not know that he was the violator, his treatment should be judged as if he were not the violator? This is a puzzle we do not have to solve for our purposes because, either way, police must answer the objections of those who are stopped for identification who are found not to be the violator ex post – the innocent tall Asian teens. If their objections can be answered, so, a fortiori, can the objections of the violator.

The objection of the innocent nonviolator subjected to race-based instrumentally rational identification is something like this: Though I have broken no law, my liberty has been infringed, my privacy violated, my dignity affronted, and my sense of security shaken. I have been selected for this treatment because of the color of my skin. If everything about me were the same, but for my skin color, I would not have been stopped and questioned. But skin color is not a relevant reason for different treatment by the police, so I am being treated unfairly.

If a reply is to succeed, it would have to show the innocent violator that, from some suitably constructed ex ante point of view, it would be reasonable for him to agree to subject himself to a general policy of properly regulated group-based identification. In part, this involves showing that all are at risk of victimization by thieves, so all should be willing to accept some burden of unwelcome police encounters in order to stop theft. Reasonable agreement is not simply a matter of an individual's calculation of self-interest, for it is reasonable for me to accept some sacrifices to prevent much greater harms to others. Nor does this involve simple utility-maximization: it is not unreasonable for me to reject great sacrifices to provide small benefits to many, many others. The reasonable burden will be lower, indeed far lower, than what an instrumentally rational search would impose. But the reasonable burden is not zero. This, roughly, is the lesson of contractualism.[5]

How much of a burden it is reasonable to accept depends on just what the nature of the burden is, and this in turn depends on whether respect for the individual is compromised in the encounter. Whether an unwelcome search by police can ever be respectful turns on the message of the encounter, and by this I do not simply mean what literally is said by police.[6] The reason an individual is picked out for police scrutiny itself carries a message of respect or disrespect. The wrong words can make an otherwise respectful encounter disrespectful, but the right words can go only so far in mitigating the message of an encounter that is predicated on disrespect.

Consider this message: "I'm sorry for interrupting your evening, sir, but a crime has been committed by someone who fits your general description. For the protection of all law-abiding members of society, the police have a policy of stopping and questioning those who resemble suspected criminals. Even though I have stopped you, I continue to presume that you are a law-abiding member of society, and so I hope that you can see that you and your neighbors are protected by such a policy. I trust that, upon reflection, you will find it reasonable to assume this burden. We do not suspect *you* of committing a crime, we suspect someone who resembles you. Help us confirm our presumption that you are yourself, and not the suspect you resemble, and we will trouble you no more. It is true that you were picked out for questioning in part because your skin color matches the described skin color of the suspect. But I am not supposing that individuals with your skin color are more likely to commit crimes, which I can well imagine would be insulting. I simply am supposing that individuals with your skin color are more likely to be the particular person for whom we are searching." Under very favorable conditions, I believe that something like this could be the message of a police identification. I am not seriously proposing that Miss Manners be hired to deliver such "Miranda apologies"; but I do think that the content of this reply involves no necessary incoherence, deception, or self-deception, and so police searches can treat persons in ways that are consistent with it. (Whether such treatment is self-defeating is another matter: perhaps the police cannot sincerely believe this about those they identify, or cannot honestly convey it, and still be effective at catching violators.)

An innocent black male teen who is stopped can accept much of this reply and still have a remaining complaint. He can grant that, looking only at the probabilities of success in a particular search, the search strategy under which the police have stopped him is both rational and reasonable, and he can grant that there is nothing inherently disrespectful about making a probabilistic inference about his identity from his appearance, which includes racial features. But even if "black male teen" when the suspect is a black male teen is equally predictive as "tall redheaded woman" when the suspect is a tall redheaded woman, an innocent black male teen might object that he fits the description of suspects with far greater frequency than do tall redheaded women. Black male teens therefore will be overburdened by unwelcome police scrutiny, and that is unfair. Even if, implausibly, police can maintain with honesty the presumption of innocence and convey a respectful message in each instance, the cumulative message of repeated searches is degrading.

Once we allow the ugly reality of American racism to intrude, this becomes a powerful objection, but I wish to keep this reality bracketed for just a while longer so that we can isolate arguments about the use of statistical generalization. Suppose a small band of tall redheaded women committed so many thefts that police efforts at identifying them placed as great a burden on the population of innocent tall redheaded women as that borne by innocent black male teens. This would be a great misfortune for the innocent redheads, but I am not sure that it would be an injustice. The rest of us owe them something – certainly gratitude, perhaps recompense – for the troubles they undergo for our benefit. But I do not think that they can reasonably ask the police not to take their appearance into account. Still, there is an important lesson here for the treatment of innocent black males who bear a disproportionate burden of police scrutiny, even when that treatment is not tainted by biased inference and racial prejudice. They are owed gratitude, at least, for their troubles, and it is especially ungrateful to punish them with lingering suspicion.

This leads us squarely to the case of group-based patrol, in which police use statistical inferences about the behavior of members of groups to search for as yet undiscovered violations or to deter violations. The examples given earlier were stopping Ozians at customs or shadowing young black males in department stores. Since we are trying to isolate the moral significance of using group-based generalizations, assume that the probabilities, benefits, and burdens are such that, if not for the fact that group characteristics are part of the search criteria, the targets of the search would have no reasonable objection. For example, suppose that if 5 percent of those who cross the border frequently are smugglers, frequent travelers would have no reasonable objection to the patrol strategy "Open the luggage of all who cross the border frequently."

Here, there are stronger objections to overcome. One could reply to those scrutinized for purposes of identification that, in the pure case of group-based identification, no inference about the propensity of the group to engage in criminal activity was made. But precisely such an inference drives group-based patrol.

What is the complaint of the Ozian subjected at customs to the search strategy "Open the luggage of all Ozians," when that Ozian is indeed a smuggler? Unlike the black speeders in the pure enforcement case, the Ozian smugglers in the pure patrol case cannot claim that there is no difference between them and the non-Ozians who are not searched. The difference is that the proportion of Ozians who are smugglers is much higher than the proportion of non-Ozians who are smugglers. The Ozian needs to show either that this is not a morally relevant difference, or that the relevance of the difference is counteracted by moral reasons to ignore that difference. Some of these objections appeal to the way that the group is viewed or treated, and others appeal to the way the individual is viewed or treated.

The Ozian smuggler might try to object on the grounds that the search strategy "Open the luggage of all Ozians" amounts to an inherently disre-spectful ethnic slur, for it supposes that all Ozians are criminals. But this misunderstands the connection between inference and action. The statisti-cal inference is simply that the proportion of Ozians who are smugglers is one in twenty, while the proportion of non-Ozians who are smugglers is about one in twenty thousand. By assumption, this inference is both well supported by evidence and true, and so cannot by itself be a slur. "Search all Ozians" is a decision rule that follows from the costs and benefits of search, not an inference about all Ozians. One may have good grounds to criticize the evaluation of costs and benefits, but not the inference itself.

The Ozian smuggler refines her objection: the inference supposes, not that every Ozian is a criminal, but that every Ozian has a higher propensity to commit a crime, and that is an ethnic slur. This is a serious objection from an innocent Ozian, and I will consider it shortly. The Ozian smug-gler, however, is estopped from making this objection. She, after all, is part of the reason that the proportion of Ozians who are smugglers is higher than the proportion of Ozians who are not – her behavior helps to make true the inference that she finds insulting to her and her group.

Consider, then, the objections of the innocent Ozian. She complains that the message of group-based patrol is inherently disrespectful, both to her as an individual and to Ozians as a group. The search is disrespectful to her as an individual because it treats her as someone who has a propensity to commit a crime for no reason other than that she is a member of a group. We cannot say, as we said in the case of group-based description, that the inference is simply about whether she is a particular person. Here, the inference is about whether she is a smuggler. The search is disrespectful to Ozians as a group because it supposes that there is some trait that Ozians have that predisposes them to criminality. We cannot say, as we said in the case of group-based description, that she has been picked out simply because her appearance matches the appearance of a suspect. Here, the inference is more than skin deep: criminality is a purposeful activity, so there is some inference being made about the motivations, character, or culture of Ozians.

As before, the response to these objections will try to find an honestly respectful message in the actions of law enforcement officers. To answer the charge that group-based patrol treats the innocent individual as someone who has a propensity towards criminality, we need to show how using statistical inference to pick a search strategy is still compatible with a presumption of innocence. When Bayesian decision analysis expresses a degree of certainty about some event occurring, it makes no commitment to any one of the many underlying causal mechanisms compatible with the statistical inference made. A Bayesian may say, loosely, something like, "I believe that the probability that an Ozian is a smuggler is 5 percent," but this does not commit the Bayesian to the belief that this particular Ozian smuggles 5 percent of the time, or that she has an inclination to smuggle that has a 5 percent chance of winning out over other inclinations, or that she would turn out to be a smuggler in 5 percent of the replays if her life could be replayed, or any other formulation. To be sure, sometimes one of these is believed to be the correct causal mechanism, but it need not be. All the Bayesian needs to say is, first, that he is justified in believing that 5 percent of the Ozians passing through customs are smugglers, and second, that he has no other justified beliefs that indicate which 5 percent. Therefore, a Bayesian police officer can sincerely maintain that he is not imputing a propensity toward criminality to any particular Ozian who is searched, and so is not treating any particular Ozian with disrespect. The innocent Ozian is burdened by a loss of privacy and by the fear that law enforcement scrutiny generates, but is not burdened by disrespect or insult. The message to the innocent Ozian is, roughly, "It's nothing personal."

The innocent Ozian finds this a small comfort. The search strategy is built on the inference that Ozians as a group are far more likely to be smugglers than non-Ozians. The message of the search can be respectful to her as an individual only by supposing some distance between this "decent" Ozian and Ozians in general. If she is to accept the message, and understand herself to have been treated with respect, she needs to adopt that distance herself. But if she is connected to or identifies with other Ozians in significant ways, this is a cruel choice.

The reply to this objection is really the same as to the previous one: because Bayesianism is agnostic about underlying causal mechanisms, it does not require enforcement officials to believe anything about "Ozians in general," and it certainly does not require them to believe that Ozians have a trait that predisposes them to criminality. Ozian smugglers and Ozian innocents may be two distinct groups, one that always smuggles and the other that never does; and the causes of smuggling among the Ozian smugglers may have nothing to do with any important component of Ozian culture or identity. Perhaps only the assimilated, alienated Ozians smuggle. Obviously, if the Bayesian law enforcement officer could make these distinctions in the field, he would be foolish not to use a more refined search strategy. But just because one does not have a more refined search strategy in hand one is not committed to the view that the underlying causal mechanisms admit no further refinement. All Ozians are insulted, and the innocent Ozian needs to alienate herself to avoid insult only if the customs official is committed to an insulting underlying mechanism. As long as the bracketing assumptions are kept in place, even group-based patrol can be given a respectful message.

To keep the bracketing assumptions in place here, however, strains credulity. In practice, it is much harder for police to believe sincerely and convey honestly the respectful message of the action when they are making inferences about criminality, rather than about identity. As the proportion of true positives picked out by a strategy rises, the cognitive discipline required to maintain respectful treatment in group-based patrol is enormous. Compare an identification case in which the search picks out two individuals who meet the description of the violator and a patrol case in which the expected rate of violation among those who fit the search criteria is one in two. A modicum of training and good will can lead police officers to recognize that at least one of the suspects in the description case is innocent, and that that should affect how both are treated. But a heroic amount of training and good will is required to get police to recognize that, in a population where half are violators, half are not, and that that should affect how all are treated.

The cognitive demand is especially great in deterrent patrol, since there is no way to confirm that one has deterred a would-be violator, and not harassed a nonviolator. Pure race-based identification, if practiced with good will, has this self-regulating feature: a false positive rate that is higher than expected prompts a reevaluation of the reasonableness and rationality of the search strategy. But in deterrent patrol, one does not know the actual false positive rate, so one never gets evidence that could weaken one's confidence in the search strategy. A department store's security guard who spends his day closely trailing young blacks is confirmed in his belief that his strategy is a good way to deter shoplifting each time an innocent kid is shamed into leaving the store.

This is a caution against all deterrent police scrutiny, on whatever criteria. But the dangers of self-confirming suspicion of racial and ethnic groups are much greater than the dangers of self-confirming suspicion of behaviors such as associating with the wrong people, hanging out in the wrong places, or wearing the wrong clothing. Though it may be unfair to be suspected because of one's clothing, one can avoid the unfairness by not wearing gang colors. One cannot avoid the unfairness of being suspected because of one's race by changing one's skin color.

CONCLUSION

Howard McGary takes contractualist justification and Bayesian inference to be in conflict. I do not. The view developed here is contractualist in that its moral evaluations appeal to the kinds of treatment it is reasonable for persons to accept. It is Bayesian in that it recognizes that the usefulness of a statistical inference for guiding action depends on what one cares about. There is no necessary conflict between contractualism and Bayesianism because, if we care to treat persons with respect, not all statistical inferences will guide action, and when inferences do guide action, they need not be disrespectful.

I have asked the reader to abstract away what may, in the end, be the most important moral reasons against the use of race-based generalizations. I have done this so that the analytic structure of the problem of statistical inference in law enforcement could stand out more clearly. Not surprisingly, the case for race-based generalization is strongest when the virulence of racism is weakest. First, I have supposed that race-based inferences are accurate, and while no doubt many are, many are not, and the injustice wrought by the use of ignorant and malevolent generalizations may be great. Second, I have supposed that the police and the rest of us can intend and convey a respectful message, when in practice the use of race-based generalizations may do the opposite: they may add insult to burden, and replace deserved gratitude with undeserved suspicion. Third, the pure cases that have been distinguished here are quite mixed in practice, and police officers face a great temptation to employ legally and morally permissible types of race-based generalization as a cover for legally and morally impermissible types. Last, and most important, I have not begun to assess the moral significance of America's long history of racism against blacks, and how that history indelibly colors the possible messages and meanings of any race-based police action.

Thus far, every introduction of the nonideal conditions of the real world has made the case for racial generalizations tougher than would be the case under more favorable conditions. There is one exception to that pattern that I cannot analyze here, but it bears mentioning: one mean circumstance of the nonideal world is that African-Americans disproportionately are the victims of crime. Though the burdens of race-based search strategies fall most heavily on law-abiding blacks, the benefits may as well. Still, no one should be forced to trade respect for safety. It is an injustice, and not simply bad luck, that many black Americans face such a bleak choice.

NOTES

1. See David Wasserman, "Racial Generalizations and Police Discretion," and Howard McGary, "Police Discretion and Discrimination," in this volume, pp. 115-44.

2. If $p(O \mid S)$ is the probability of being an Ozian conditional on being a smuggler, $p(S)$ is the probability of being a smuggler, $p(O)$ is the probability of being an Ozian, and $p(S \mid O)$ is the probability of being a smuggler conditional on being an Ozian, then

$$p(O \mid S) * p(S) / p(O) = p(S \mid O).$$

In the numerical example,

$$.5 * .0001 / .001 = .05.$$

3. For the development of Bayesian decision theory, see Howard Raiffa, *Decision Analysis* (Reading, MA: Addison-Wesley, 1968).

4. In actuality, descriptions are often inaccurate or accurate only by accident. Witnesses may, willfully or unwittingly, substitute their own inferences about the proportion of violators who have a characteristic, instead of describing the characteristics of a particular suspect.

5. For the development of contractualism, see Thomas M. Scanlon, "Contractualism and Utilitarianism," in *Utilitarianism and Beyond*, ed. Amartya Sen and Bernard Williams (Cambridge: Cambridge University Press, 1982), pp. 103-28.

6. For the moral importance of an action's message, see Thomas E. Hill, Jr., "The Message of Affirmative Action," in *Autonomy and Self Respect* (Cambridge: Cambridge University Press, 1991), pp. 189-211.

Chapter 6

Police, Prosecutors, and Discretion in Investigation

Candace McCoy

In 1936, Jerome Frank published what is today regarded as a manifesto of legal realism,[1] and in 1949 he wrote a book using that philosophy to critique court structure and the tenets of trial procedure. Appropriately titled *Courts on Trial*,[2] the work was an overview of the common law and court processes from the point of view of a trial judge. In it, he summarized the realist argument that black-letter law wrenched from its social context is meaningless, and he suggested consequent court reforms. One of those reforms – a requirement that both parties provide broad discovery of all evidence and witnesses prior to trial – is now universally applied in the United States. Frank's opposition to closed discovery stemmed from his fundamental critique of one of the most cherished standards of Anglo-American law: adversarial trial procedure.

Frank despised "the fight theory" of law – the assumption "that the best way for a court to discover the facts in a suit is to have each side strive as hard as it can, in a keenly partisan spirit, to bring to the court's attention the evidence favorable to that side."[3] In theory, "zealously partisan lawyers [will] bring into court evidence which, in a dispassionate inquiry, might be overlooked . . . [or] illuminate for the court niceties of the legal rules which the judge might otherwise not perceive." But in practice, this approach degenerates into a situation

> whereby the lawyer considers it his duty to create a false impression . . . [t]he purpose of these tactics – often effective – is to prevent the trial judge or jury

from correctly evaluating the trustworthiness of witnesses and to shut out
evidence the trial court ought to receive in order to approximate the truth.[4]

Contemporary examples of this problem abound and, despite procedural
reforms, the game playing and one-upmanship of trial tactics continue
under new rules. Nevertheless, there are excellent reasons for supporting
the adversary system, and in any event the approach is so ingrained in the
structure of American trial procedure that to call for its abolition would be
quixotic. But we must fully understand its consequences, some of which
are intended and beneficial, while others may foster an unethical work
environment.

Prosecutorial discretion – and, under different assumptions and constraints, police discretion – in finding, evaluating, and preparing evidence
for trial is exercised in the context of a profoundly adversarial framework.
The "sporting theory of law" encourages police and prosecutors to regard
evidence as poker chips with which to play a winning game, not as facts to
be thoroughly and dispassionately investigated. Furthermore, police carry
out investigations not only under these adversarial assumptions, but within
a professional subculture in which the bad motives and criminal guilt of
suspects are simply assumed. In investigation, the essence of discretion is
the decision whether to suspend belief in the suspect's guilt, press forward
to find exculpatory evidence, and act objectively on the facts as found – or
so to interpret the facts as to detain a suspect and obtain a conviction even
if those facts permit varied interpretations. The latter approach is more
likely, because the choice itself is socially constructed within the working
environment of the police officer.

THE ADVERSARY SYSTEM IN TRIAL COMPARED TO INVESTIGATION

The policy reasons for adversarial trials do not transfer well to the investigatory stage. Applying the logic of the former to the practices of the latter
invites injustice. A brief consideration of the historical and still functional
roots of the adversary system helps to assess its advantages as well as its
dysfunction. Following many historians of the common law, Frank believed that adversarial trials originated in England as a civilized alternative to feud and blood vendetta.[5] To this he added another, more practical
explanation – that self-interest prompts each litigant to seek out all relevant evidence, thus providing excellent fact-finding for the neutral court.[6]

> The fighting theory of justice is a sort of legal laissez-faire. It assumes that,
> in a law suit, each litigious man in the court-room competitive strife, will,
> through his lawyer, intelligently and energetically try to use the evidential

resources to bring out the evidence favorable to him and unfavorable to his court-room competitor.[7]

This mention of laissez-faire and its mandate that government stay out of the individual's personal sphere highlights another fundamental value of American criminal procedure: distrust of government. We simply do not trust the state to stand up for the rights of the criminally accused, and adversary procedure reflects that.

One of the most revered modern scholars of the sociological and political functions of courts has taken this notion further. Martin Shapiro notes that "it must always be remembered that the basic aim of a trial is to resolve a conflict or impose social controls, not to find the facts."[8] People with any experience at all of the criminal justice system will readily agree that it is designed to maximize social control no matter what the facts of a particular case. But insofar as the adversarial trial provides an opportunity to resist the state, its social control function is mitigated. The reason for this, says Shapiro, is to serve particular policy goals at the expense of single-minded pursuit of the truth as the sole end of the criminal trial:

> Presumptions, burdens of proof, and per se rules are the standard form for manipulating factual issues to achieve policy goals. The easiest example is the presumption of innocence and the burden to prove beyond a reasonable doubt in modern Anglo-American criminal law. . . . The presumption of innocence is not some fixed truth but a declaration of social policy. For various reasons we prefer to make it easier for the criminal accused than for the state.[9]

Those reasons for adversarial as opposed to inquisitorial or bureaucratic procedures have stood the test of time; few seriously propose that we abandon them. Thus, recent proposals to reform criminal procedure concentrate not on changing the standards that embody the adversary relationship between the accused and the government, but on tinkering with particular rules about admitting evidence into consideration at trial, all within the existing structure of adversarial procedure. (One of these proposals from the "truth school" – reforming the exclusionary rule – is discussed below.)

It is an entirely different question, however, whether the social policies that explain a trial court's willingness to encourage adversarial procedure, even to the point of obscuring truth, should apply at pretrial stages, particularly at the level of police and prosecutorial discretionary decision making. Though the broadest goal of a trial may be to resolve a conflict or impose social controls rather than to find the truth, surely the basic aim of investigation has no purpose other than fact-finding. What other purpose could there be? The social control function that Shapiro highlights should not apply to people whose personal guilt has not been established – unless we baldly admit that police and prosecutors would regard everybody as guilty, apparently on the assumption that anyone connected to a situation in which a crime took place belongs to a suppressible criminal underclass.

If fact-finding is the essence of investigation but is not the only goal of the trial, adversarial assumptions appropriate at trial might not apply to pretrial investigations. Whatever the contemporary pathologies of the adversary system at the trial stage, the rationales that support the system – trial as a proxy for blood feuds, the behavioral assumption that truth emerges from a searing fight, and the fundamental distrust of governmental power that prompts us to require the state to meet a heavy burden of proof – explain as a matter of social policy why we retain the adversary structure at trial. But the rationales do not apply *pre*trial. An investigation is not a substitute for a feud. Nor is it likely that evidence will come to light by fighting with its sources – in fact, the opposite is true.

Although the first two of these rationales for adversary trial procedure are completely inappropriate to investigation, at first glance it would seem that the third (that is, distrust of state power) does indeed apply equally to pretrial and trial stages. The adversarial posture between the defendant and the state must prevail at trial, and it is surely equally important at pretrial – especially considering that only a small percentage of criminal cases ever get to the trial stage. But maintaining an adversarial relationship in investigation is necessary only in the broadest sense of adversarialness. At early stages of prosecution, it simply means that the defendant has the right to conduct his own investigation and does not have an obligation to aid the government in its work. (The Fifth Amendment prohibition of uncounseled confessions is an apt example.)

Prosecutors are in the unusual position of serving both as investigators and trial lawyers. Thus their adversarial assumptions about trial can begin to infect their investigatory work. It is often said, however, that as officers of the court prosecutors have an ethical obligation to pursue the truth first and trial advantage second – a standard that applies both at investigation and trial. The non-truth-seeking policies of trial are left to the judge.

If in the course of investigation a prosecutor finds that an innocent person has been charged with a crime, it is a legal as well as ethical imperative that the charges be dropped.[10] Nobody would disagree with this standard, though in practice it can be interpreted very broadly.[11]

Many prosecutors admit to one common situation in which they will keep charges open against a defendant who, investigation has since proven, is innocent: the defendant who has knowledge that could convict the guilty party. The result is that few people who are completely uninvolved in criminal activity are charged with serious crimes.[12] Most people charged are indeed guilty, but the germane issue almost invariably is: guilty of *what?* Often, in the course of investigation, police and prosecutors find that the criminal defendant's level of culpability is not as high as originally charged. The prosecutor under these circumstances should certainly refrain from taking the case to trial on the original charges – a fact which may explain the bulk of guilty pleas to lesser charges.

The problem is that the role of the advocate overshadows that of the magistrate with many if not most prosecutors. This is a common, almost inevitable, psychological accommodation to the requirements of trial advocacy. Where evidence is ambiguous or at least may develop in unexpected ways at trial, the temptation is to overinterpret and assume the highest degree of wrongdoing.[13] Here, there is no reason to continue to investigate so as to find exculpatory evidence. That is left to the defense in plea negotiation or trial.

But injecting adversarial assumptions into the conditions under which police and prosecutors investigate cases sends the message that social control, not objective fact-finding, is the purpose of pretrial as well as trial procedures. The pressure to win in court may prompt prosecutors to regard evidence not as objective proof but as facts to be interpreted and marshaled so as to produce a winning outcome for the state despite the ambiguities of the situation. Furthermore, insofar as a prosecutor's main goal is to win, he or she might encourage other law enforcement officers in the jurisdiction – the police – to investigate and present evidence primarily so as to win at trial or in a guilty plea, where "winning" is not necessarily defined as arriving at an outcome based on the truth but as arriving at an outcome detrimental to the defense.

The point where the prosecutor's role in fact-finding and adjudication meets the police role in investigation is problematic. Like prosecutors, police are officers of the court, bound to its ethics and values but further removed from the courtroom and backroom give-and-take. But police have to do more primary investigation than prosecutors do, and it is the cases that require development over time – as opposed to on-the-spot arrests in street crimes – in which police adversarialness is often even more pronounced than is adversarialness among prosecutors. Scholars of the police have consistently commented that police are habitually suspicious, a psychological trait that is surely the inevitable result of the task required of them:

> The process by which this [police] "personality" is developed may be summarized: the policeman's role contains two principal variables, danger and authority, which should be interpreted in the light of a "constant" pressure to appear efficient. The element of danger seems to make the policeman especially attentive to signs indicating a potential for violence or lawbreaking. As a result, the policeman is generally a "suspicious" person.[14]

Here, Skolnick is speaking of the patrol officer, whose job on the street combines the pressures of potential danger and the need to appear authoritative in order to gain suspects' compliance. For different reasons, the detective is equally suspicious. Detectives start their careers as patrol officers and develop the suspicious habit of mind there. In addition, the nature of their task fosters an attitude of suspicion and a tendency to attribute guilt to any suspect under investigation. After all, detectives are required to probe the details of people's activities, to suspect their motives, and to arrest and prove the guilty to be, in fact, exactly that: guilty. It is hardly surprising that a detective's working assumption is that everyone is guilty unless proven innocent; after all, someone is guilty, or there wouldn't be a crime for the detective to investigate. There are few institutional incentives to prove innocence and many incentives to prove guilt.

The strongest incentive to prove innocence is the fact that if the suspect is not guilty, then someone else is. If investigation stops because a police investigator mistakenly assumes an innocent person to be guilty, the real guilty person is still on the street, possibly victimizing others. But in the pressure to clear cases and obtain convictions – the usual departmental measures of detectives' successes – it is easier to believe that the suspect is the bad guy and to take the credit than to keep digging and perhaps come up empty-handed. This tendency is especially evident in cases that require extended investigations involving several suspects – drug dealing, burglary rings, automobile "chop shops," and so forth. In a criminal conspiracy, everyone involved is usually guilty, but the degrees of culpability and the available proof might vary significantly. It is easy to believe that those conspirators on whom facts can be pinned are the ones with the greatest criminal involvement and moral culpability.

To these institutional and organizational conditions that breed the habit of suspiciousness and willingness to assume guilt, add the almost indefinable but palpable police attitude: what many observers call "us versus them." The Christopher Commission, the 1991 investigative body established to probe the circumstances of the Rodney King beating and subsequent riots, found that the Los Angeles Police Department's emphasis on aggressive crime control served to train officers in a "siege mentality," in which citizens came to be regarded as "the enemy" in "a war on crime."[15] The adversarial mind-set applies not only to investigation but also to the very bedrock assumptions of police role and function that most police officers learn on the job.

When a case proceeds from the police station to the office of the prosecutor, the pressures of trial adversarialness are added to these occupational conditions of policing. Taken together, these factors assure that police will exercise their discretion from the starting point of an organizational culture that is paradoxically antithetical to the dispassionate investigation of fact.

MAKING CHOICES UNDER ADVERSARIAL ASSUMPTIONS

The essence of police discretion is the legal capacity to make a choice between equally permissible alternatives.[16] Broadly, the same could be said of prosecutorial discretion. The main point here is that the context in which a decision is made will itself mold how the decision maker understands the available choices. Put another way, discretion is exercised within an occupational and ideological mind-set. Applied to police and prosecutorial powers, the discretion we are discussing here shapes both the activity of gathering facts and the analysis of their meaning.

Making a choice, of course, presumes a rational model of decision making, in which the actor considers the alternatives under an assumption of complete information and objective cost/benefit reasoning. As any deterrence theorist knows, the problem with this model is that many decision makers are not rational. For example, many criminals engage in expressive rather than instrumental behavior, ignoring the costs of possible punishments and eschewing the possible benefits of a stable lifestyle in favor of emotive "acting out." Typical methods of deterring police misconduct also presume a rational officer. The assumption is that illegal searches and seizures will be prevented if a rational officer decides that the costs in having evidence excluded at trial outweigh the benefits of an illegal search. We also assume that officers will not engage in brutality if they know they can be sued for civil damages and lose substantial amounts of money in court judgments. More realistic believers in the rational-decision-maker model say that the exclusionary rule and/or civil lawsuits fail to deter police misconduct because the officer rationally decides to avoid the costs of misconduct by committing perjury – attempting thus to assure that evidence is not excluded or that a jury will not believe a civil plaintiff's version of events.

Furthermore, many who embrace the rational model of deterring police misbehavior are nevertheless likely to point out the same weakness highlighted by critics of the rational-criminal model: even assuming that the subject engages in a rational cost/benefit calculation, the costs are remote and speculative. For deterrence to work, it is said, it is more important for punishment to be swift and certain than severe.

These criticisms of the rational-decision model simply amend it so as to describe more realistically the operation of presumed costs and benefits. They do not reject the assumption of rationality itself. But a more fundamental criticism of the model of rational choice and its corollary, deterrence, is that rationality is moot when the conditions under which decisions are made present false choices to decison makers.

When an investigator looks at facts, under conditions of adversarialness, the moment of exercising discretionary choice is the moment that he or she decides whether the evidence adds up to guilt. But this misapprehends the alternatives. Under conditions of objectivity, the moment of choice should be the moment the detective or prosecutor decides whether the "facts" are true. Whether the true facts signify guilt is a different matter, and it is a decision to be made much later in the process, at the trial stage.

The danger of conflating the adversarial approach at trial with the fact-finding requirements of pretrial procedures is that the law enforcement officer is encouraged to presume guilt, and to act on this presumption, because he wants to win. The adversary system itself molds a context for the discretionary decision so that it is made under conditions in which the decision maker does not fully apprehend the alternatives. The great benefit is to win; the great cost is to lose – that is how the rational officer understands the conditions of choice. Discretionary actions made under this cost/benefit assumption will invariably tend toward presumption of guilt in assessing the meaning of facts.

A recent article by Mark Cooney perfectly summarizes the point.[17] "The social process by which events are transformed into legally relevant information is neither random nor inscrutable," he says.[18] Establishing a distinction, similar to this essay's, between trial proceedings in which adversarialness is appropriate and investigatory proceedings in which it is not, Cooney notes that "while scholars have analyzed the second phase of fact-finding – evaluation of evidence – they have rarely explored the prior stage – the production of evidence . . . ,"[19] in which production is defined as "the effort legal officials put into generating evidence through investigation of facts."[20]

Cooney's main goal is to demonstrate that the volume and quality of evidence thus produced varies with the social status of the victims and witnesses and the degree of social relation between them and the police.[21] He seeks to identify social indicators that explain why some cases get investigated thoroughly and others do not. Consider, too, that organizational factors intrinsic to the police culture can also explain variation in outcomes of the most fundamental decisions by police and prosecutors. Cooney believes that his approach provides "a body of 'evidence scholarship'" that is concerned with "the manner in which legal officials construct legal proof."[22]

Ordinarily, we hope, there is no material difference in the decision to get a conviction because it is simply attainable – a desirable win – and the decision to seek a conviction because the evidence shows the defendant to be truly guilty. Convictions should be attainable only because the volume of evidence adds up to factual and legal guilt. But the match is not perfect, and under conditions of adversarialness police and prosecutors are not encouraged to make it so.

ILLUSTRATIONS

None of this is intended to allege that police regularly arrest and prosecute people they know to be innocent. But, given a moment or two, we could all think of examples of cases in which the police have objectively focused upon a possible suspect and then readily accepted interpretations of fact congruent with conviction, rejecting those pointing to acquittal. One scenario springs to mind: the situation in which a heinous crime is committed, police focus quickly upon an unpopular person, evidence is gathered, and a conviction obtained – on the basis of a mostly circumstantial case against the resourceless defendant. The person goes to prison but, after many years, a new scientific test of evidence – DNA testing – becomes available. The convict's blood is subjected to DNA tests and matched to DNA obtained at the crime scene, and a person who evidence supposedly indicated was "stone cold guilty" is proven in fact to have been innocent beyond a statistical certainty.[23]

Rapes often receive extensive adversarial attention because the evidence usually hinges on the testimony of the victim. If she can be impeached, the state's case withers. Once police and prosecutors make the decision that the prosecutrix is truthful, they have invested in the case and will do all they can to support her version of events. The adversarial pressures to help the victim to withstand cross-examination in court, and to obtain satisfaction that a bad guy is behind bars, encourage investigators to look no further than the suspect named in the initial police report.

Rape investigations are particularly stark examples of the pathological results of adversarial investigation, because a new kind of evidence (DNA) has recently been added to the investigatory arsenal, and use of it has highlighted how evidentiary judgments made without objective checks were often simply wrong. The great bulk of felony processing, however, relies on witness testimony and circumstantial evidence about the suspect's motives and connections to the crime scene rather than on scientific tests. For illustrative purposes, consider investigation of a "modal" crime: burglary.

The hypothetical facts are these. A homeowner calls the police after finding his condominium ransacked and looted. He provides the police with descriptions and serial numbers of the television, personal computer, and tape deck/CD player equipment stolen, and he files for reimbursement with his insurance company. The police have no leads. Weeks later, the police arrest a burglar caught red-handed in a nearby apartment building. In return for consideration in sentencing, he provides the name and address of his fence – that is, the person to whom he sells his stolen goods and who then resells them in the underground market.

Based on this tip, the criminal records of the fence so named, and their past knowledge of this person's activities in the neighborhood, the police obtain a search warrant. They go to the apartment of the alleged fence, enter it, but find nobody home and no stolen goods. But they do see in plain view on the kitchen counter a note saying "Angela – I'll see you at your place tonight after 8:00." They know that Angela is the suspect's girlfriend and they know where she lives. They go to her apartment and find her home. They show her the warrant, although it is for a different apartment and different suspect, and she allows them to come inside. They then see in plain view several personal computers stacked in a corner. After checking serial numbers on the computers and ascertaining that one of them matches the number given by the victim, they arrest Angela for receiving stolen property. When the suspected fence arrives at Angela's apartment at 8:00 p.m., they arrest him, too.

What is the truth about factual guilt in this case? Perhaps Angela and her boyfriend are both involved in fencing stolen property. Perhaps the boyfriend is the major dealer and Angela, however naive, is involved only because he uses her apartment to store stolen goods. Perhaps Angela is the major dealer and the boyfriend is not involved, assuming the informant was lying about the true identity of the fence. On the facts presented, any of these scenarios is possible. More investigation is needed.

By contrast, it is a different question to ask: What is the legal guilt in this case? The prosecutor must connect the stolen computer to an intentional "receiving" on the part of one of the suspects. Since the computer was physically present in Angela's apartment, they can connect it to her, and they can connect it to the boyfriend by introducing evidence that he regularly used her apartment. (His note to her, obtained as part of a legal search, will accomplish that.) But there will be a "swearing contest" between the police and Angela as to how they gained entrance to her apartment. She will say they tricked her into believing there was a warrant for her arrest and a search of her apartment. They will say she gave them consent to enter the apartment after they explained they were investigating a crime, and that once inside they saw the computer equipment in plain view. The truth here might indeed depend on the viewpoint of the observer, an ambiguity that could be settled at trial.

It is certain, however, that using the evidence obtained in Angela's apartment will be possible only after a fight. But that evidence is essential to sustain a conviction against Angela and also against her boyfriend because, without more, the informant's tip is insufficient proof that the boyfriend was receiving stolen goods.

It is at this point that discretionary decisions about the meaning of evidence occur. The police detectives' and the prosecutor's interpretation of the facts will be conditioned by their ultimate goal – convicting the bad guy – and by how they will obtain a conviction in court. On the facts presented, they have the choice of pursuing Angela, her boyfriend, or both. A decision determined by adversarial assumptions would be to seek to convict only the boyfriend. The facts of his criminal record, the informant's tip, and gender stereotypes holding that the ringleader of a criminal conspiracy must be the male would lead police to concentrate only on him. They would also pursue Angela, especially since the goods were physically present in her apartment, but there are legal problems in her case. Legally, they must connect each defendant to the stolen goods. The prosecutor, acting under current Fourth Amendment case law in that state, notes that the boyfriend has no standing to challenge the legality of the search; only the owner of the apartment does. Legally, the prosecutor could seek to introduce evidence of the stolen computer against the boyfriend but not against Angela, if she wins a motion to suppress the evidence and it is specific to her case. But it will probably not be specific to her case. If she wins the motion to suppress (which she probably will not, since police usually win swearing contests), then the police cannot use the computer as evidence against either her or her boyfriend, since it is fruit of a poisoned search.

The prosecutor, in order to be assured of a win, could refrain from prosecuting Angela at all. If Angela is not prosecuted, there will be nobody with standing to challenge the legality of the search in a motion to suppress. With no suppression motion, the stolen computer will be admitted as evidence, as will the fact that it is common knowledge that Angela is the girlfriend of the suspect and, as the note in his own handwriting said, he had access to her apartment. If the prosecutor is really lucky, he can convince Angela to testify against the boyfriend in return for his promise not to pursue the charges against her (which he wouldn't have done, anyway). The result? Probably the boyfriend's guilty plea to receiving stolen property, with jail time part of the resulting sentence because of his criminal record.

But what if the truth is that Angela is really the fence? If we remove from the equation the stereotypical assumption that women are not primary culprits in street crimes, and do not rely on the further assumption that the boyfriend must be guilty because he has a criminal record whereas Angela does not, the only objective evidence that the boyfriend is the fence is the informant's tip. A nonadversarial investigator – one who does not simply accept the win of convicting the boyfriend – would backtrack and probe the informant. The detective would also try to find out what happened to the other equipment stolen in the condominium burglary. But the informant is under pressure to produce a win, too, because this will reduce his own sentence. And in fact he may have reason to frame the boyfriend. Without more investigation, we cannot know whether Angela is truly the criminal.

Note the combination of factual and legal assumptions as they developed in this hypothetical case. Factually, suspicion fixed on the boyfriend and there was little reason to upset the assumption that he was a bad guy. Legally, a conviction was easier to obtain against him than against his girlfriend, and that is because of the operation of the exclusionary rule. Given a system in which the work of investigators and prosecutors is regarded as good only if it ends in conviction, it is hardly surprising that police and prosecutors would decide to pursue the convictable suspect, untroubled by the factual possibility that some other person was really the criminal.

This is an example of police discretion in practice because police, like judges, must find the meaning of facts. How hard they are obliged to dig for that meaning determines how well the discretion is exercised. The point of discretionary decision making for a police detective is the time at which the investigator must make a choice – whether to continue looking for more evidence and explanations or mentally to close the case because the person under suspicion is most probably guilty. There is a rough parallel in jurisprudence: Dworkin's Herculean judge and his decision making in hard cases. A case is hard "when no settled rule dictates a decision either way."[24] Dworkin used the phenomenon of the hard case as a jumping-off point for his critique of judicial activism and his resolution of its dilemmas by reference to arguments of principle versus policy. But it is also instructive as a behavioral description of judges' discretionary decisions.

Dworkin's judge would devote only to the hard cases detailed arguments about judicial policy making through case interpretation. From the start, to know whether "no settled rule dictates a decision either way," the judge would have to search diligently in precedent and statute. The great majority of cases would be settled by reference to established law, and the judge would have no discretion to do otherwise. Only after a thorough, panoptic review of applicable law would a judge be confident that no established standard applied to the case at hand.[25] It is only then that the judge has discretion to decide the case on extralegal grounds. And even then, Dworkin says, the judge is morally justified in deciding only with reference to principles, not policies. Without delving into the distinctions between the two, and Dworkin's careful unpacking of what a principle itself would be, suffice it to say that the judge relies ultimately on "institutional rights" to decide the hard case. The judge determines what those rights are by reference to political morality – surely a discretionary decision.

The parallel to discretion in investigation is that the Herculean detective must search for facts, facts, facts – just as the judge searched for law, law, law – and not be satisfied that the case is appropriate for discretionary decision making until all avenues are exhausted. At that point, the decision is made with creative reference to institutional morality, which – to a detective as well as a judge – is that the case is submitted to the established decision maker for a judgment about the truth. In the detective's situation, the case goes to a court. Dworkin's judge must take it a step further, to appellate decision making, in which the judge has discretion in interpreting the constitutional background upon which it must be based.

We can all create our own hypotheticals or even appeal to exact examples from actual police and court files. The point is that a fundamental
postulate upon which the entire criminal justice system operates – that is,
the adversary system – molds the operation of investigation so that legal
officials' discretionary decisions about the meaning of facts are conditioned as much upon convictability as upon objective fact.

CONNECTIONS TO THE TRUTH SCHOOL OF EVIDENCE

Having progressed this far in the argument, the reader is probably musing
about how commonsense understandings built up into epistemological
and sociological frameworks are nevertheless still just common sense. Of
course police want to catch bad guys; of course prosecutors want to win in
court; and of course the system is adversarial and not necessarily truth
seeking. We do not have to talk about "the social construction of meaning"
to know that police detectives are suspicious and put together facts so that
they will add up to conviction in court, or that prosecutors tailor evidence
to fit the legal theory that will convict.

But sometimes common sense is so decisively a description simply of
things as they are, and not of things as they ought to be, that we forget
there is any other possibility. The adversarial mind-set, for instance, is so
deeply ingrained in the occupational framework of the criminal justice
system that we regard it as a natural empirical reality, not as a configura-
tion of social conditions that grew over time. A reconceptualization of
adversarialness would question whether the policies behind its presence at
the trial stage of the criminal process are equally compelling at the investigatory stage. To the degree that adversarialness encourages police to
assume guilt and truncate fact-finding, and prosecutors to interpret facts
only in light of prospective trial outcome, it is an inappropriate factor in
discretionary decision making.

An alternative, of course, is somehow to emphasize the objectivity of
fact-finding rather than the adversarial use of evidence in the trial courtroom. This observation may seem worthy of Pollyanna, but such optimistic rethinking of fundamental assumptions in criminal justice is well under
way among legal scholars. A small but vocal group of law professors and
scholars comprise what some call the "truth school" of evidence and trial
procedure.[26] Its primary tenet is to sweep away restrictive rules that
prevent relevant evidence from being introduced at trial, even though the
policies behind not introducing the evidence may be compelling.[27] The
truth school deems the truth of the fact to be paramount over any consider-

ations of policy. "If you have a truth-seeking model of criminal law, and if you have incriminating evidence, the point is to let the jury hear all that evidence and let them decide what really happened."[28]

A statutory exemplar of the group's thinking is the "Right to Truth-in-Evidence" provision of California's Proposition 8, which was passed by popular initiative ballot in 1982 and has withstood several constitutional challenges in that state. It reads: "Relevant evidence shall not be excluded in any criminal proceeding, including pretrial and post conviction motions and hearings, or in any trial. . . ."[29] Without aligning myself with the political impulses that sparked some of these proposals,[30] it is fair to note that they spring from frustration with mindless adversarial trial sparring. Getting rid of the exclusionary rule may be ill-advised on other grounds, but as an example of how the trial system clouds truth in pursuit of other objectives, it is a proposal to be entertained.

The current of thought the truth school represents has recently seeped into the popular press because of the bizarre twists in the O. J. Simpson trial. The well-known scholar of comparative criminal procedure, John Langbein, opined in *Newsweek:*

> There are two defining (and interconnected) characteristics of American criminal justice that set it apart from the smooth-functioning systems of other advanced Western countries. . . . One is the failure to have a thorough, impartial, judge-supervised investigation of the facts in the pretrial process. The other is the license that we give lawyers to engage in truth-defeating distortion and trickery at trial.[31]

Although, for the reasons set out above, adversarial assumptions are generally appropriate at trial, for jury trials at least scholars of the law are challenging the commonsense assumptions of adversarial procedure. Surely this would be even more possible at the investigatory stages, where Langbein's "impartial, judge-supervised investigation of the facts" would do much to dispel the expectation of guilt and conviction so prevalent in contemporary police discretionary decision making.

POLICY IMPLICATIONS

If adversarial assumptions are inevitable in investigations, how can they at least be minimized? The answer is so broad as to seem, again, somehow Pollyanna-ish. We must change the conceptual conditions under which discretionary decisions about the adequacy of evidence are made.

It is crucial for this change to be accomplished internally, within the organization: pressure from outside only hardens the adversarial mind-set. This may partly explain some of the consequences of the exclusionary rule (namely, widespread police perjury and continued widespread police misconduct). But internal constraints on detectives' and prosecutors' discretionary choices, and more fundamentally on the context which frames those choices, are minimal. Essentially, those constraints are abstract professional ethical standards that are assumed to hold great power (and, in fact, probably do hold great power) but that are enforced only informally in the workplace itself and formally in court only in cases of egregious misconduct.

The best approach to the improvement of discretionary decisions is to be sure that the organization itself provides the conditions under which particular choices are encouraged. It seems that prosecutors are more likely to mitigate their adversarialness than police, because they do not have to cope with the daily suspiciousness and elements of danger, nor necessarily with the "us versus them" mentality, as do police. Although they are practiced in the adversarialness of trial, their organizational role and subculture are more likely to be amenable to nonadversarial investigation than police.

What prosecutors think of the police with whom they work matters to police detectives, both organizationally and professionally. If prosecutors communicate to police that convictions are the only goal or that fact-finding may be sloppy, the organizational conditions for limitless police discretion in investigation are exacerbated. Police will simply assume every arrestee is guilty if prosecutors regard an acquittal as a negative reflection on the detective's abilities and judgments. Prosecutors must communicate to detectives that clearing the name of a suspect at the investigation phase is as exemplary of good police work as convicting at trial would be. And this is a task for the prosecutor, since many police managers frequently overlook what happens to arrestees' cases once they leave the police bailiwick – were it otherwise, the exclusionary rule would have much more bite.

So how do you get prosecutors to change their consideration of evidence? You change the conditions under which they work. You do not reward them for quick guilty pleas based on minimal evidence. You sanction anybody who prosecutes an innocent person. Most importantly, you encourage the prosecutors to communicate this nonadversarial approach to the police when they work together. A habit of mind that is investigative, thorough, and objective will eventually supplant a contentious approach concerned only with social control if prosecutors themselves demand objective facts – and lots of them – from the police with whom they work.

NOTES

1. Jerome Frank, *Law and the Modern Mind* (New York: Tudor, 1936).
2. Jerome Frank, *Courts on Trial* (Princeton: Princeton University Press, 1949).
3. Ibid., p. 80.
4. Ibid., pp. 82 and 85.
5. Ibid., p. 91, quoting Wigmore.
6. Parenthetically, note that this fact-finding is also inexpensive for the government. If the defendant is responsible for finding exculpatory evidence and bringing it to the attention of the court, the government does not have to pay to conduct that part of the investigation. In an era when the majority of lower-level street criminals are represented by public defenders whose investigators are paid with public money, however, this rationale disappears. But the concern may reemerge if the defense investigators are not paid enough to do a thorough job. In that case, the adversary system rationale of inexpensive fact-finding is actually unjust, because it leaves the poor without adequate defense while wealthier defendants can afford good investigations. See, generally, Mark Cooney, "Evidence as Partisanship," *Law and Society Review* 28, no. 4 (1994) pp. 833-58, discussed in other contexts below.
7. Frank, *Courts on Trial*, p. 92.
8. Martin Shapiro, *Courts: A Comparative and Political Analysis* (Chicago: University of Chicago Press, 1981), p. 44.
9. Ibid., p. 47.
10. The ethical tenet that it is wrong for a prosecutor to charge a person with a crime unless convinced of guilt is well understood and surely well followed in practice. See, generally, John Kaplan, "The Prosecutorial Discretion – A Comment," *Northwestern Law Review* 60 (1965), pp. 174-93, explaining the situations in which the issue arises in federal prosecution. Here, consider the more common situation in which a prosecutor is initially convinced that the suspect committed the crime, but in which further investigation casts doubt on the degree of culpability.
11. Prosecutors regularly offer to drop charges in such cases, but only in exchange for testimony or information that can be used to convict. If the accused does not cooperate, charges usually will not be dismissed.
12. The dynamics under discussion here apply to serious street crimes and white collar crimes, in which extended detective work and prosecutorial digging are often necessary. Adversarialness manifests itself in less serious crimes too, of course, and surely many more completely innocent and uninvolved people are arrested for minor charges than for serious crimes. This is a serious matter in any consideration of police discretion, but the point here is to illuminate common discretionary dilemmas of police and prosecutors – and this usually involves serious crimes that will not quickly end in guilty pleas, as less serious ones usually do.
13. Of course, it is often said also that prosecutors know from the start whether they are likely to get a conviction only for a lesser included offense, so they overcharge as a bargaining tool. From the prosecutor's point of view, "upping the ante" this way is an attempt to get a conviction on the highest possible charge. It is also a way for police officers to demonstrate to their bosses that they are locking up very bad actors. This is important because the only thing that most police agencies

evaluate is the original charge lodged against arrestees, rather than what was actually tried or the eventual charge of conviction.

14. Jerome H. Skolnick, *Justice without Trial: Law Enforcement in Democratic Society*, 1st ed. (New York: Wiley, 1966), p. 44. The observation is constantly confirmed in other times and places by a variety of police sociologists. See, for example, Robert M. Fogelson, *Big-City Police* (Cambridge: Harvard University Press, 1977) and Peter K. Manning, *Police Work: The Social Organization of Policing* (Cambridge: MIT Press, 1977).

15. Christopher Commission Report, p. 95, quoted in Jerome Skolnick and James Fyfe, *Above the Law: Police and the Excessive Use of Force* (New York: Free Press, 1993), p. 106.

16. Kenneth Culp Davis, *Police Discretion* (St. Paul: West, 1975).

17. Cooney, "Evidence as Partisanship."

18. Ibid., p. 834.

19. Ibid., p. 835.

20. Ibid., p. 838.

21. The argument is quite clearly based on the work of Donald Black. The part of Black's work Cooney cites as most germane is *The Social Structure of Right and Wrong* (San Diego: Academic Press, 1993). Cooney summarizes his proposition: "The quantity of supporting evidence increases with the principal parties' social status and the number of intimate ties they have, and the quality of supporting evidence increases with the principal parties' social status and the number of distant ties they have" (Cooney, "Evidence as Partisanship," p. 852).

22. Cooney, "Evidence as Partisanship," p. 835.

23. Examples drawn from the popular press include the case of Gary Dotson, convicted of rape in 1979. The prosecutrix eventually recanted her false testimony upon which Dotson had been convicted; but only after DNA profile evidence proved he could not have been the rapist did a court order his release. The story was reported nationwide in October of 1989; for a legal angle on it, see D. C. Moss, "Free at Last," *ABA Journal* 75 (October 1989). Many similar cases began to be reported in the 1990s, when DNA testing slowly became widely available. I. Fisher, "Ruling Allows DNA as Evidence," *New York Times*, 30 March 1994, p. B1; "DNA Proves Innocence of Man Imprisoned Ten Years for Rape," *Jet* (October 1994), p. 40. Almost all involved charges of rape, probably because rape investigation procedures must include gathering semen samples from the victim's body if they are available. It is thus possible to extract DNA from a bodily fluid found at the crime scene and compare it to a sample taken from the convicted person. Crimes in which there is no blood, semen, or human tissue from which DNA can be extracted are of course pursued with more traditional evidentiary measures of guilt, and therefore there is no objective "truth test" by means of which we can check the discretionary decisions of police and prosecutors about the meaning of evidence gathered.

24. Ronald Dworkin, "Hard Cases," *Harvard Law Review* 88, no. 6 (April 1975), p. 1060.

25. Ibid., pp. 1083-88, describing how "Hercules" works through and finds constitutional principles, statutes, and precedents not to be applicable before he determines that the case could appropriately be decided by reference to some other authority.

26. From the popular press, see Jeffrey Toobin, "Ito and the Truth School," *The*

New Yorker, 27 March 1995, pp. 42-48.

27. For example, a defendant's prior criminal record is usually not permitted to be introduced into court in front of the jury, on the assumption that it unduly prejudices the case at bar. The most contentious rule, perhaps, is the exclusionary rule which prohibits evidence from illegal searches or seizures to be brought into the trial courtroom, on the assumption that police misconduct will be deterred if police do not benefit from their misdeeds and that court integrity will thereby be preserved.

28. Akhil Reed Amar, professor at Yale Law School, quoted in Toobin, "Ito and the Truth School," p. 46.

29. California Constitution, art. 1, sec. 28(d). For comments, see Kenneth J. Melilli, "Exclusion of Evidence in Federal Prosecutions on the Basis of State Law," *Georgia Law Review* 22 (1988) and Frederic Ron Krausz, "Comment: The Relevance of Innocence: Proposition 8 and the Diminished Capacity Defense," *California Law Review* 71 (1983).

30. The drafters of Proposition 8, far from being disinterested truth seekers, were most probably right-wing moral entrepreneurs who used the crime issue as a way to sweep away liberal state supreme court law and even justices that they opposed. An account of the long saga is found in Candace McCoy, *Politics and Plea Bargaining: Victims' Rights in California* (Philadelphia: University of Pennsylvania Press, 1994).

31. John Langbein, "Money Talks, Clients Walk," *Newsweek*, 17 April 1995, p. 32.

Response

Robert Jackall

Procrustes, the legendary Attic highwayman, had an iron bed on which he either stretched his victims or lopped off their limbs until, one way or the other, they fit his contraption. Procrustes' ancient device has become a metaphor for hard-and-fast conceptual frameworks into which one forces empirical realities.

Consider the nub of Professor McCoy's argument, briefly outlined here. The adversarial nature of our justice system, regrettable but unavoidable at trial since the principal purpose of trials is to resolve conflicts or impose social control, contaminates pretrial investigation. Adversarialness fosters win-at-any-cost habits of mind in prosecutors, who are virtually indistinguishable from police. Constables, moreover, are habitually suspicious, and this base view of suspects affects prosecutors as well since they work closely with police. All of this causes prosecutors and, of course, police to overinterpret often marginal evidence and to issue higher than warranted counts in an effort to coerce suspects into admitting some guilt in return for a reduced charge. The search for truth is the first casualty of such a process. It goes without saying that the lack of objective fact-finding most drastically affects vulnerable, marginal members of our society, those without the financial or cultural resources to resist state power. The matter becomes still more complicated by entrenched "us versus them" attitudes among police, who see all citizens as potential criminals, especially citizens who don't fit police stereotypes of respectability. Happily, Professor McCoy argues, there is a way out of this bind. If our society were to adopt a truth-in-evidence approach to pretrial investigation (without, of course, countenancing the right-wing impulses that led to its being instituted in California), things would be much better. In the meantime, prosecutors must control widespread police perjury and other forms of misconduct by communicating to detectives a truth-seeking ethos, instead of making convictions the measure of good investigative work.

What evidence does Professor McCoy offer for her argument? Surely such a sweeping thesis, one that casually impugns the integrity of two occupational groups, must rest on years of careful observation of actual investigative work by police detectives, coupled with scrutiny of the operations of prosecutorial offices. But, alas, one finds nothing of the sort in her paper. Instead, the paper offers only warmed-over, secondhand sociologies of uniformed police, none of which treat detective work in any detail; yet the paper claims to understand such work, arguing that detectives' habits of mind are simply an extension of attitudes learned during their years in uniform. There is no material whatsoever on prosecutors, the analysis of whose work proceeds entirely by analogy to police work. Professor McCoy does invent a hypothetical case to illustrate her argument and then treats her invention as if it were factual and, indeed, paradigmatic. Readers can judge for themselves the plausibility of her fiction. They can also judge the merits of a paper about evidence that cites no evidence.

I can make only a few general comments here. First, any analysis of the occupational ethics of detectives, on the one hand, and prosecutors, on the other, particularly regarding the issue of evidence, must take account of (1) the extraordinarily bureaucratic framework of both detective and prosecutorial work, and (2) the radically different attitudes of police and prosecutors toward the bureaucratic procedures that frame their work. Put briefly, detectives are both in and sometimes of the streets, a frequently chaotic world, though one with its own peculiar rationality. Although detectives use all available bureaucratic nets in their investigations, their effectiveness as investigators depends principally on their abilities and willingness to circumvent and transcend bureaucratic procedures. Indeed, such transgressiveness is a prerequisite to understanding and, especially, to controlling the streets. Prosecutors, however, are officers of the court[1] and therefore become the guardians and enforcers of legal procedures that are often quite rarified. One constant contest, then, is between detectives' knowledge of criminality, often obtained by bypassing procedures, and prosecutors' (and the courts') demands for legal proof, that is, convincing demonstrations of waywardness that adhere strictly to established and legitimate procedures. At times – when, say, a crime has been committed behind closed doors, as it were, or when witnesses to a public crime have been effectively silenced – legal proof is simply not available. In such cases, detectives can sometimes trick suspects into admissions (for example, the Central Park jogger case) or solicit lies contradicted by some tangible evidence, thus undermining criminals' credibility before juries.

But trickery makes prosecutors uncomfortable because it often hurts the state at trial.

Even when there is mountainous evidence of guilt, defense attorneys can successfully put the police on trial, charging unfair applications or violations of fixed procedures, or arguing that detectives' occupational deviousness makes them, rather than their clients, unworthy of belief. The strategy here is to divert jurors' attention from the particulars of a case by fashioning a moral drama in which the police, as representatives of the state, oppress citizens. Of course, when some police do cross the line and engage in outright lawbreaking – when, for instance, New York State police fabricate fingerprint evidence, or anticrime cops in New York City's Thirtieth Precinct or in Philadelphia's Thirty-ninth District shake down drug dealers – the gleeful, though ostensibly solemn, media reports provide yet more materials for defense attorneys, or moralizing pundits, or academics, to tar all police.[2] Moreover, many defense attorneys specialize in race-mongering. They inflame the long-standing and, one must say, carefully nurtured hurts of blacks and other minorities on juries, direct their rage against police as the most visible symbol of societal authority, and appeal to the most primitive, particularistic standards of reckoning, instead of to the universalistic norms on which our law presumably rests.

Detectives recognize the dilemma. The aphorism in their world is: It's always the detective who's on trial. It is only detectives' transgressiveness and their willingness constantly to place their very lives in jeopardy that makes an overbureaucratized system work at all. Prosecutors, who depend on police investigators for their own work, understand this and often do not want to know what happens on the streets or in station houses, even as they try to work through the law's thickets to exact justice in particular cases. The very anomaly and moral ambiguity of detectives' work, and the secret knowledge of worlds apart that they possess (detectives have, after all, a front-row ticket to the raw, coarse, yet vital world of the streets), make many middle-class citizens, including many prosecutors, uncomfortable and ambivalent about what detectives do, even as they are fascinated by it, and even as they benefit from the public order that detectives' hard-won knowledge helps to create.

For their own part, detectives often see prosecutors as adversaries. They become impatient with prosecutors' necessary preoccupation with legal technicalities insofar as it is part of what they see as the whole criminal justice system's bend-over-backwards attentiveness to defendants' rights, often at the expense of victims' rights. Although closing and, it is to be hoped, clearing cases, outfoxing sometimes wily opponents, and besting the bully boys of the street in personal confrontations are all extremely important to detectives, the deepest meaning of detective work, hidden behind the gallows humor and gruff façade of their world, is the championing of victims, preferably innocent victims or victims who can, in some way, be construed to be innocent. Detectives often note the savage irony of our system of justice. Dead victims, to take the extreme case, have no civil rights precisely because they are dead, while those who made them dead, at least until they are convicted of murder and sometimes even long afterwards, enjoy remarkable constitutional protections. Indeed, justice itself often falls victim to the intricacies of the law – an outcome that erodes the significance of work that is all too often thankless in the first place.

Professor McCoy's essay illustrates what detectives as well as many prosecutors have come to expect from middle-class academics, preoccupied as the latter typically are with professional and disciplinary dialogues that are out of touch with the hard realities of the streets or prosecutorial offices.[3] Its unwarranted assumptions, bald assertions, and non sequiturs create an unyielding framework on which the author seems determined to fit a sprawling, fabulously complicated social world.

NOTES

1. Contrary to Professor McCoy's statement in this volume (p. 163), police are *not* officers of the court.

2. There can be no acceptable excuses for police corruption of any sort. Yet one should note that only certain kinds of corruption normally draw the ire of the media and assorted pundits. To an observer who spent two years with the NYPD, the most pervasive corruption in that organization is the laziness and incompetence of about a fifth of its personnel (not necessarily the lowest-ranking fifth), an observation backed by veteran police officers' own estimates. Goldbricking, sloughing off work on others, dumping cases, and avoiding responsibility wherever possible are behavioral patterns that one finds in any bureaucracy, especially one of more than 38,000 people, although large civil service bureaucracies, with their public-trough character and their nearly total separation of work and reward, may be singular in this regard. In the NYPD, of course, such normal, and officially sanctioned, corruption ebbs and flows depending on political pressures on the department from city hall.

3. I showed Professor McCoy's essay to two high-ranking assistant district attorneys in the Homicide Investigation Unit of the Manhattan District Attorney's Office. They found her characterizations of their world unrecognizable, though they acknowledge that courts increasingly resemble the academy in entertaining unfounded assertions. The prosecutors were particularly unimpressed by her notion that "anybody who prosecutes an innocent person" should be sanctioned (p. 174). They wondered exactly how Professor McCoy proposes to determine wrongful prosecution.

Chapter 8

Structuring Police Discretion

James J. Fyfe

Unlike most line workers in hierarchical organizations, police officers enjoy more professional discretion than do the leaders of their institutions. Police officers' decisions generally take place before limited audiences and, especially when they involve the choice to refrain from taking formal action – as in decisions not to ticket motorists, or not to arrest juvenile offenders or abusive spouses – rarely leave any objective documentation of why officers have done what they did. Police chiefs' decisions, by contrast, typically are documented in written orders or press releases, where they are subject to review, comment, and criticism by elected officials, the public, the media, special interest groups, police labor groups, and all those who are affected by public policy decisions.

Several justifications for this peculiar situation have been offered, most of which involve the need to allow officers to tailor enforcement decisions in ways that best achieve police goals without overtaxing police resources.[1] There is some validity to this reasoning, but it would hold more water if there were less confusion and more consensus about *which* goals police policy and police actions should serve.

The absence of consensus concerning police goals is an omission of major dimensions. With Peter Manning, I believe that this default generally can be attributed to the same police leaders who complain about the inverted distribution of police discretion in their organizations.[2] Certainly, the variety and urgency of field situations encountered by police officers dictate that, like emergency room personnel, they enjoy the grant of some discretion: but discretion in any profession can be justified only if it serves to accomplish some broadly agreed upon purpose. The end sought by emergency room personnel is clear and unequivocal: save the patient! In many field situations, however, the goal to be sought by the police is defined only hazily or not at all. This confusion is attributable largely to the failure of police leaders to take the initiative in carefully identifying the goals (and order of priority among them) that should be served during police actions, and their failure to specify with any precision the best means of accomplishing these goals.

In the absence of substantive attempts by police leaders to define their occupation's goals and priorities, the police mission has often been reduced to meaningless homilies – "To protect and to serve" applies to condom manufacturers as well as it does to police – especially by those with narrow partisan or ideological agendas. When expedient, for example, law-and-order politicians and the police leaders they choose have often given officers thinly veiled authorization to violate citizens' rights.[3] In at least one other case, the purpose of police work has been defined in narrow, but overly complex, terms that do not reflect commitment to either a consistent goal or the concerns of those most affected by the phenomenon involved: victims of domestic violence.

DOMESTIC VIOLENCE

Nothing illustrates better the confusion concerning police goals than the history of police practice related to domestic violence. Police often describe themselves as law enforcement officers, but neither they nor the public have always regarded domestic violence as an activity that called for enforcing laws. Instead, for generations, police treated both criminal domestic violence and simple noncriminal domestic arguments in the same way: by attempting to avoid doing anything that might cause or accelerate the disintegration of families.[4] Giving such primacy to the goal of family solidarity meant that arrest was generally to be avoided even when serious crimes had been committed. This was supported by the reasoning that nothing was more likely to precipitate family dissolution than the spectacle of Dad being taken from the house in handcuffs before his children and neighbors. This conclusion probably is accurate, but there were other costs to failing to arrest Dad when he had committed crimes against Mom. It gave him a license to continue his abusive ways, perpetuated family dysfunction, and made it more likely that his children would also become abusers.[5]

The conventional wisdom is that this approach to domestic violence has endured uninterrupted over several centuries,[6] but Lawrence Sherman musters convincing evidence that U.S. policies and attitudes toward wife beating have not been unvaryingly tolerant.[7] Instead, he indicates, the American Puritan colonists' strong moral condemnation of domestic violence found its way into seventeenth-century law. Later, the Enlightenment era's distinction between public and private conduct weakened this legalistic approach, but it subsequently came back to life with the creation of modern, enforcement-oriented police departments in the mid-nineteenth century. In the late nineteenth century, elite reformers' concern that immigrants conform to American standards of conduct led to enactment of much stringent anti-domestic violence legislation, along with provisions for legal assistance for victims. Like most of the causes of the Progressive reformers, wife beating faded as a policy issue during the 1920s, when the most recent period of official tolerance of wife beating began. Then in the 1970s the current swing back toward stringent enforcement of assault laws in domestic violence cases began.

In serving the goal, or ideal, of family solidarity that prevailed until the late seventies, police adopted a variety of crisis intervention strategies.[8] This approach was viewed with antipathy by many officers, who regarded the crisis intervention movement as a naive ivory-tower attempt to involve them in social work.[9]

By the 1980s, women's advocates and plaintiffs in class actions had compelled the police to reconsider domestic violence policy. In 1979, the New York City Police Department stipulated in *Bruno v. Codd* that it would treat domestic violence in the same manner that it treated other violence: by arresting.[10] A few years later, abused spouse Tracey Thurman won access to the federal courts to argue that the police department of Torrington, Connecticut, had violated her right to equal protection of law by repeatedly failing to arrest her abusive estranged spouse. His continued violence against her, Ms. Thurman argued, was tolerated by the police only because it occurred within a domestic relationship. She prevailed and won a $2.6 million verdict against the police.[11] Her case, in essence, was an affirmation of the primacy of the police obligation to provide equal protection over the ideal of family solidarity - of the law enforcement method over the social work approach.

As *Bruno* and *Thurman* were being argued, police and scholars began collaboration on a series of experiments related to police domestic violence policy.[12] Although the methods and results of these studies have varied somewhat, all tested some variant of the same question: Are arrests in misdemeanor domestic violence cases more likely than such less formal alternatives as mediation to achieve specific deterrence of future violence? In other words, should the police favor a law enforcement approach over a social work approach in dealing with misdemeanor family assaults? According to Sherman and Cohn,[13] the positive answer to this question provided by the Minneapolis Domestic Violence Experiment has caused major change in police policy and practice throughout the United States.[14]

Others have argued that the effects of the Minneapolis experiment have been overstated.[15] Three questions related to this line of research, however, are more basic and more relevant to this discussion of police goals and discretion:

1. Is the research responsive to the concerns of feminists and to the issues raised in courtrooms by plaintiffs like Bruno and Thurman?
2. Should econometric analyses of deterrence in reported misdemeanor domestic violence cases drive criminal justice policy?
3. If the answer to question 2 is no, then what should drive criminal justice policy related to domestic violence?

Question 1: Is the research responsive?

When Ms. Bruno and Ms. Thurman took their cases to court, their concern was not the minor, *misdemeanor* violence studied by researchers. Rather, they demanded compensation for what had happened because the police had declined to arrest spouses who had inflicted serious, *felonious* violence upon them. Thus, these cases have not hinged on the econometric question of whether arrest was the best way of producing a statistically significant decrease in future misdemeanor violence. Instead, plaintiffs have argued that the final acts of violence visited upon them would have been impossible if the police had jailed their assailants for earlier attacks or, in the case of Tracey Thurman, if they had taken him to court so that he could be incarcerated or exiled from town as the terms of his probation required. In short, these cases have involved questions of incapacitation and of access to the law in felony victimizations rather than deterrence of such misdemeanors as simple assault and harassment.

Thus, the answer to our first question is that, despite all the effort and funds devoted to this line of police domestic violence research, it has not addressed the issue as it generally has been defined by victims and their advocates. This is an important disjunction: researchers and the progressive police executives who have cooperated with their studies have focused on the fine points of police response to such relatively minor – but still deplorable – domestic violence as slaps, kicks, and threats. In doing so, they apparently have assumed that the big issue – what do police do about such really serious domestic violence as shootings, stabbings, and rapes? – has been resolved, and that officers arrest in such cases.

There is little reason to believe that this is so. By definition, the departments studied by experimental social science researchers are atypical and probably unrepresentative of U.S. police experience. Consequently, it is risky to generalize from them to agencies that have not been confident enough to expose their books and practices to research scrutiny. Further, as evidence presented later in this paper suggests, it may not even apply to the agencies that have been studied. Three cases illustrate this point.[16]

Hynson v. City of Chester.[17] On 15 October 1984, Alesia Hynson's estranged common-law husband, Jamil Gandy, culminated a long series of attacks and threats against her by shooting and killing her. Prior to her death, Ms. Hynson had notified police in both her hometown (Chester, Pennsylvania) and at least one other nearby jurisdiction of these attacks. Despite Hynson's repeated pleas for help, police took no action against Gandy. A few days before her death, Hynson successfully sought renewal of a court order of protection against Gandy. She had not obtained physical possession of this order by late the following night, when her teenage babysitter called the Chester police to report that a man she did not recognize (Gandy) was attempting to break into Hynson's apartment through a window. Confused, the sitter gave police what the officers who had been dispatched immediately recognized as a wrong address; these officers informed the dispatcher that the address could not be correct and conducted no further investigation.

In the meantime, Gandy realized that Hynson was not at home and proceeded to a neighborhood bar, where he found her and threatened her with a gun. While a bouncer restrained Gandy, Hynson left the bar, returned home, and found the distraught babysitter. Hynson then summoned Chester police and asked them to go to the bar to arrest Gandy for violating the order of protection, for attempting to break into her house, for threatening her, and for carrying a concealed weapon. The police refused. First, they claimed to have no record of either the current or the expired order;[18] second, Hynson declined to leave her home and infant daughter (who had been fathered by Gandy) in order to accompany them to the bar to identify Gandy. A day later – and several hours after he had been scheduled to surrender to prison authorities in order to begin a sentence for an unrelated matter – Gandy went to Hynson's place of work, where he used his gun to shoot and kill her.

In their litigation against Chester, Hynson's survivors introduced an analysis I had prepared on their behalf. This suggested that the police nonresponses to Hynson's requests for help were not isolated events and that the Chester police response to violence depended heavily on the relationship between offender and victim, as well as upon victim characteristics.

The data analyzed for the case consisted of all Chester Police Department reports of felonious acquaintance and domestic assaults by adults for approximately fifteen months immediately prior to Ms. Hynson's death (18 July 1983 – 14 October 1984). These cases were classified as domestic if reports indicated that they involved victims and assailants who shared the same household, and/or who were related by blood or marriage, and/or who shared a present or past intimate relationship (for example, parentage of a child). Nondomestic cases, in which victims or other witnesses had identified assailants, or had given police other information reasonably likely to lead to identification of suspects (for example, first names; nicknames; addresses or reasonably specific areas of residence or work; descriptions and vehicle license numbers) were classified as acquaintance crimes. The files were complete and indicated whether arrests were made, regardless of whether they occurred on-site or as the result of follow-up investigations.[19]

The most salient part of the resulting analysis is shown in Table 1. It demonstrates that, even when the Chester police had strong evidence concerning assailant identity, arrest was unlikely: only 21.5 percent of all assailants were arrested. More to the point of this discussion, the table also shows that arrests were less likely in domestic situations (15.9 percent) than in nondomestic acquaintance crimes (26.6 percent). The table also shows that the percentage arrested among domestic victimizers of men (20.8 percent) was higher than for those who victimized women (12.4 percent), and that arrest was more than twice as likely when women were victimized by nondomestic acquaintances (27.3 percent) as when they were victimized by those with whom they shared domestic relationships (12.4 percent). The likelihood of arrest was lowest in cases of domestic violence against black women like Ms. Hynson (10.4 percent).

Again, these were all felony assaults, none of which was trivial or unworthy of arrest. Included among domestics in which assailants were not arrested, for example, there were two cases in which handguns were used as weapons; two involved rifles; thirty-eight involved knives or other cutting instruments, including axes; twenty-seven featured clubs or similar weapons, usually baseball bats or hammers. One victim whose assailant was not arrested had been shot; several others were shot at or threat-

TABLE 1: **Victim Race and Gender and Case Disposition in Domestic and Acquaintance Felony Assaults.**

| Victim Characteristics* | Assault Type Percentage Resulting in Arrest | | TOTALS |
	Domestic	Acquaintance	
White female	12.5%	29.4%	19.5%
Total/arrests	24/3	17/5	41/8
Black female	10.4%	25.0%	15.7%
Total/arrests	77/8	44/11	121/19
White male	18.8%	20.5%	20.0%
Total/arrests	16/3	39/87	55/11
Black male	21.7%	29.3%	26.3%
Total/arrests	60/13	92/27	152/40
All females	12.4%	27.3%	18.1%
Total/arrests	105/13	66/18	171/31
All males	20.8%	26.3%	24.3%
Total/arrests	77/16	133/35	210/51
All whites	15.0%	23.2%	19.8%
Total/arrests	40/6	56/13	96/19
All blacks	15.3%	27.9%	21.6%
Total/arrests	137/21	136/38	273/59
TOTALS	15.9%	26.6%	21.5%
Total/arrests	182/29	199/52	381/82

Domestic/Acquaintance p = .02

*Subcells exclude cases with Hispanic victims.

ed with guns; forty were stabbed or cut; thirty-two were struck by objects, including television sets, flashlights, and belts; three were raped; one was struck by a car; several were thrown down stairs; one was held by her feet over a second-floor landing and dropped to the floor below where she landed on her head; and one lost the tip of a finger to a bite. Ten victims were kept at hospitals, and one hundred were released after treatment.

The case was settled before trial.

Smith v. City of Elyria.[20]   This suit, brought by the survivors of Karen Guerrant, alleged that she had become a domestic murder victim because of the failure of the Elyria, Ohio, police to respond to repeated calls from Guerrant, her sister (Dorice Smith), and Guerrant's nine-year-old daughter, Elaine, to intervene in fights between the female victim and her ex-husband, Alfred Guerrant. Karen called the police at 6:22 p.m., 6 March 1989, and asked the police to keep Alfred out of the home she alone owned. Officers Altheide and Charles were sent to the home by a radio dispatcher, who told them that Karen and Alfred had been divorced since 1986. When Altheide and Charles arrived at the Guerrant home, they found Alfred standing on the front steps of the house, holding a plastic trashbag that contained his belongings. Instead of asking or requiring Alfred to leave, the police walked him into the house. Once inside, the police told Karen that she could not order Alfred to leave: Officer Charles testified at deposition that the police had carried Alfred's bag into the house, and would not order Alfred out of the house because the weather was cold and because Karen had previously allowed him to stay temporarily in a guest room after he had been released from a prison sentence for assaulting her and forging her checks. It was true that Karen had allowed Alfred into the house, she and Dorice complained, but that had occurred before Alfred had refused to return to Karen the only key to the house. While the police were there, Karen threw Alfred's plastic bag out a window. The police told him to "throw [it] back in," and left after spending three minutes at the house.

At 6:47 p.m., Elaine called the police to report that "my daddy's beating up my mom . . . I want the police . . . Mommy told me to." Dorice took the phone to confirm this. When the dispatcher asked, "Is he beating her now?" Dorice said, "He has." When the question was repeated, she said, "No." The dispatcher then told her that the police would not respond because "this is a civil matter." Dorice asked to speak to a supervisor; Lieutenant Michael Adkins took the phone and hung up on Dorice when she protested his conclusion that this was a civil matter and that she needed an attorney. At 6:54 p.m., Dorice called the local sheriff's office and asked them to respond. The tape of this call discloses the background noise of fighting. The sheriff's office referred the call to the Elyria police and was told by the Elyria operator that "these people are pissing . . . making me mad!" The sheriff's telephone operator replied, "Well, they just called me and they're beating the shit [out] of each other, so whatever you guys, you want to do."

At 6:59 p.m., the Elyria operator called Altheide and Charles, and found that they were out to lunch. She declined to interrupt their lunch for what she regarded as a "basic disturbance." At 7:00 p.m., a neighbor called to tell the police that Dorice had run to her house to report a stabbing. At 7:02 p.m., Elaine called to report that her father had cut off part of her ear and had stabbed her mother, and that her two-year-old sister was frightened but uninjured. At 7:03 p.m., Elaine called back to report that her mother was dead. At 7:08 p.m., Officers Miller and Folley arrived at Guerrant's home, while Altheide and Charles apparently finished their lunch.

The captain in charge of an internal investigation of this incident reported to his chief that he had found "no problem with what had transpired. We handled this Domestic dispute as we would any other." The Elyria police chief then signed off on this, approving the officers' actions, and the case was settled before trial after the presiding judge rejected the City of Elyria's motion for summary judgment.

Sinthasomphone v. City of Milwaukee.[21] At about 2 a.m., 27 May 1991, two young black women called the Milwaukee police to report that a naked and incoherent boy was wandering about a street corner, bleeding from the rectum. When Officers Balcerzak and Gabrish responded, they found fourteen-year-old Konerak Sinthasomphone, a Laotian immigrant. Although he was by then covered with a blanket that had been furnished by a paramedic, he was otherwise as described, and was in the company of Jeffrey Dahmer, who was to be disclosed as a serial murderer two months later. Dahmer later testified that he had lured the youth to his home under the guise of doing some work. There, he had drugged the youth, stripped him, and taken Polaroid photos of him as he lay on Dahmer's couch. Dahmer then drilled two holes in the top of Sinthasomphone's head, and filled them with a mixture of acid and hot water. He then left the apartment to purchase some beer, expecting to find that Sinthasomphone would have expired by the time he returned home. Instead, he was shocked to see that Sinthasomphone had left the apartment and was on a street corner with a small crowd of black people.

Dahmer tried to pull Sinthasomphone back to his apartment, attempting to convince the bystanders that he and Sinthasomphone were homosexual lovers who had had a spat. Dahmer was not entirely convincing, however, because he reportedly called the boy by two separate names, both of which were incorrect. As this proceeded, a fire department ambulance and Balcerzak and Gabrish arrived. The officers spoke to Dahmer (warning the black bystanders to be quiet or be arrested), while a young woman probationary firefighter and paramedic covered Sinthasomphone with a blanket before beginning to examine him. She found him incoherent and unresponsive, but was almost immediately called off her work by her lieutenant, who advised her that it was a "gay thing," and that the police would handle it. With misgivings to which she later testified, she left the scene.

According to Balcerzak's deposition testimony, Dahmer told the police that Sinthasomphone "was his roommate of the past few weeks." Several citizen witnesses confirm that they heard Dahmer make this statement. With the assistance of a third young officer, Balcerzak and Gabrish then walked to Dahmer's apartment with Dahmer and Sinthasomphone, who remained incoherent and had to be half carried. In the apartment, Dahmer showed the police Sinthasomphone's clothes and the photos he had just taken, and reassured the police that Sinthasomphone was actually "John Hmung," his adult live-in lover. A strong odor pervaded the apartment. The police testified that they assumed that someone had left a "bowel movement" on the floor but, as Dahmer later attested, it came from a dead body in an adjoining room. The police left Sinthasomphone without ever speaking to him or getting identification.

Minutes later, the mother of one of the two young women called the police to inquire about why they had left a young boy, whom she had known from the neighborhood, with Dahmer. Fortuitously, she was connected to Balcerzak, who wrongly assured her several times that the police had identified Sinthasomphone, that he was an adult, that he had been involved in a domestic argument with his lover, and that "he's got belongings at the house where, ah, he came from. He's got very ah nice pictures of himself and his boyfriend and so forth, so . . . ." Dahmer testified that he murdered the boy after the police left. He then sexually assaulted and dismembered the body, ate parts of it, and preserved the skull.

A few days later, the same woman saw a photograph of Sinthasomphone in a Milwaukee newspaper, atop a story that identified him as missing and that solicited information about his whereabouts. She called the police and spoke at length to a detective, who (like all the other police personnel to whom she and her daughter spoke) never identified her and never conducted any investigation of the information she gave. Later, when Dahmer had been arrested, she called back and the police role in this became public. Both conversations are memorialized on Milwaukee police tapes.

The Milwaukee Board of Police Commissioners dismissed Balcerzak and Gabrish. They subsequently were reinstated with full pay by a judge who concluded that their actions and inactions were justifiable, because they had been misled by Dahmer. The City of Milwaukee declined to appeal this reversal, and the Milwaukee Police Association named the two officers "Cops of the Year" in 1994.

The case brought by Sinthasomphone's survivors was settled before trial shortly after the presiding judge rejected the City of Milwaukee's motion for summary judgment.

Lessons of these three cases.   What do these three cases say about police decision making and about the responsiveness of the domestic violence research to the concerns of domestic violence victims and their advocates? The circumstances and data of *Hynson* suggest that Alesia Hynson was merely the most grievously injured among a long list of victims of repeated felonious domestic violence on whose behalf the Chester police took no formal action. In *Smith*, the Elyria police compelled a divorced woman to keep an unwelcome ex-husband in her home and failed to respond to repeated reports of an assault – some from a nine-year-old – that culminated in a death and two nonfatal stabbings. This action, the police investigation concluded, was consistent with the department's prescribed manner of handling domestic violence.

Although many factors are involved in the police nonaction in the Sinthasomphone matter, three are most salient to this discussion. First, when the police left Sinthasomphone with Dahmer, they claimed to have done so because they were under the wrongful impression that he was drunk and that he lived, at least part-time, in a homosexual relationship with Dahmer in Dahmer's apartment.[22] By that time, several people had told, or tried to tell, the police that Sinthasomphone was a child, that he had been injured, and that he had resisted Dahmer. The police knew that Sinthasomphone was incoherent, never were able to communicate with him, and never obtained any documentation of the false name Dahmer used for him. They called short a paramedic's examination of Sinthasomphone, and then left him with Dahmer.

Second, the police did this in one of the few cities that has been the site of domestic violence research,[23] where police purportedly

were required to make arrests *when the suspect was present at the scene* in misdemeanor battery cases involving anyone currently or formerly in a

cohabiting relationship, including males who had fathered children with a
female.[24]

It appears that this policy was not followed in the Sinthasomphone case
or, at least, that the police investigation was so shoddy that the police did
not discover the *felony* assault by Dahmer on a person the police believed
to be his roommate. None of the charges lodged against the officers,
however, involved such a violation. Thus, Sherman's claim that there was
an extraordinarily high degree of compliance with the mandatory arrest
policy because the Milwaukee Police Department had "one of the strictest
organizational climates among big-city police agencies,"[25] seems to have
been contradicted by this incident.

Third, like the officers in *Hynson* and *Smith*, Balcerzak and Gabrish
ultimately suffered no penalty for their actions. Their chief and commissioners fired them but, in what can only be labeled a bizarre opinion, a
court reinstated them with full pay for the period in which they were out of
work. Subsequently, their municipal legislature declined to appeal their
reinstatement and the Sinthasomphone family resolved their suit without
recovering anything from the officers.

Further, though several provisions of Wisconsin law apparently were
applicable to the police actions in the Sinthasomphone incident, Balcerzak
and Gabrish were not subjected to very strict review at that level, either.
One of the most confusing and confused documents in this case file is
Wisconsin Attorney General James Doyle's written explanation of his
decision not to prosecute the officers for misconduct in public office. A
prosecution under the state law prohibition of failure to take action to
protect an abused child was impossible, Doyle asserted, because Balcerzak
had "firmly stated his belief that Sinthasomphone was an adult." Doyle
reached this decision even though Balcerzak had not documented
Sinthasomphone's age, and several witnesses had insistently and repeatedly told him that Sinthasomphone was a child. Later in his report, Doyle
explained that he could not prosecute the officers for failing to take action
in a case of domestic abuse because the law applies only to adults sharing
residences. Doyle reached this conclusion despite Balcerzak's claimed
firm belief that Dahmer and Sinthasomphone were adults sharing a domestic relationship. Doyle also declined to prosecute the officers for
failing to take action to protect a person incapacitated by alcohol. Even
though the record is replete with references to the claimed police belief
that Sinthasomphone was incoherently drunk, Doyle explained this decision on two grounds. First, the law does not apply to people who are

merely intoxicated short of incapacitation – though all the evidence indicates that Sinthasomphone was naked, unresponsive, and unable to walk without assistance. Second, Doyle pointed out that after his arrest Dahmer had told authorities that Sinthasomphone's state was the result of drugging rather than alcohol. But the attorney general then declined to prosecute the officers for failing to render first aid because

> [w]hile there is evidence to believe that the officers had reason to believe that Sinthasomphone was intoxicated, there was no evidence that at the time the officers saw Sinthasomphone he needed CPR, or that he had any wounds that needed attention to stop bleeding. Furthermore, there is no evidence that the officers at the time were aware, as Dahmer later admitted to the police, that Dahmer had drugged Sinthasomphone. In short, the evidence does not support a finding that the officers were confronted with a medical emergency.[26]

Doyle's report does not mention the two holes that had been drilled in Sinthasomphone's head or the acid that had been poured into them. It does note that

> The investigation developed conflicting evidence as to Sinthasomphone's appearance during the May 27 incident. As noted previously, one of the eyewitnesses stated that she tried to tell the officers about the blood she had observed on Sinthasomphone's buttocks prior to the officers' arrival, but that she felt the police listened to Dahmer and did not listen to her. We note that in a statement Dahmer later made to the police after his arrest, he stated that he did not have anal intercourse with Sinthasomphone before he killed him. The civilian eyewitnesses give different descriptions of Sinthasomphone's physical condition with respect to possible injury or bleeding, which may be explained in part by the distance from which each witness observed him, when they observed him, and the [several months'] lapse of time between their observations and when they were interviewed by police. We note that some witnesses reported seeing Sinthasomphone stumble and fall. Some of the descriptions are summarized as follows: no injuries or blood observed; bruised lower right side back, right shoulder, no injuries to face; blood on buttocks, shoulder and knee scraped up; bleeding in area of buttocks, dried blood on testicles and pubic hair; blood on left shoulder, scraped buttocks; scraped knees, buttocks, and right shoulder, with darker blood running down inner thigh from buttocks. Finally, two of the officers interviewed in the Dahmer investigation reported that Sinthasomphone showed no sign of any physical injury.[27]

In sum, these three cases suggest that researchers may be looking at and drawing conclusions about one aspect of a problem while a far larger feature has gone unexamined and unaffected by empirical attempts to influence policy. Like Tracey Thurman before them, Alesia Hynson, Karen Guerrant, and Konerak Sinthasomphone were victimized not because of anything related to police deterrence of misdemeanor domestic violence, but because the police had failed to lock up people who had committed serious felony violence against them. These cases all emanated from events that occurred long after publication of the Minneapolis findings and the outcomes of *Bruno* and *Thurman*. Consequently, they raise questions about the representativeness and prevalence of the police performance studied in the domestic violence literature. Among these issues, two are especially important here:

- Given this reason to suspect that police may not take felony domestic violence seriously unless someone is looking closely over their shoulders, what do studies of the manner in which police dispose of misdemeanor domestic violence really tell us about the way police see their role?
- What sort of commitment to either the general thrust or specific implications of the domestic violence research can be expected from line police officers when the officers in these three cases ultimately were found to have acted appropriately by the officials who reviewed their conduct?

The absence of admissions aside, large pretrial settlements to the survivors of Hynson, Guerrant, and Sinthasomphone seemed to indicate official recognition that police had behaved wrongly, but no officer was ever held to account for any wrongdoing. On this score, the case of Milwaukee – where arrest was presumably mandated in domestic violence cases – provides especially strong food for thought. When Milwaukee declined to appeal the reinstatement of the officers who had handled the Sinthasomphone case, it paid them in full for the period in which they had been off the police payroll. The Milwaukee Police Department also claimed not to have been able to identify the officers who failed to respond appropriately to a witness's attempts to provide information about Sinthasomphone's disappearance. Despite clear audiotapes of the conversations involved, complete with dates, times, and the units that received the calls, the department did no voice comparisons. Instead, its investigation consisted only of asking officers if they had been involved in the phone calls that had caused the department international embarrassment, that had preceded the deaths of additional victims of Dahmer, and that were sure to result in dismissal of anyone who admitted them. With the predictable denials, the investigation closed.

Question 2: Should the deterrence research drive domestic violence policy?

Consider again the question addressed by the domestic violence research: Are arrests in misdemeanor domestic violence cases more likely than such less formal alternatives as mediation to achieve specific deterrence of future violence?

This is an interesting question, but it is far from the most important issue to be resolved in policy formulation, and has been asked only by researchers. Indeed, it is hard to imagine that it would be raised at all where other types of offenses are concerned. Should policy concerning police disposition of shoplifters and other petty thieves, of people who assault strangers or use their telephones to harass neighbors, of jostlers and nonviolent sex offenders, or of drunk drivers be determined by statistical findings comparing recidivism rates among arrestees with those of offenders who have been merely counseled and released by officers?

Even if it could be empirically demonstrated that on-the-spot counseling of shoplifters was a better deterrent than arrest, few police departments could get away with promulgating policies dictating such actions. This is so because for most offenses specific deterrence is not the only goal of the police. The processes begun by police action in these cases are also required to give victims access to the law, to achieve general deterrence, to incapacitate potential offenders, and, frankly, to punish and express society's condemnation of the behavior involved. Consequently, the general presumption for virtually all victimizing criminal behavior is that police will arrest so that the wheels of justice eventually may find their way to the path that best achieves these goals.

The police domestic violence research and its suggestion that arrest/no-arrest policy should be formulated largely – or exclusively – on the basis of which alternative better accomplishes specific deterrence is a demonstration that this presumption does not hold for domestic violence. Indeed, the mere existence of this work and the current state of the debate about which alternatives are the best specific deterrents should offend those who believe that the criminal law is a means of giving the weak parity with the strong, and that police should not discriminate between domestic violence and other forms of violence. Consider, for example, policy recommendations that might have followed a finding in the Minneapolis research that mediation was a better deterrent than arrest. Consider also the convoluted policy implications that could arise from the findings of the domestic violence research, as summarized here by Sherman:

- Arrest increases domestic violence among people who have nothing to lose, especially the unemployed.

- Arrest deters domestic violence in cities with higher proportions of white and Hispanic suspects.
- Arrest deters domestic violence in the short run, but escalates violence later on in cities with higher proportions of unemployed black suspects.
- A small but chronic portion of all violent couples produce the majority of domestic violence incidents.
- Offenders who flee before police arrive are substantially deterred by warrants for their arrest, at least in Omaha.[28]

It is difficult to see how any of these findings concerning misdemeanants have meaning for victims like Thurman, Hynson, Guerrant, and Sinthasomphone, all of whom would have been spared injury or death had police arrested the felons who had victimized them when their crimes were first reported. Instead, the importance with which some apparently view these findings suggests that we have lost the forest for the trees in consideration of what police intervention in domestic violence should accomplish.

Question 3: What should drive domestic violence policy?

The short answer to this question is that domestic violence policy should be determined by commitment to the same goals which should – but do not – drive all police policy. Domestic violence is the most extreme example of confusion over police goals and formulation of policies to achieve these goals, but it is not the only such case. In most police agencies, officers are given little more instruction in handling such crises as robberies and burglaries, encounters with the emotionally disturbed, and vehicle pursuits than to use caution and to do the best they can.

Domestic violence has been a particular nightmare for the police because, for the last several generations, they have attempted to take upon themselves the task of holding together families rather than simply looking for guidance to some first principles of policing. Instead of applying these principles to domestic violence – and, typically, locking up husbands who beat their wives – police have ceded their management prerogatives to social workers and social scientists anxious to test theory.

These principles are not nearly so complex as those implied in social science research. Indeed, with some variation, they are found in the front pages of almost all police department manuals: It is the job of the police to protect life, rights, and property. When police are called to intervene in violent confrontations, the police should protect life, rights, and property by exercising the monopoly on the legitimate use of coercive force upon which Bittner first commented.[29] In other words, by using or threatening to use the power of the state against predators, the police are an official equalizer between the weak and the strong.

To go from the abstract to the concrete, then, formulation and enforcement of police policy related to domestic violence should be based, first and foremost, on the principle that police action should protect life, rights, and property— in that order. The police should do this just as they do with violence of other types: by using whatever force may be necessary to put an immediate end to whatever violence may be in progress; and by using the law to protect the weak and to hold predators to account for whatever violence they have committed before the police intervened. These are not duties that require any predictive skills.

In addition, police must be held closely accountable for abiding by the guidelines that are defined for them. Throughout my work in these three cases – and several other matters, some of which are pending and all of which are egregious – I have been struck by an enormous inconsistency. On the one hand, there exist toothless policies and laws that require arrests in minor cases; on the other hand, officers have been free to ignore felony violence without any penalties.

DISCUSSION AND IMPLICATIONS

Formulating and enforcing policy in this manner, and thereby directing officers' broad discretion toward protection of life, rights, and property – goals with which nobody can seriously take issue – is a job that must be begun by police chiefs, their agencies' chief executive officers, operating managers, and leaders. Certainly, in doing this, chiefs must take into account the views of citizens, elected leaders, line officers, and other stakeholders in police service, but they cannot afford to follow the current pattern of allowing narrow interests (of employee groups, for example) or theory testers to alter the historical priorities of the police or to determine the best methods of achieving them.

When police chiefs have taken the lead in formulation and enforcement of policy to define and limit line officers' discretion, their efforts have usually been rewarded with great success. Two extremely critical operational areas – response to hostage and barricade situations, and use of deadly force – are illustrative.

Hostage and barricade situations. Until the early 1970s, police policy for dealing with armed persons who barricaded themselves and/or took hostages and resisted law enforcement personnel was virtually nonexist-ent. Instead, officers and agents were encouraged only to assess situations and to do their best to resolve them. This ad hoc approach resulted in such disasters as the 1971 New York State Police invasion of Attica Prison, which resulted in the deaths of thirty-nine inmates and corrections offi-cers, and the German attempt to overpower hostage takers at the 1972 Munich Olympics, which resulted in the deaths of nine Israeli athletes.[30]

Since the early 1970s, when hostage and barricade protocols were devel-oped by the New York City Police Department and became standard police operating procedure, violent endings to such situations have be-come the exception. This is so because the protocols and those who apply them strive tenaciously to achieve one goal: protection of life. As hostage team leader George Maher notes:

> First it has to be recognized that the life of the subjects involved, whether they be hostages, hostage takers, barricaded subjects, or a person attempting suicide, is of foremost concern. For example, the apprehension of a perpetra-tor who uses a hostage to further his escape has to be secondary to the life and safety of the hostage. This concept has to be recognized and instilled in the mind of each police officer who may be used as a negotiator.[31]

Deadly force. As one might expect, there is a considerable amount of research evidence that the frequency with which police employ deadly force is closely associated with such measures of public violence as rates of public homicide, violent crime, and arrests for violent crime.[32] As a rule, police who work in high-crime areas are more likely to encounter situa-tions calling for deadly force than officers who work in low-crime areas.

During the last two decades, however, this relationship certainly has not held: our increased murder, violent crime, and arrest rates attest that we have become a much more violent society, but every indication is that police use of deadly force has decreased dramatically.[33]

The major reason for this change is that police administrators have promulgated administrative policies that emphasize the value of human life, and that limit police officers' authority to use deadly force.[34] The great influence of such policies on police deadly force rates was first suggested by Gerald Uelmen, who reported that the major determinant of police deadly force rates among Los Angeles County police agencies was the personal philosophies and policies of the department's chiefs.[35] Subse-quently, I found that the 1972 implementation and enforcement of a re-strictive deadly force policy reduced the number of police shootings in New York, especially those involving little danger to police, without any negative effects on crime rates, police safety, or effectiveness.[36] Since then, other researchers have reported similar findings in other jurisdictions.[37]

In short, police administrators' recent experience in controlling line discretion at hostage and barricade situations and in the use of deadly force demonstrates that policies reflecting unwavering commitment to the protection of life can achieve that purpose. It is now time to follow the same route where other issues are concerned.

Discretion may be narrow at the tops of police agencies, but it is not nonexistent. If policing is to improve, police leaders must exercise their authority to more carefully structure line-level police discretion in ways that best serve to protect life, rights, and property.

NOTES

I wish to thank the participants at this workshop, especially Diana Gordon, Candace McCoy, and Jeffrey Reiman, for their comments on this essay.

1. See, for example, Kenneth Culp Davis, *Police Discretion* (St. Paul: West, 1975).

2. Peter K. Manning, *Police Work: The Social Organization of Policing* (Cambridge: MIT Press, 1977).

3. Sometimes these authorizations are not veiled at all. Consider the following colloquy between a reporter and the Superintendent of the New Jersey State Police. It occurred during a 1989 television news series concerning allegations that police drug interdiction efforts included hundreds of unconstitutional stops and searches of vehicles driven by black and Hispanic motorists:

Q. Some people feel that, as though they've had their rights violated. Is that a serious concern?

A. It's of serious concern. But nowhere near the concern that I think we have got to look to in trying to correct some of the problems we find with the criminal element in this state.

4. International Association of Chiefs of Police, *Training Key 245: Wife Beating* (Gaithersburg, MD: International Association of Chiefs of Police, 1976); Nancy Loving, *Responding to Spouse Abuse and Wife Beating* (Washington, DC: Police Executive Research Forum, 1980); D. Martin, *Battered Wives* (San Francisco: Glide Publications, 1976). Certainly, as many critics have suggested, casual police treatment of domestic violence has also involved sexism and the view of women as property. Both my experience and my research, however, suggest that the primary goal of police domestic violence policy of the 1960s and 1970s was preservation of the family, the primary American social unit.

5. See, for example, Eva Buzawa and Carl Buzawa, *Domestic Violence: The Criminal Justice Response* (Newbury Park, CA: Sage, 1990); J. David Hirschel, Ira W. Hutchison, Charles W. Dean, and Ann-Marie Mills, "Review Essay on the Law Enforcement Response to Spouse Abuse: Past, Present, and Future," *Justice Quarterly* 9 (1992), pp. 247-84.

6. See, for example, Robert Calvert, "Criminal and Civil Liability in Husband and Wife Assaults," in *Violence in the Family*, ed. Suzanne R. Steinmetz and Murray A. Straus (New York: Dodd, Mead, 1974), pp. 88-91.

7. Lawrence W. Sherman, *Policing Domestic Violence* (New York: Free Press, 1992), pp. 45-48.

8. Morton Bard, *Training Police as Specialists in Crisis Intervention* (Washington, DC: U.S. Department of Justice, National Institute of Law Enforcement and Criminal Justice, 1970); Morton Bard and Joseph Zucker, *The Police and Interpersonal Conflict: Third Party Intervention Approaches* (Washington, DC: Police Foundation, 1976).

9. It is not so clear, however, that champions of police crisis intervention were all naive about the police. The most visible of their number, Morton Bard, was a former police officer, and there is some reason to believe that he and his colleagues overcame police resistance to their message by spreading the fiction that "domestics" were the most dangerous of all police assignments (James J. Fyfe, *Shots Fired: An Analysis of New York City Police Firearms Discharge* [Ann Arbor, MI: University Microfilms, 1978]; David Konstantin, "Homicides of American Law Enforcement Officers," *Justice Quarterly* 1 [March 1984], pp. 29ff.; Joel Garner and E. Clemmer, *Danger to Police in Domestic Disturbances: A New Look* [Washington, DC: National Institute of Justice, 1986]), and that mastery of crisis intervention skills was the best way for officers to avoid injury at these situations.

10. *Bruno v. Codd*, 90 Misc. 2d 1047, 396 N.Y.S. 2d 974 (Sup. Ct. 1977) *rev'd in part, appeal dismissed in part*, 407 N.Y.S. 2nd 165 (App. Div. 1978), *aff'd* 47 N.Y.S. 2d 582, 393 N.E. 2nd 976, 419 N.Y.S. 2d 901 (1979).

11. *Thurman v. City of Torrington*, 595 F. Supp. 1521 (D. Conn. 1984). Over the preceding eight months, I learned as Tracey's expert consultant and witness in the case, police had been notified of approximately a dozen occasions on which Buck Thurman had attacked his wife, some of which involved forced entries into her home, and abduction of their infant child. In each instance, the police either did not report the event or indicated that Tracy wanted a "report only," rather than an arrest. This claim was vigorously denied by Tracey and several family members, who could document that they had also gone to the police station to request Buck's arrest for his attacks on Tracey. In addition, as Torrington police had been advised, Buck's mere presence in town was a violation of the terms of his probation for an earlier attack on Tracey.

12. See Lawrence W. Sherman and Richard A. Berk, "The Minneapolis Domestic Violence Experiment," *Police Foundation Reports* (Washington, DC: Police Foundation, 1984), pp. 1ff.; idem, "The Specific Deterrent Effect of Arrests for Domestic Assault," *American Sociological Review* 49 (1984), pp. 261-72; Franklyn Dunford, David Huizinga, and Delbert S. Elliott, *The Omaha Domestic Violence Experiment: Final Report to the National Institute of Justice* (Washington, DC: National Institute of Justice, 1989); J. David Hirschel, Ira W. Hutchison, and Charles W. Dean, *Charlotte Spouse Abuse Replication Project: Final Report* (Washington, DC: National Institute of Justice, 1990); Antony Pate, Edwin E. Hamilton, and Sampson Annan, *Metro-Dade Spouse Abuse Replication Project: Draft Final Report* (Washington, DC: Police Foundation, 1991); Lawrence W. Sherman, Janell D. Schmidt, Dennis P. Rogan, Patrick R. Gartin, Ellen G. Cohn, Dean J. Collins, and Anthony C. Bacich, "From Initial Deterrence to Long-Term Escalation: The Effects of Short-Custody Arrest for Poverty Ghetto Domestic Violence," *Criminology* 29 (1991), pp. 821-50.

13. Lawrence W. Sherman and Ellen G. Cohn, "The Impact of Research on Legal Policy: The Minneapolis Domestic Violence Experiment," *Law and Society Review* 23 (1989), pp. 117-44.

14. Sherman and Berk, "The Minneapolis Domestic Violence Experiment";

idem, "The Specific Deterrent Effect of Arrests for Domestic Assault."

15. Richard Lempert, "Humility Is a Virtue: On the Publicization of Policy Relevant Research," *Law and Society Review* 23, no. 1 (1989), pp. 146-61. In depicting the state of affairs prior to the Minneapolis experiment, for example, Sherman has sometimes overlooked changes that had already occurred. In writing about the New York City *Bruno* case, he argued that this

> lawsuit was, ironically, more a symbolic victory for the plaintiffs than a substantive success. Rather than agreeing to make arrests upon probable cause in domestic violence cases, the police merely stipulated that they would not take gender or relationship to the offender into account in decisions to make arrests. Since we have seen that the criminal law is widely underenforced, New York's consent decree barely amounted to any change in practice at all. (pp. 52-53)

This claim is not supported by a reading of the New York City Police Department directive issued as a result of the *Bruno* litigation:

1. In dealing with husband and wife disputes, members of the service shall observe the following guidelines;

   a. A member of the service will respond to every request for assistance sought by persons alleging that a violation or crime, or a violation of an Order of Protection, has been committed against such person by a spouse.

   b. Where probable cause exists for a police officer to believe that a spouse has committed a misdemeanor against his/her mate; or where a spouse has committed a violation against his/her mate in the officer's presence, the officer shall not refrain from making an arrest without justification. In making such a determination, an officer shall not rely on any of the following:

    (1) The parties are married;

    (2) The aggrieved spouse has not sought or obtained an Order of Protection;

    (3) The aggrieved spouse has instituted prior pending legal proceedings;

    (4) The officer prefers to reconcile the parties despite the aggrieved spouse's determined insistence that an arrest be made;

    (5) The aggrieved spouse intends to institute a proceeding in Court based on the current incident.

   c. Where probable cause exists that a spouse has committed a felony against his/her mate or has violated an Order of Protection, the arrest of such spouse will be made. An officer shall not attempt to reconcile the parties or to mediate the situation.

   d. Where probable cause exists that a spouse has committed a crime or violation against his/her mate, but such spouse is not present at the scene, normal procedures should be followed by members of the service;

   e. Assistance in obtaining medical aid will be given, if requested, or if need is apparent;

   f. A member of the service shall temporarily remain at the scene until reasonably satisfied that the danger of a recurrence of the incident has subsided. (NYPD, 1978)

In short, *Bruno* created a strong presumption in favor of misdemeanor arrests, and mandated arrest in felony cases and violations of protective orders. This was a dramatic change in New York, and one that apparently put its police practice in line with any recommendations that flowed from the subsequent Minneapolis research.

16. I consulted and testified as plaintiffs' expert in each of these cases.

17. *Hynson v. the City of Chester*, U.S.D.C. (E.D. Pennsylvania, Civil Action No. 86-2913).

18. Police claims that they possessed no record of the earlier court order were contradicted in documents that the City of Chester made available, apparently inadvertently, during discovery proceedings.

19. Despite the experience with the order of protection in the Hynson murder, cases in which such orders existed were excluded from analysis on grounds that, on paper at least, such orders eliminated police discretion by mandating arrest.

20. *Smith v. City of Elyria*, 857 F. Supp. 1203 (N.D. Ohio 1994).

21. *Sinthasomphone v. City of Milwaukee* (U.S.D.C., E.D. Wisconsin, Civil Action 91-C-1124).

22. Sherman states that the police "were apparently persuaded by [Dahmer] that the naked male was an adult lover with whom he had been involved in a dispute, although not cohabitating" and that "[t]he absence of cohabitation apparently exempted the case from the policy" (*Policing Domestic Violence*, pp. 121-22). As suggested above, these claims are only partially accurate. Balcerzak, who was the de facto police leader at the incident, testified that he "believed [Dahmer] to be [Sinthasomphone's] roommate at the time," and clearly left that impression with many witnesses.

23. See Sherman, *Policing Domestic Violence*; Sherman, Schmidt, Rogan, Gartin, Cohn, Collins, and Bacich, "From Initial Deterrence to Long-Term Escalation."

24. Sherman, *Policing Domestic Violence*, p. 118, emphasis in original.

25. Ibid., p. 121.

26. James Doyle, Wisconsin Attorney General's Report, "Re: Milwaukee Police Department and Jeffrey Dahmer," 29 August 1991, and attached report to Attorney General Doyle from Assistant Attorneys General Matthew J. Frank, Douglas Haag, and Diane M. Hicks, 28 August 1991.

27. Ibid.

28. Sherman, *Policing Domestic Violence*, p. 247.

29. Egon Bittner, *The Functions of the Police in Modern Society* (Rockville, MD: National Institute of Mental Health, 1970).

30. See Frank Bolz and Edward Hershey, *Hostage Cop* (New York: Rawson, Wade, 1979), pp. 239-301, for detailed accounts of both the Attica and Munich incidents.

31. George F. Maher, "Hostage Negotiations," in *The Encyclopedia of Police Science*, ed. William C. Bailey (New York: Garland, 1989), p. 274. Three widely publicized disasters emanating from hostage or barricade situations – the 1985 Philadelphia Police Department encounter with the radical group MOVE headquarters and the FBI's more recent encounters with extremists in Ruby Ridge, Idaho, and Waco, Texas – should not be viewed as failures of prevailing practice to achieve the goal of protecting life. The police bombing of MOVE headquarters and the assaults on the Weaver family and the Branch Davidians were undertaken by officials who cast aside existing policy and standards in favor of ill-advised and untested rules of engagement that were devised on the spot.

32. See Richard R. E. Kania and Wade C. Mackey, "Police Violence as a Function of Community Characteristics," *Criminology* 15 (May 1977), pp. 27-48; James J. Fyfe, "Geographic Correlates of Police Shooting: A Microanalysis," *Journal of Research in Crime and Delinquency* 17 (January 1980), pp. 101-13; William Geller, and Kevin Karales, *Split-Second Decisions: Shootings of and by Chicago Police* (Chicago: Chicago Law Enforcement Study Group, 1981); Kenneth R. Matulia, *A Balance of Forces*, 2d ed. (Gaithersburg, MD: International Association of Chiefs of Police, 1985).

33. See, for example, William A. Geller and Michael S. Scott, *Deadly Force: What We Know* (Washington, DC: Police Executive Research Forum, 1992), pp. 29-49.

34. Certainly, the United States Supreme Court's declaration that the legal rule allowing police officers to shoot to apprehend any fleeing felony suspects (*Tennessee v. Garner*, 471 U.S. 1 [1985]) was also a major intervention on police authority to use deadly force. As the *Garner* majority noted, however, by that time almost all major U.S. police departments – who apparently account for the lion's share of police shootings – had already issued rules prohibiting such shooting (see Police Foundation et al., amici curiae brief in *Tennessee v. Garner*, United States Supreme Court Numbers 83-1035, 83-1070 [1984]).

35. Gerald Uelmen, "Varieties of Public Policy: A Study of Police Policy Regarding the Use of Deadly Force in Los Angeles County," *Loyola of Los Angeles Law Review* 6 (1973), pp. 1-55.

36. James J. Fyfe, "Administrative Interventions on Police Shooting Discretion: An Empirical Examination," *Journal of Criminal Justice* 7 (winter 1979), pp. 309-24.

37. See, for example, Geller and Scott, *Deadly Force: What We Know,* pp. 248-67.

Response

Diana R. Gordon

James Fyfe's essay examines the reality that the criminal law remains unenforced in many felonious domestic violence situations, despite the widespread belief that lessons learned from studies of misdemeanor cases have altered policy and made arrest mandatory in most police departments. His analysis of case disposition in felonious domestic and acquaintance assaults in Chester, Pennsylvania, suggests some predictable biases of the criminal justice system and the society in general: greater likelihood of the arrest of victimizers of men than of women, greater likelihood that black victimizers would be arrested than white victimizers. His concerns are not limited to preventing present and future harm to victims, but include, more broadly, the recognition of women's (and other victims') rights to equal enforcement of the criminal laws. Furthermore, since he urges giving equal weight to criminal behavior within and without the domestic context and recognizes a role for police in protecting the weak against the strong, he would presumably constrain many other exercises of police discretion. But law enforcement (and perhaps society in general) lacks a consensus on police goals, and that is at the heart of the problem as he sees it.

Fyfe attributes the persistence of police passivity in the face of felonious domestic violence to a failure of professional leadership. It is certainly beyond argument that lines of communication along the chain of command should be precise and unequivocal, but reducing ambiguity is much less complicated than conquering ambivalence within the profession (at the levels of both commissioners and beat cops). I have less faith than Fyfe does in supervisors' commitment to the rights of battered wives and other victims and in the ability of even the most well-meaning professional leadership to dispel deeply rooted beliefs and attitudes that are powerful influences on behavior even in less tightly knit groups than police.[1]

Fyfe's prescriptions rely on an overly simple analysis of political and social behavior. Fyfe responds to evidence that domestic violence is still treated differently from other violence by calling for police managers to make law enforcement goals and priorities – the protection of life, rights, and property, in that order – absolutely clear. He relies on committed police leadership to reorient the rank-and-file officer from placing priority on family preservation to placing priority on victims' rights. As evidence that leadership can turn around practice, he cites successful policy developments with regard to hostage situations and the use of deadly force.

First, I am not convinced that reform in handling domestic violence is as amenable to change as the two areas he cites. In both of those situations the officer is being directed in the negative: what he or she is *not* supposed to do can be communicated with relative ease. Even if the wished-for consensus about goals existed at the top of the police hierarchy, adaptation and even defiance of those goals, as in other organizations, would be likely to persist farther down the ladder,[2] especially in cases where the command is for taking an affirmative step (for example, arrest or shoot). Given that some amount of discretion is a daily reality in the lives of all street-level bureaucrats,[3] police decisions will always be driven by a variety of influences: police may identify with perpetrators as well as victims; they may choose to comply with directives that reflect budgetary or personnel problems rather than professional ideals (for example, arrest only the worst cases); they may cling to traditional ideologies about family governance (the legal right of chastisement died at the end of the nineteenth century, but its legacy may prevail in the broader cultures to which both police and perpetrators belong). Finally, the "violence-prone officers" who exist in many departments may simply not hear directives from above.[4]

To counter these influences and become axiomatic in police practice, the message needs to come from a broader range of sources. One potentially powerful influence is the judiciary. In the Sinthasomphone case, where two police officers found a fourteen-year-old victim of the serial murderer Jeffrey Dahmer naked, bleeding, and incoherent in the street and dismissed the incident as a "gay thing," a judge reinstated them with full pay after they were dismissed by the Milwaukee Board of Police. It is evident that the legal climate in many jurisdictions is not conducive to major civil damage awards against the police; in each of Fyfe's case studies, law suits brought by survivors of the victims were settled before trial. Prosecutors, too, must participate in establishing a standard of professional behavior for police in domestic violence cases; Fyfe notes that the state attorney general cited several flimsy reasons for not charging the officers in the Sinthasomphone case.

Mayors and other political leaders are as important as criminal justice officials in what is essentially a culture-molding, not just a rule-making task. Indeed, rules appear to be of limited value; for example, Fyfe has noted elsewhere the range of evasions and manipulations of which police are capable in order to get around the Miranda warnings required at a defendant's arrest.[5] As with acceptance of community policing as a major alternative to conventional law enforcement, a serious effort to reduce domestic violence requires well-publicized commitment from elected politicians. Several cities have tied the two campaigns – against domestic violence and in favor of community policing – together in a strategy endorsed at the highest political level.[6]

So far I have examined some impediments to realizing the consensus on police goals that Fyfe proposes (protect life, rights, property, in that order). For the purpose of that discussion, I have assumed, as Fyfe does, that such a set of goals would be clear and comprehensible in most police departments. But the formulation still allows lots of room for interpretation – what is life-threatening, whose rights predominate where there are multiple claimants or a mutual deprivation of rights, can one be certain who the predator is in every situation, and so forth. An effort to eradicate all discretion in family conflicts will surely lead to accusations of false arrest and subsequent litigation. And I am not sure the conventional concerns about family disruption will vanish altogether, especially on those occasions – admittedly rare, when felonious assault is at issue – when victims express a strong preference for nonenforcement.

Fyfe's essay has a secondary theme, a justified expression of pique that the widely publicized research of the early 1980s dealt with misdemeanor domestic violence and was therefore not responsive to the victims with the greatest need – those who were threatened with severe injury or death. He fails to state whether the initial catalyst for the Minneapolis Domestic Violence Experiment was the availability of a tidy methodology (econometric research on the deterrent value of various dispositions, including arrest) or a resource allocation decision that took into consideration the greater likelihood of the lesser crime. In any case, his criticism should be taken as a serious indictment of disseminating research that tests intervention strategies in only one jurisdiction and at one level in a manner that permits practitioners to implement them partially and then to claim a major policy reform. Others have criticized the publicity for the Minneapolis experiment as premature,[7] but only Fyfe has given us such a troubling and poignant glimpse of the human consequences of studying only the easier cases.

NOTES

1. Perhaps the best recent documentation of the secretive, protective, and suspicious culture of police is Fyfe's own work in Jerome H. Skolnick and James J. Fyfe, *Above the Law: Police and the Excessive Use of Force* (New York: Free Press, 1993), esp. chs. 5, 6, and 7.

2. Donald S. Van Meter and Carl E. Van Horn, "The Policy Implementation Process: A Conceptual Framework," *Administration and Society* 6, no.4 (1975).

3. Michael Lipsky, *Street-level Bureaucracy: Dilemmas of the Individual in Public Services* (New York: Russell Sage Foundation, 1980).

4. Skolnick and Fyfe, *Above the Law.*

5. Ibid.

6. Janet Quist, *Nation's Cities Weekly* 18, no. 38 (1995).

7. Richard Lempert, "Humility Is a Virtue: On the Publicization of Policy-Relevant Research," *Law and Society Review* 23, no.1 (1989).

Index of Names

Index of Names

Index of Subjects

ABF survey, 1-2
accountability, 9, 20, 42-43, 73, 92, 97
administrative rule making, 2, 10, 96-97
adversarialness, 6, 10, 159-75, 179, 181-82
age discrimination, 138-39, 141
arrest, 68, 71-83, 85, 132, 141, 185-88, 193, 197-98, 203n. 15, 204n. 19
 alternatives to, 32, 184, 193
assault, 5, 88-89, 90n. 4, 185-99
authority, 8, 38-39, 48, 53, 76-77, 79

barricades, 199-200, 204n. 31
Bayesian decisions, 139-42, 146-57
bureaucrats, 22, 33n. 22, 39-40, 98-99, 180, 208

code of conduct, 54-55
coercion, 79
community, 7, 10, 59-62, 66-67, 102, 104, 110-12
community policing, 10, 35, 40-41, 94-95, 98-105, 107-12, 123, 126, 143, 209
competence, 19, 65-66
consent, 39, 78
consequentialism, 45, 133
corruption, 11, 96, 181-82
Critical Legal Studies, 51-52
crowd control, 31
cynicism, 30

deadly force; *see* use of force
debriefing, 30, 45
decisions about priority, 6-7, 88
detectives, 14, 166, 171-72, 174, 175n. 12
discovery, 159
discretion
 defined, 2-3, 16-26, 49, 51-52, 65, 68, 81, 131, 165

 to disobey, 24-25, 28, 34n. 30
 history of, 1-2, 31-32, 69
 justifying, 8-9, 61, 71-83, 85-89, 92, 183
 kinds of, 3-4, 17-26, 41-44, 49-50, 65, 68, 115
 limiting, 2, 9-10, 97
 managerial, 55, 183, 200-201
 normative dimension of, 3, 47, 52-53, 65-66
 relativity of, 66
 strong, 3, 42-43, 50, 68
 weak, 3, 42, 50, 53
discrimination, 45, 52, 54, 59, 65, 79, 83n. 16, 104, 108, 116, 121, 132, 135-36, 142-43
domestic disputes, 5-6, 47, 57-58, 61-62, 96, 183-99, 201n. 4, 202nn. 9, 11, 203n. 15, 207

enforcement, 28, 68, 71, 103
equality, 59, 61, 75, 97, 103, 109, 112, 133
equity, 27-29
exclusionary rule, 161, 165, 177n. 27

fairness; *see* justice
force; *see* use of force
full enforcement, 16, 85, 89

general will, 101-4

handcuffing, 21, 116, 184
hard cases, 41, 50, 171
hassling, 143
hostage negotiations, 199-200

individualization, 45
injustice, 2, 11, 45, 86, 97, 109, 140, 142, 153, 156, 160
interests, 61, 67, 102-104, 109

Notes on Contributors

ARTHUR ISAK APPLBAUM is associate professor of public policy at Harvard University's John F. Kennedy School of Government, where he is director of graduate fellowships in ethics. His work on official discretion and professional roles has appeared in *Philosophy & Public Affairs* and *Harvard Law Review*. Applbaum has been a Rockefeller Fellow at the Princeton University Center for Human Values and a fellow in ethics at the Harvard University Program in Ethics and the Professions. He is completing a book on the morality of roles in politics and the professions, titled *Ethics for Adversaries*.

HOWARD COHEN is provost/vice chancellor for academic affairs and professor of philosophy at the University of Wisconsin-Green Bay. He is coauthor of *Power and Restraint: The Moral Dimension of Police Work* (1991), *Equal Rights for Children* (1980), and several articles on police authority and police ethics. Professor Cohen has worked as a consultant and trainer with police organizations around the country. Between 1979 and 1984 he was on the staff of the Law Enforcement Trainers Institute and the Institute for Humanities and Law Enforcement Training.

MICHAEL DAVIS is senior research associate at the Center for the Study of Ethics in the Professions, Illinois Institute of Technology. Before coming to IIT in 1986, he taught at Case-Western Reserve, Illinois State, and the University of Illinois at Chicago. In 1985-86, he held a National Endowment for the Humanities fellowship. He has received a number of grants, including one from the National Science Foundation to integrate ethics into technical courses (1991-95). Davis has published more than seventy articles, authored *To Make the Punishment Fit the Crime* (1992), and coedited *Ethics and the Legal Profession* (1986) and *AIDS: Crisis in Professional Ethics* (1994). His recent work in criminal justice ethics includes the entry "Codes of Ethics" in *The Encyclopedia of Police Science* (2d ed., 1995), and "Hands across the Border: Ethical Guidelines for Transnational Law Enforcement," in *The Globalization of Law Enforcement* (forthcoming). Davis received his Ph.D. in philosophy from the University of Michigan in 1972.

JAMES J. FYFE is professor of criminal justice and senior public policy research fellow at Temple University. He holds a Ph.D. in criminal justice from the State University of New York–Albany, and his major professional interest is street-level police discretion. Fyfe served for sixteen years as a New York City police officer and has testified as an expert witness in more than two hundred police misconduct court actions. With Jerome H. Skolnick, he is coauthor of *Above the Law: Police and the Excessive Use of Force* (1993), and he has recently completed coauthoring *Police Administration* (forthcoming, 1996).

DIANA R. GORDON is professor of political science at City College of New York, City University of New York. She has served as president of the National Council on Crime and Delinquency. Her writings have focused on various aspects of crime and, most recently, on drug policy. Her recent books include *The Justice Juggernaut: Fighting Street Crime, Controlling Citizens* (1990) and *The Return of the Dangerous Classes: Drug Prohibition and Policy Politics* (1994). Gordon received her J.D. from Harvard Law School in 1964.

VIDAR HALVORSEN is a member of the Research and Development Unit at the National Police College, Norway. He is currently working on his doctoral project, "The Legitimacy of Force," as a research fellow at the Institute for Sociology of Law, University of Oslo. The project, financed by the Norwegian Research Council, is part of the council's comprehensive research program in ethics. In 1995, Halvorsen spent seven months as a visiting scholar at the Institute for Criminal Justice Ethics, John Jay College of Criminal Justice.

WILLIAM C. HEFFERNAN is associate professor of law at John Jay College of Criminal Justice and the Graduate Center of the City University of New York. His articles on constitutional criminal procedure have appeared in numerous law reviews. He is also an editor of *Criminal Justice Ethics*, a journal published by John Jay's Institute for Criminal Justice Ethics.

ROBERT JACKALL is Willmott Family Professor of Sociology and Social Thought at Williams College. He is author of, among other works, *Moral Mazes: The World of Corporate Managers* (1989), and is editor of *Propaganda* (1995), a book in the Main Trends in the Modern World series that he coedits with Arthur J. Vidich. From 1991 to 1993, Professor Jackall did intensive fieldwork with police detectives in the New York City Transit Police and the New York City Police Department. He spent nearly a year and a half of this time with the 34 Squad in upper Manhattan. During the same period, he worked with Trial Bureau 50 of the Manhattan District Attorney's Office (DANY), observing prosecutorial work from ECAB (Early Case Assessment Bureau) through trial. He spent the summer of 1995 with the Homicide Investigation Unit of DANY.

JOHN KLEINIG is professor of philosophy in the Department of Law and Police Science, John Jay College of Criminal Justice, City University of New York, and director of the Institute for Criminal Justice Ethics. He is an editor of *Criminal Justice Ethics*. Among his publications are *Punishment and Desert* (1973), *Paternalism* (1984), *Valuing Life* (1991), *Professional Law Enforcement Codes: A Documentary Collection* (with Yurong Zhang, 1993), and *The Ethics of Policing* (1996). He is currently doing research on the topic of loyalty.

CANDACE McCOY is assistant professor of criminal justice at the Graduate School of Criminal Justice, Rutgers, State University of New Jersey, Newark. At Rutgers she teaches graduate seminars in courts, sentencing, and criminal justice politics, and undergraduate courses in policing and criminal justice ethics. She holds an undergraduate degree in political science from Hiram College in Ohio, a law degree from the University of Cincinnati, and a Ph.D. in jurisprudence and social policy from the University of California, Berkeley. Author of several articles and a book on plea bargaining, McCoy is currently researching the moral and empirical dimensions of the trial penalty.

HOWARD McGARY is professor of philosophy at Rutgers, State University of New Jersey. He has also taught at the University of Arizona, the University of Illinois–Chicago, and Oxford University. His areas of specialization are African-American philosophy, ethics, and social philosophy. He has published numerous articles on questions of distributive justice, moral responsibility, and philosophical issues raised by racism. He is the coauthor of *Between Slavery and Freedom: Philosophy and American Slavery* (1992), and he serves on the editorial boards of *The Philosophical Forum, Encyclopedia of Ethics,* and *Social Identities*.

JOAN McGREGOR is associate professor of philosophy at Arizona State University. She received her Ph.D and J.D. from the University of Arizona. Included among her research interests are philosophical issues in criminal law and criminal justice, feminist jurisprudence, and problems in political philosophy and environmental ethics.

JOHN P. PITTMAN teaches philosophy at John Jay College of Criminal Justice, City University of New York. He edited *African-American Perspectives and Philosophical Traditions* – a special triple issue of *Philosophical Forum* (1992-1993) – and is currently coediting, with Tommy L. Lott, the *Blackwell Companion to African-American Philosophy.*

JEFFREY REIMAN is William Fraser McDowell Professor of Philosophy at American University in Washington, D.C. He is the author of *In Defense of Political Philosophy: A Reply to R. P. Wolff's* In Defense of Anarchism (1972), *Justice and Modern Moral Philosophy* (1990), *The Rich Get Richer and the Poor Get Prison: Ideology, Class, and Criminal Justice* (4th ed., 1995), and numerous articles in moral philosophy.

DAVID WASSERMAN is a research associate at the University of Maryland's Institute for Philosophy and Public Policy, and also teaches in the University of Maryland's law school and philosophy department. He is author of *A Sword for the Convicted: Representing Indigent Defendants on Appeal* (1990), and articles in *Michigan Law Review, Cardozo Law Review, Maryland Law Review,* and *Philosophy & Public Affairs.*